||||| |||||||||||||||||||||||||||||||||||
W9-AXN-280

# Rick Steves'

# SPANISH & PORTUGUESE

## Phrase Book & Dictionary

### 4th Edition

John Muir Publications
Santa Fe, New Mexico

Thanks to the team of people at *Europe Through the Back Door*
who helped make this book possible: Dave Hoerlein, Colleen
Murphy, Mary Romano, and . . .

Spanish translation: Gloria Villaraviz Weeden with Julio Villaraviz
    and John Weeden
Spanish proofreading: Angelina Saldaña de Gibbons
Portuguese translation: Luis F. Gonçalves Conde and Maria
    Antonia Campota
Phonetics: Risa Laib
Layout: Rich Sorensen and Colleen Murphy
Maps: David C. Hoerlein
Edited by Risa Laib and Rich Sorensen

John Muir Publications, P.O. Box 613, Santa Fe, NM  87504

Copyright © 1999, 1996, 1995, 1993 by Rick Steves
Cover copyright © 1999 by John Muir Publications
All rights reserved.

Printed in the U.S.A. by Banta Company
Fourth edition.  First printing March 1999

ISBN 1-56261-479-7

Cover photos: Cathedral, Segovia, Spain; © Leo de Wys Inc./
                Charles Bowman
                Foreground photo: Rick Steves

Distributed to the book trade by
Publishers Group West
Berkeley, California

*While every effort has been made to keep the content of this
book accurate, the author and publisher accept no responsibility
whatsoever for anyone ordering bad beer or getting messed up in
any other way because of the linguistic confidence this phrase
book has given them.*

**JMP travel guidebooks by Rick Steves**

*Europe 101: History and Art for the Traveler* (with Gene Openshaw)
*Rick Steves' Mona Winks: Self-guided Tours of Europe's Top Museums* (with Gene Openshaw)
*Rick Steves' Postcards from Europe*
*Rick Steves' Best of Europe*
*Rick Steves' Europe Through the Back Door*
*Rick Steves' France, Belgium & the Netherlands* (with Steve Smith)
*Rick Steves' Germany, Austria & Switzerland*
*Rick Steves' Great Britain & Ireland*
*Rick Steves' Italy*
*Rick Steves' Russia & the Baltics* (with Ian Watson)
*Rick Steves' Scandinavia*
*Rick Steves' Spain & Portugal*
*Rick Steves' London* (with Gene Openshaw)
*Rick Steves' Paris* (with Steve Smith and Gene Openshaw)
Rick Steves' Phrase Books for: French, German, Italian, Spanish/Portuguese, and French/Italian/German
*Asia Through the Back Door*

Rick Steves' company, *Europe Through the Back Door*, provides many services for budget travelers, including a free quarterly newsletter/catalog, budget travel books and accessories, Eurailpasses (with free video and travel advice included), free-spirited European tours, on-line travel tips, and a Travel Resource Center in Edmonds, WA. For a free newsletter, call, write, or e-mail:

**Europe Through the Back Door**
120 Fourth Avenue N., Box 2009
Edmonds, WA 98020 USA
Tel: 425/771-8303, Fax: 425/771-0833
Web: http://www.ricksteves.com
E-mail: rick@ricksteves.com

iv

# Contents

## Hi, I'm Rick Steves.

I'm the only mono-lingual speaker I know who's had the nerve to design a series of European phrase books. But that's one of the things that makes them better.

You see, after 25 summers of travel through Europe, I've learned first-hand: (1) what's essential for communication in another country, and (2) what's not. I've assembled the most important words and phrases in a logical, no-frills format, and I've worked with native Europeans and seasoned travelers to give you the simplest, clearest translations possible.

But this book is more than just a pocket translator. The words and phrases have been carefully selected to help you have a smarter, smoother trip in Spain and Portugal without going broke. Spain used to be cheap and chaotic. These days it's neither. It's better organized than ever—and often as expensive as France or Germany. The key to getting more out of every travel dollar is to get closer to the local people, and to rely less on entertainment, restaurants, and hotels that cater only to foreign tourists. This book will not only help you order a meal at a locals-only Sevilla restaurant—it will help you talk with the family who runs the place . . . about their kids, social issues, travel dreams, and favorite *música*. Long after your memories of museums have faded, you'll still treasure the personal encounters you had with your new Iberian friends.

A good phrase book should help you enjoy your Iberian experience—not just survive it—so I've added a healthy dose of humor. But please use these phrases carefully, in a self-effacing spirit. Remember, one ugly American can undo the goodwill built by dozens of culturally-sensitive ones.

To get the most out of this book, take the time to internalize and put into practice my Spanish and Portuguese pronunciation tips. Don't worry too much about memorizing grammatical rules, like the gender of a noun—the important thing is to communicate!

You'll notice this book has a handy dictionary and a nifty menu decoder. You'll also find tongue twisters, gestures, international words, telephone tips, and handy tear-out "cheat sheets." Tear them out and keep them in your pocket, so you can easily memorize key phrases during otherwise idle moments. As you prepare for your trip, you may want to read this year's edition of my *Rick Steves' Spain & Portugal* guidebook.

The Spanish and Portuguese speak less English than their European neighbors. But while the language barrier may seem a little higher, the locals are happy to give an extra boost to any traveler who makes an effort to communicate.

My goal is to help you become a more confident, extroverted traveler. If this phrase book helps make that happen, or if you have suggestions for making it better, I'd love to hear from you. I personally read and value all feedback. My address is Europe Through the Back Door, P.O. Box 2009, Edmonds, WA 98020, tel. 425/771-8303, fax 425/771-0833, e-mail: rick@ricksteves.com.

Happy travels,

# Getting Started

## Spanish

...opens the door to the land of siestas and fiestas, fun and flamenco. Imported from the Old World throughout the New, Spanish is the most widely spoken romance language in the world. With its straightforward pronunciation, Spanish is also one of the simplest languages to learn.

Here are some tips for pronouncing Spanish words:

*C* usually sounds like C in cat.
> But *C* followed by *E* or *I* sounds like TH in think.

*D* sounds like the soft D in soda.

*G* usually sounds like G in go.
> But *G* followed by *E* or *I* sounds like the guttural
> J in Baja.

*H* is silent.

*J* sounds like the guttural J in Baja.

*LL* sounds like Y in yes.

*Ñ* sounds like NI in onion.

*R* is trrrilled.

*V* sounds like B in bit.

*Z* sounds like TH in think.

Spanish vowels:

*A* sounds like A in father.

*E* can sound like E in get or AY in play.

*I* sounds like EE in seed.

*O* sounds like O in note.

*U* sounds like OO in moon.

## 2 Spanish

Spanish has a few unusual signs and sounds. The Spanish add extra punctuation to questions and exclamations, like this: *¿Cómo está?* (How are you?) *¡Fantástico!* (Fantastic!) You've probably seen and heard the Spanish *ñ*: think of *señor* and *mañana*. Spanish has a guttural sound similar to the J in Baja California. In the phonetics, the symbol for this clearing-your-throat sound is the italicized *h*.

Spanish words that end in a consonant are stressed on the last syllable, as in *Madrid*. Words ending in a vowel are generally stressed on the second-to-last syllable, as in *amigo*. To override these rules, the Spanish sometimes add an accent mark (ʹ) to the syllable that should be stressed, like this: *rápido* (fast) is pronounced **rah**-pee-doh.

When you're speaking a romance language, sex is unavoidable. Even the words are masculine or feminine, and word endings can change depending on gender. A man is *simpático* (friendly), a woman is *simpática*. In this book, we show gender-bender words like this: *simpático[a]*. If you're speaking of a woman (which includes women speaking about themselves), use the *a* ending. It's always pronounced "ah." Words ending in *r*, such as *doctor*, will appear like this: *doctor[a]*. A *doctora* is a female doctor. Words ending in *e*, such as *amable* (kind), apply to either sex.

The endings of Spanish nouns and adjectives agree. Cold weather is *tiempo frío*, and a cold shower is a *ducha fría*.

Plurals are a snap. Add *s* to a word that ends in a vowel, like *pueblo* (village) and *es* to a word that ends in a consonant, like *ciudad* (city). Visit a mix of *pueblos* and *ciudades* to get the full flavor of Spain.

In northern and central Spain, Spanish sounds as if it's spoken with a lisp. *Gracias* (thank you) sounds like grah-thee-ahs. As you head farther south, you'll notice a difference in pronunciation. In southern Spain, along the coast, people thpeak without the lisp: *Gracias* sounds like grah-see-ahs. Listen to and imitate the Spanish people around you.

You'll often hear the Spanish say, *"Por favor"* (Please). The Spanish are friendly, polite people. *Por favor* use *por favor* whenever you can.

*¡Buen viaje!* Have a good trip!

Here's a quick guide to the phonetics we've used in this book:

| | |
|---|---|
| ah | like A in father. |
| ay | like AY in play. |
| ee | like EE in seed. |
| eh | like E in get. |
| ehr | sounds like "air." |
| g | like G in go. |
| *h* | like the guttural J in Baja. |
| ī | like I in light. |
| oh | like O in note. |
| or | like OR in core. |
| oo | like OO in moon. |
| ow | like OW in now. |
| oy | like OY in toy. |
| s | like S in sun. |

# Spanish Basics

## Greeting and meeting the Spanish:

| | | |
|---|---|---|
| Hello. | **Hola.** | **oh**-lah |
| Good morning. | **Buenos días.** | **bway**-nohs **dee**-ahs |
| Good afternoon. | **Buenas tardes.** | **bway**-nahs **tar**-days |
| Good evening. | **Buenas tardes.** | **bway**-nahs **tar**-days |
| Good night. | **Buenas noches.** | **bway**-nahs **noh**-chays |
| Mr. | **Señor** | sayn-**yor** |
| Mrs. | **Señora** | sayn-**yoh**-rah |
| Miss | **Señorita** | sayn-yoh-**ree**-tah |
| How are you? | **¿Cómo está?** | **koh**-moh ay-**stah** |
| Very well, thanks. | **Muy bien, gracias.** | **moo**-ee bee-**yehn grah**-thee-ahs |
| And you? | **¿Y usted?** | ee oo-**stehd** |
| My name is... | **Me llamo...** | may **yah**-moh |
| What's your name? | **¿Cómo se llama?** | **koh**-moh say **yah**-mah |
| Pleased to meet you. | **Mucho gusta.** | **moo**-choh **goo**-stah |
| Where are you from? | **¿De dónde es usted?** | day **dohn**-day ays oo-**stehd** |
| See you later. | **Hasta luego.** | **ah**-stah loo-ay-**goh** |
| Goodbye. | **Adiós.** | ah-dee-**ohs** |
| Good luck! | **¡Buena suerte!** | **bway**-nah **swehr**-tay |
| Have a good trip! | **¡Buen viaje!** | bwayn bee-**ah**-*hay* |

## Survival phrases

Ernest Hemingway fought in the Spanish Civil War using only these phrases. They're repeated on your tear-out cheat sheet near the end of this book.

## The essentials:

| | | |
|---|---|---|
| Hello. | **Hola.** | **oh**-lah |
| Do you speak English? | **¿Habla usted inglés?** | **ah**-blah oo-**stehd** een-**glays** |
| Yes. / No. | **Sí. / No.** | see / noh |
| I don't speak Spanish. | **No hablo español.** | noh **ah**-bloh ay-spahn-**yohl** |
| I'm sorry. | **Lo siento.** | loh see-**ehn**-toh |
| Please. | **Por favor.** | por fah-**bor** |
| Thank you. | **Gracias.** | **grah**-thee-ahs |
| It's (not) a problem. | **(No) hay problema.** | (noh) ī proh-**blay**-mah |
| Very good. | **Muy bien.** | **moo**-ee bee-**yehn** |
| You are very kind. | **Usted es muy amable.** | oo-**stehd** ays **moo**-ee ah-**mah**-blay |
| Goodbye. | **Adiós.** | ah-dee-**ohs** |

## Where?

| | | |
|---|---|---|
| Where is a...? | **¿Donde hay un...?** | **dohn**-day ī oon |
| ...hotel | **...hotel** | oh-**tehl** |
| ...youth hostel | **...albergue de juventud** | ahl-**behr**-gay day hoo-behn-**tood** |
| ...restaurant | **...restaurante** | ray-stoh-**rahn**-tay |
| ...supermarket | **...supermercado** | soo-pehr-mehr-**kah**-doh |
| ...bank | **...banco** | **bahn**-koh |
| Where is the...? | **¿Dónde está la...?** | **dohn**-day ay-**stah** lah |
| ...pharmacy | **...farmacia** | far-mah-**thee**-ah |
| ...train station | **...estación de trenes** | ay-stah-thee-**ohn** day **tray**-nays |
| ...tourist information office | **...Oficina de Turismo** | oh-fee-**thee**-nah day too-**rees**-moh |

| Where are the toilets? | ¿Dónde están los aseos / servicios? | **dohn**-day ay-**stahn** lohs ah-**say**-ohs / sehr-**bee**-thee-ohs |
| men / women | **hombres / mujeres, caballeros / damas** | **ohm**-brays / moo-**heh**-rays, kah-bah-**yay**-rohs / **dah**-mahs |

## How much?

| How much is it? | ¿Cuánto cuesta? | **kwahn**-toh **kway**-stah |
| Write it? | ¿Me lo escribe? | may loh ay-**skree**-bay |
| Cheap(er). | (Más) barato. | (mahs) bah-**rah**-toh |
| Cheapest. | El más barato. | ehl mahs bah-**rah**-toh |
| Is it free? | ¿Es gratis? | ays grah-**tees** |
| Is it included? | ¿Está incluido? | ay-**stah** een-kloo-**ee**-doh |
| Do you have...? | ¿Tiene...? | tee-**ehn**-ay |
| Where can I buy...? | ¿Dónde puedo comprar...? | **dohn**-day **pway**-doh kohm-**prar** |
| I want... | Quiero... | kee-**ehr**-oh |
| We want... | Queremos... | kehr-**ay**-mohs |
| ...this. | ...esto. | **ay**-stoh |
| ...just a little. | ...un poquito. | oon poh-**kee**-toh |
| ...more. | ...más. | mahs |
| ...a ticket. | ...un billete. | oon bee-**yeh**-tay |
| ...a room. | ...una habitación. | **oo**-nah ah-bee-tah-thee-**ohn** |
| ...the bill. | ...la cuenta. | lah **kwayn**-tah |

## How many?

| one | uno | **oo**-noh |
| two | dos | dohs |
| three | tres | trays |
| four | cuatro | **kwah**-troh |

| five | **cinco** | **theen**-koh |
| six | **seis** | says |
| seven | **siete** | see-**eh**-tay |
| eight | **ocho** | **oh**-choh |
| nine | **nueve** | **nway**-bay |
| ten | **diez** | dee-**ayth** |

You'll find more to count on in the Numbers chapter.

## When?

| At what time? | **¿A qué hora?** | ah kay **oh**-rah |
| Just a moment. | **Un momento.** | oon moh-**mehn**-toh |
| Now. | **Ahora.** | ah-**oh**-rah |
| Soon. | **Pronto.** | **prohn**-toh |
| Later. | **Más tarde.** | mahs **tar**-day |
| Today. / Tomorrow. | **Hoy. / Mañana.** | oy / mahn-**yah**-nah |

Be creative. You can combine these survival phrases to say: "Two, please," or "No, thank you," or "I'd like a cheap hotel," or "Cheaper, please?" Please is a magic word in any language. If you want something and you don't know the word for it, just point and say, *"Por favor"* (Please).

## Struggling with Spanish:

| Do you speak English? | **¿Habla usted inglés?** | ah-blah oo-**stehd** een-**glays** |
| A teeny weeny bit? | **¿Ni un poquito?** | nee oon poh-**kee**-toh |
| Please speak English. | **Hable en inglés, por favor.** | ah-**blay** ayn een-**glays** por fah-**bor** |
| You speak English well. | **Usted habla bien el inglés.** | oo-**stehd** ah-**blah** bee-**yehn** ehl een-**glays** |

| I don't speak Spanish. | No hablo español. | noh **ah**-bloh ay-spahn-**yohl** |
| I speak a little Spanish. | Hablo un poco de español. | **ah**-bloh oon **poh**-koh day ay-spahn-**yohl** |
| What is this in Spanish? | ¿Cómo se dice esto en español? | **koh**-moh say **dee**-thay **ay**-stoh ayn ay-spahn-**yohl** |
| Repeat? | Repita? | ray-**pee**-tah |
| Please speak slowly. | Por favor hable despacio. | por fah-**bor** ah-blay day-**spah**-thee-oh |
| Slower. | Más despacio. | mahs day-**spah**-thee-oh |
| I understand. | Comprendo. | kohm-**prehn**-doh |
| I don't understand. | No comprendo. | noh kohm-**prehn**-doh |
| Do you understand? | ¿Comprende? | kohm-**prehn**-day |
| What does this mean? | ¿Qué significa esto? | kay sig-**nee**-fee-kah **ay**-stoh |
| Write it? | ¿Me lo escribe? | may loh ay-**skree**-bay |
| Does someone there speak English? | ¿Habla alguien inglés? | **ah**-blah **ahl**-gee-ehn een-**glays** |
| Who speaks English? | ¿Quién habla inglés? | kee-**ehn ah**-blah een-**glays** |

## Common questions in Spanish:

| How much? | ¿Cuánto? | **kwahn**-toh |
| How many? | ¿Cuánto? | **kwahn**-toh |
| How long...? | ¿Cuánto tiempo...? | **kwahn**-toh tee-**ehm**-poh |
| ...is the trip | ...es el viaje | ays ehl bee-**ah**-*hay* |
| How many minutes? | ¿Cuántos minutos? | **kwahn**-tohs mee-**noo**-tohs |
| How many hours? | ¿Cuántos horas? | **kwahn**-tohs oh-rahs |
| How far? | ¿A qué distancia? | ah kay dees-**tahn**-thee-ah |
| How? | ¿Cómo? | **koh**-moh |
| Is it possible? | ¿Es posible? | ays poh-**see**-blay |
| Is it necessary? | ¿Es necesario? | ays nay-thay-**sah**-ree-oh |
| Can you help me? | ¿Me puede ayudar? | may **pway**-day ah-yoo-**dar** |

| What? | ¿Qué? | kay |
|---|---|---|
| What? (didn't hear) | ¿Cómo? | **koh**-moh |
| What is this? | ¿Qué es esto? | kay ays **ay**-stoh |
| What is better? | ¿Qué es mejor? | kay ays may-*hor* |
| What's going on? | ¿Qué pasa? | kay **pah**-sah |
| When? | ¿Cuándo? | **kwahn**-doh |
| What time is it? | ¿Qué hora es? | kay **oh**-rah ays |
| At what time? | ¿A qué hora? | ah kay **oh**-rah |
| On time? Late? | ¿Puntual? ¿Tarde? | poon-too-**ahl** / **tar**-day |
| What time does this...? | ¿A qué hora...? | ah kay **oh**-rah |
| ...open | ...abren | **ah**-brehn |
| ...close | ...cierran | thee-**ay**-rahn |
| Do you have...? | ¿Tiene...? | tee-**ehn**-ay |
| Anything else? | ¿Algo más? | **ahl**-goh mahs |
| Where is...? | ¿Dónde está...? | **dohn**-day ay-**stah** |
| Where are...? | ¿Dónde están...? | **dohn**-day ay-**stahn** |
| Where can I find / buy...? | ¿Dónde puedo encontrar / comprar...? | **dohn**-day **pway**-doh ayn-kohn-**trar** / kohm-**prar** |
| Who? | ¿Quién? | kee-**ehn** |
| Why? | ¿Por qué? | por kay |
| Why not? | ¿Por qué no? | por kay noh |
| Yes or no? | ¿Sí o no? | see oh noh |

To prompt a simple answer, ask, "*¿Sí o no?*" (Yes or no?). To turn a word or sentence into a question, ask it in a questioning tone. A simple way to ask, "Where are the toilets?" is to say, "*¿Aseos?*"

# El yin and yang:

|  |  |  |
|---|---|---|
| cheap / expensive | barato / caro | bah-**rah**-toh / **kah**-roh |
| big / small | grande / pequeño | **grahn**-day / pay-**kayn**-yoh |
| hot / cold | caliente / frío | kahl-**yehn**-tay / **free**-oh |
| open / closed | abierto / cerrado | ah-bee-**yehr**-toh / thehr-**rah**-doh |
| entrance / exit | entrada / salida | ayn-**trah**-dah / sah-**lee**-dah |
| arrive / depart | llegar / salir | yay-**gar** / sah-**leer** |
| early / late | temprano / tarde | tehm-**prah**-noh / **tar**-day |
| soon / later | pronto / más tarde | **prohn**-toh / mahs **tar**-day |
| fast / slow | rápido / despacio | **rah**-pee-doh / day-**spah**-thee-oh |
| here / there | aquí / allí | ah-**kee** / ah-**yee** |
| near / far | cerca / lejos | **thehr**-kah / **lay**-hohs |
| indoors / outdoors | dentro / afuera | **dayn**-troh / ah-foo-**ehr**-ah |
| good / bad | bueno / malo | **bway**-noh / **mah**-loh |
| best / worst | mejor / peor | may-**hor** / pay-**or** |
| a little / lots | un poco / mucho | oon **poh**-koh / **moo**-choh |
| more / less | más / menos | mahs / **may**-nohs |
| mine / yours | mío / suyo | **mee**-oh / **soo**-yoh |
| everybody / nobody | todos / nadie | **toh**-dohs / **nah**-dee-ay |
| easy / difficult | fácil / difícil | **fah**-theel / dee-**fee**-theel |
| left / right | izquierda / derecha | eeth-kee-**ehr**-dah / day-**ray**-chah |
| up / down | arriba / abajo | ah-**ree**-bah / ah-**bah**-hoh |
| above / below | encima / debajo | en-**thee**-mah / day-**bah**-hoh |
| young / old | joven / viejo | **hoh**-behn / bee-**ay**-hoh |
| new / old | nuevo / viejo | noo-**ay**-boh / bee-**ay**-hoh |
| heavy / light | pesado / ligero | pay-**sah**-doh / lee-**hehr**-oh |
| dark / light | oscuro / claro | oh-**skoo**-roh / **klah**-roh |
| happy / sad | felice / triste | fay-lee-chay / **tree**-stay |

| beautiful / ugly | bonito / feo | boh-**nee**-toh / **fay**-oh |
| nice / mean | simpático[a] / antipático[a] | seem-pah-**tee**-koh / ahn-tee-**pah**-tee-koh |
| smart / stupid | listo / estúpido | **lee**-stoh / ay-**stoo**-pee-doh |
| vacant / occupied | libre / ocupado | **lee**-bray / oh-koo-**pah**-doh |
| with / without | con / sin | kohn / seen |

## Big little words in Spain:

| I | yo | yoh |
| you (formal) | usted | oo-**stehd** |
| you (informal) | tú | too |
| we | nosotros | noh-**soh**-trohs |
| he / she | él / ella | ehl / ay-yah |
| they | ellos / ellas | ay-yohs / ay-yahs |
| and | y | ee |
| at | a | ah |
| because | porque | **por**-kay |
| but | pero | **pay**-roh |
| by (via) | por | por |
| for | para | **pah**-rah |
| from | de | day |
| here | aquí | ah-**kee** |
| if | si | see |
| in | en | ayn |
| not | no | noh |
| now | ahora | ah-**oh**-rah |
| only | solo | **soh**-loh |
| or | o | oh |
| this | esto | ay-stoh |
| to | a | ah |
| very | muy | **moo**-ee |

## Alphabet:

In case you want to spell your name out loud or participate in a spelling bee...

| | | | | | | | | |
|---|---|---|---|---|---|---|---|
| **A** | ah | **H** | **ah**-chay | **O** | oh | **V** | bay |
| **B** | bay | **I** | ee | **P** | pay | **W** | bay **doh**-blay |
| **C** | thay | **J** | *hoh*-tah | **Q** | koo | **X** | **ay**-*h*ees |
| **D** | day | **K** | kah | **R** | **ayr**-ay | **Y** | ee-**gryay**-gah |
| **E** | ay | **L** | **ayl**-yay | **S** | **ays**-ay | **Z** | **thay**-tah |
| **F** | **ayf**-fay | **M** | **aym**-ay | **T** | tay | | |
| **G** | gay | **N** | **ayn**-yay | **U** | oo | | |

## Spanish names for places:

| Spain | **España** | ay-**spahn**-yah |
|---|---|---|
| Madrid | **Madrid** | mah-**dreed** |
| Seville | **Sevilla** | seh-**vee**-yah |
| Gibraltar | **Gibraltar** | *h*ee-brahl-**tar** |
| Portugal | **Portugal** | por-too-**gahl** |
| Lisbon | **Lisboa** | lees-**boh**-ah |
| Austria | **Austria** | **ow**-stree-ah |
| France | **Francia** | **frahn**-thee-ah |
| Germany | **Alemania** | ah-lay-**mahn**-yah |
| Great Britain | **Gran Bretaña** | grahn bray-**tahn**-yah |
| Italy | **Italia** | ee-**tah**-lee-ah |
| Morocco | **Marruecos** | mar-**way**-kohs |
| Switzerland | **Suiza** | soo-**ee**-thah |
| United States | **Estados Unidos** | ay-**stah**-dohs oo-**nee**-dohs |
| Canada | **Canadá** | kah-nah-**dah** |
| Mexico | **Méjico** | **may**-*h*ee-koh |
| the world | **el mundo** | ehl **moon**-doh |

# Numbers

| | | |
|---|---|---|
| 0 | cero | theh-roh |
| 1 | uno | oo-noh |
| 2 | dos | dohs |
| 3 | tres | trays |
| 4 | cuatro | kwah-troh |
| 5 | cinco | theen-koh |
| 6 | seis | says |
| 7 | siete | see-eh-tay |
| 8 | ocho | oh-choh |
| 9 | nueve | nway-bay |
| 10 | diez | dee-ayth |
| 11 | once | ohn-thay |
| 12 | doce | doh-thay |
| 13 | trece | tray-thay |
| 14 | catorce | kah-tor-thay |
| 15 | quince | keen-thay |
| 16 | dieciséis | dee-ay-thee-says |
| 17 | diecisiete | dee-ay-thee-see-eh-tay |
| 18 | dieciocho | dee-ay-thee-oh-choh |
| 19 | diecinueve | dee-ay-thee-nway-bay |
| 20 | veinte | bayn-tay |
| 21 | veintiuno | bayn-tee-oo-noh |
| 22 | veintidós | bayn-tee-dohs |
| 23 | veintitrés | bayn-tee-trays |
| 30 | treinta | trayn-tah |
| 31 | treinta y uno | trayn-tah ee oo-noh |

| | | |
|---|---|---|
| 40 | **cuarenta** | kwah-**rehn**-tah |
| 41 | **cuarenta y uno** | kwah-**rehn**-tah ee **oo**-noh |
| 50 | **cincuenta** | theen-**kwehn**-tah |
| 60 | **sesenta** | say-**sehn**-tah |
| 70 | **setenta** | say-**tehn**-tah |
| 80 | **ochenta** | oh-**chehn**-tah |
| 90 | **noventa** | noh-**behn**-tah |
| 100 | **cien** | thee-**ehn** |
| 101 | **ciento uno** | thee-**ehn**-toh **oo**-noh |
| 102 | **ciento dos** | thee-**ehn**-toh dohs |
| 200 | **doscientos** | dohs-thee-**ehn**-tohs |
| 1000 | **mil** | meel |
| 2000 | **dos mil** | dohs meel |
| 2001 | **dos mil uno** | dohs meel **oo**-noh |
| 10,000 | **diez mil** | dee-**ayth** meel |
| million | **millón** | mee-**yohn** |
| billion | **mil millones** | meel mee-**yoh**-nays |
| first | **primero** | pree-**may**-roh |
| second | **segundo** | say-**goon**-doh |
| third | **tercero** | tehr-**thehr**-oh |
| half | **mitad** | mee-**tahd** |
| 100% | **cien por cien** | the-**ehn** por thee-**ehn** |
| number one | **número uno** | **noo**-may-roh **oo**-noh |

*Once* (eleven) is considered a lucky number in Spain. It's the word you'll see on booths that sell tickets for the national lottery, run by and for the blind.

# Money

|  |  |  |
|---|---|---|
| Can you change dollars? | ¿Me puede cambiar dólares? | may pway-day kahm-bee-ar doh-lah-rays |
| What is your exchange rate for dollars...? | ¿A cuanto pagan el dólar...? | ah kwahn-toh pah-gahn ehl doh-lar |
| ...in traveler's checks | ...en cheques de viajero | ayn chay-kays day bee-ah-hay-roh |
| What is the commission? | ¿Cuánto es la comisión? | kwahn-toh ays lah koh-mee-see-ohn |
| Any extra fee? | ¿Tiene cuota extra? | tee-ehn-ay kwoh-tah ayk-strah |
| I want... | Quiero... | kee-ehr-oh |
| ...small bills. | ...billetes pequeños. | bee-yeh-tays pay-kayn-yohs |
| ...large bills. | ...billetes grandes. | bee-yeh-tays grahn-days |
| ...coins. | ...monedas. | moh-nay-dahs |
| Is this a mistake? | ¿Es esto un error? | ays ay-stoh oon ehr-ror |
| I'm rich / poor. | Soy rico[a] / pobre. | soy ree-koh / poh-bray |
| I'm broke. | No tengo dinero. | noh tayn-goh dee-nay-roh |
| 55 pesetas | cincuenta y cinco pesetas | theen-kwehn-tah ee theen-koh peh-say-tahs |
| euro | euro | yoo-roh |
| Where is a cash machine? | ¿Dónde está el cajero automático? | dohn-day ay-stah kah-hay-oh ow-toh-mah-tee-koh |

## Key money words:

|  |  |  |
|---|---|---|
| bank | banco | bahn-koh |
| money | dinero | dee-nay-roh |

| | | |
|---|---|---|
| change money | **cambio de moneda** | kahm-bee-oh day moh-**nay**-dah |
| exchange | **cambio** | **kahm**-bee-oh |
| buy / sell | **comprar / vender** | kohm-**prar** / bayn-**dehr** |
| commission | **comisión** | koh-mee-see-**ohn** |
| traveler's check | **cheque de viajero** | **chay**-kay day bee-ah-**hay**-roh |
| credit card | **tarjeta de crédito** | tar-**hay**-tah day **kray**-dee-toh |
| cash advance | **adelanto de dinero** | ah-day-**lahn**-toh day dee-**nay**-roh |
| cash machine | **cajero automático** | kah-**hay**-roh ow-toh-**mah**-tee-koh |
| cashier | **cajero** | kah-**hehr**-oh |
| cash | **efectivo** | ay-fehk-**tee**-voh |
| bills | **billetes** | bee-**yeh**-tays |
| coins | **monedas** | moh-**nay**-dahs |
| receipt | **recibo** | ray-**thee**-boh |

Banks are open 9:00-2:00 p.m. Monday through Friday. Traveler's checks are widely accepted, but commissions are steep (starting around $5). Big department stores like *El Corte Inglés* in Madrid exchange money at decent rates during their business hours. *Casas de cambio* (exchange offices) are open long hours, but you'll pay for the convenience with a lousy rate or sky-high commission.

You'll get the best rates by using an ATM or debit card to withdraw money from cash machines. When using a *cajero automático* (cash machine), you'll probably see these words: *anotación* (enter), *continuar* (enter), *retirar* (withdraw), *confirmar* (affirm), *corregir* (correct), *borrar* (erase), and *cancelar* (cancel). Your PIN number is a *número clave*.

Spain's currency, the *peseta*, will go extinct in July, 2002, when the common currency throughout Europe's 11-country Euroland will be the *euro* (€ ).

# Time

| What time is it? | ¿Qué hora es? | kay **oh**-rah ays |
|---|---|---|
| It's... | Son las... | sohn lahs |
| ...8:00 in the morning. | ...ocho de la mañana. | **oh**-choh day lah mahn-**yah**-nah |
| ...16:00. | ...dieciséis. | dee-ay-thee-**says** |
| ...4:00 in the afternoon. | ...4:00 de la tarde. | kwah-troh day lah tar-day |
| ...10:30 (in the evening). | ...diez y media (de la noche). | dee-**ayth** ee may-dee-ah (day lah noh-chay) |
| ...a quarter past nine. | ...nueve y cuarto. | nway-bay ee kwar-toh |
| ...a quarter to eleven. | ...once menos cuarto. | ohn-thay **may**-nohs kwar-toh |
| ...noon. | ...doce / mediodia. | **doh**-thay / may-dee-oh-**dee**-ah |
| ...midnight. | ...doce de la noche. | **doh**-thay day lah **noh**-chay |
| It's... | Es... | ays |
| ...sunrise. | ...amanecer. | ah-mah-nay-**thehr** |
| ...sunset. | ...puesta de sol. | **pway**-stah day sohl |
| ...early / late. | ...temprano / tarde. | tehm-**prah**-noh / **tar**-day |
| ...on time. | ...puntual. | poon-too-**ahl** |

In Spain, the 24-hour clock (military time) is used mainly for train, bus, and ferry schedules. Friends use the same "clock" we do. You'd meet a friend at 3:00 *de la tarde* (in the afternoon) to catch a train at 15:15. You'll hear people say *"Buenas tardes"* (Good afternoon/evening) starting about 2:00 p.m. You won't hear *"Buenas noches"* (Good night) until around 10 p.m.

## Timely words:

| | | |
|---|---|---|
| minute | **minuto** | mee-**noo**-toh |
| hour | **hora** | **oh**-rah |
| in the morning | **por la mañana** | por lah mahn-**yah**-nah |
| in the afternoon | **por la tarde** | por lah **tar**-day |
| in the evening | **por la noche** | por lah **noh**-chay |
| night | **noche** | **noh**-chay |
| day | **día** | **dee**-ah |
| today | **hoy** | oy |
| yesterday | **ayer** | ah-**yehr** |
| tomorrow | **mañana** | mahn-**yah**-nah |
| tomorrow morning | **mañana por la mañana** | mahn-**yah**-nah por lah mahn-**yah**-nah |
| anytime | **a cualquier hora** | ah kwahl-kee-**ehr oh**-rah |
| immediately | **inmediatamente** | een-may-dee-ah-tah-**mehn**-tay |
| in one hour | **dentro de una hora** | **dehn**-troh day **oo**-nah **oh**-rah |
| every hour | **cada hora** | **kah**-dah **oh**-rah |
| every day | **cada día** | **kah**-dah **dee**-ah |
| last | **último** | **ool**-tee-moh |
| this | **este** | **ay**-stay |
| next | **próximo** | **prohk**-see-moh |
| May 15 | **15 de mayo** | **keen**-thay day **mah**-yoh |
| high season | **temporada alta** | taym-poh-**rah**-dah **ahl**-tah |
| low season | **temporada baja** | taym-poh-**rah**-dah **bah**-*h*ah |
| in the future | **en el futuro** | ayn ehl foo-**too**-roh |
| in the past | **en el pasado** | ayn ehl pah-**sah**-doh |

| week | **semana** | **say-mah**-nah |
| Monday | **lunes** | **loo**-nays |
| Tuesday | **martes** | **mar**-tays |
| Wednesday | **miércoles** | mee-ehr-koh-lays |
| Thursday | **jueves** | *h*way-bays |
| Friday | **viernes** | bee-**ehr**-nays |
| Saturday | **sábado** | **sah**-bah-doh |
| Sunday | **domingo** | doh-**meen**-goh |
| | | |
| month | **mes** | mays |
| January | **enero** | ay-**nay**-roh |
| February | **febrero** | fay-**bray**-roh |
| March | **marzo** | **mar**-thoh |
| April | **abril** | **ah**-breel |
| May | **mayo** | **mah**-yoh |
| June | **junio** | *h*oon-yoh |
| July | **julio** | *h*ool-yoh |
| August | **agosto** | ah-**goh**-stoh |
| September | **septiembre** | sehp-tee-**ehm**-bray |
| October | **octubre** | ohk-**too**-bray |
| November | **noviembre** | noh-bee-**ehm**-bray |
| December | **diciembre** | dee-thee-**ehm**-bray |
| | | |
| year | **año** | **ahn**-yoh |
| spring | **primavera** | pree-mah-**bay**-rah |
| summer | **verano** | bay-**rah**-noh |
| fall | **otoño** | oh-**tohn**-yoh |
| winter | **invierno** | een-bee-**ehr**-noh |

TIME

## Spanish holidays and happy days:

| holiday | **festivo** | fay-**stee**-boh |
|---|---|---|
| national holiday | **festivo nacional** | fay-**stee**-boh nah-thee-oh-**nahl** |
| religious holiday | **día religioso** | **dee**-ah ray-lee-_hee_-oh-soh |
| Is today / tomorrow a holiday? | **¿Es hoy / mañana un día festivo?** | ehs oy / mahn-**yah**-nah oon **dee**-ah fay-**stee**-boh |
| What is the holiday? | **¿Qué fiesta es?** | kay fee-**eh**-stah ehs |
| Easter | **Pascuas** | **pahs**-kwahs |
| Merry Christmas! | **¡Feliz Navidad!** | fay-**leeth** nah-bee-**dahd** |
| Happy new year! | **¡Feliz Año Nuevo!** | fay-**leeth** ahn-yoh **nway**-boh |
| Happy anniversary! | **¡Feliz aniversario!** | fay-**leeth** ah-nee-behr-**sah**-ree-oh |
| Happy birthday! | **¡Feliz cumpleaños!** | fay-**leeth** koom-play-**ahn**-yohs |

The Spanish sing "Happy birthday" to the same tune we do, but they don't fill in the person's name. Here are the words: _Cumpleaños feliz, cumpleaños feliz, te deseamos todos cumpleaños, cumpleaños feliz._

Other happy days in Spain include _Semana Santa_ (Holy Week), leading up to Easter. It's a festive time throughout Iberia, especially in Sevilla. _Corpus Christi_ comes early in June, _Ascensión de María_ on August 15th, and _Día de la Hispanidad_, Spain's national holiday, is on October 12th.

# Transportation

**TRANSPORTATION**

## Trains:

| Is this the line for...? | ¿Es esta la fila para...? | ays **ay**-stah lah **fee**-lah **pah**-rah |
| ...tickets | ...billetes | bee-**yeh**-tays |
| ...reservations | ...reservas | ray-sehr-bahs |
| How much is a ticket to...? | ¿Cuánto cuesta el billete a...? | **kwahn**-toh **kway**-stah ehl bee-**yeh**-tay ah |
| A ticket to ___. | Un billete para ___. | oon bee-**yeh**-tay **pah**-rah |
| When is the next train? | ¿Cuándo es el siguiente tren? | **kwahn**-doh ays ehl seeg-ee-**ehn**-tay trayn |
| I want to leave... | Quiero salir... | kee-**ehr**-oh sah-**leer** |
| I want to arrive... | Quiero llegar... | kee-**ehr**-oh yay-**gar** |
| ...by ___. | ...a las ___. | ah lahs |
| ...in the morning. | ...por la mañana. | por lah mahn-**yah**-nah |
| ...in the afternoon. | ...por la tarde. | por lah **tar**-day |
| ...in the evening. | ...por la noche. | por lah **noh**-chay |
| Is there a...? | ¿Hay un...? | ī oon |
| ...earlier train | ...tren más temprano | trayn mahs tehm-**prah**-noh |
| ...later train | ...tren más tarde | trayn mahs **tar**-day |

| | | |
|---|---|---|
| ...overnight train | ...tren nocturno | trayn nohk-**toor**-noh |
| ...supplement | ...suplemento | soo-play-**mehn**-toh |
| Does my railpass cover the supplement? | ¿Mi eurorail incluye el suplemento? | mee **yoo**-roh-rayl een-**kloo**-yay ehl soo-play-**mehn**-toh |
| Is there a discount for...? | ¿Tienen descuento para...? | tee-**ehn**-nehn days-**kwehn**-toh **pah**-rah |
| ...youths | ...jovenes | **h**oh-beh-nays |
| ...seniors | ...la tercera edad | lah tehr-**thay**-rah ay-**dahd** |
| Is a reservation required? | ¿Se requiere reserva? | say ray-kee-**eh**-ray ray-**sehr**-bah |
| I'd like to reserve... | Quiero reservar... | kee-**ehr**-oh ray-sehr-**bar** |
| ...a seat. | ...un asiento. | oon ah-see-**ehn**-toh |
| ...a berth (couchette). | ...una litera. | **oo**-nah **lee**-tay-rah |
| ...a first-class sleeper. | ...una coche cama. | **oo**-nah **koh**-chah **kah**-mah |
| Where does (the train) leave from? | ¿De dónde sale? | day **dohn**-day **sah**-lay |
| What track? | ¿Qué vía? | kay **bee**-ah |
| On time? Late? | ¿Puntual? ¿Tarde? | poon-too-**ahl** / **tar**-day |
| When will it arrive? | ¿Cuándo tiene su llegada? | **kwahn**-doh tee-**ehn**-ay soo yay-**gah**-dah |
| Is it direct? | ¿Es directo? | ays dee-**rehk**-toh |
| Must I transfer? | ¿Tengo que cambiar? | **tayn**-goh kay kahm-bee-**ar** |
| When? Where? | ¿Cuándo? ¿Dónde? | **kwahn**-doh / **dohn**-day |
| Which train to...? | ¿Qué tren para...? | kay trayn **pah**-rah |
| Which train car to...? | ¿Qué vagón para...? | kay bah-**gohn pah**-rah |
| Where is first class? | ¿Dónde está primera clase? | **dohn**-day ay-**stah** pree-**may**-rah **klah**-say |
| ...front / middle / back | ...frente / centro / detrás | **frayn**-tay / **thayn**-troh / day-**trahs** |
| Is this (seat) free? | ¿Está libre? | ay-**stah lee**-bray |

| | | |
|---|---|---|
| Save my place? | ¿Guardeme mi asiento? | **gwar**-day-may mee ah-see-**ehn**-toh |
| Where are you going? | ¿A dónde va? | ah **dohn**-day vah |
| I'm going to... | Voy a... | boy ah |
| Tell me when to get off? | ¿Digame cuándo tengo que bajarme? | **dee**-gah-may **kwahn**-doh **tayn**-goh kay bah-**har**-may |

## Ticket talk:

| | | |
|---|---|---|
| ticket window | Venta de Billetes | **bayn**-tah day bee-**yeh**-tays |
| reservations window | Reservas | ray-**sehr**-bahs |
| national / international | Nacional / Internacional | nah-thee-oh-**nahl** / een-tehr-nah-thee-oh-**nahl** |
| ticket | billete | bee-**yeh**-tay |
| one way | de ida | day **ee**-dah |
| roundtrip | ida y vuelta | **ee**-dah ee **bwehl**-tah |
| first class | primera clase | pree-**may**-rah **klah**-say |
| second class | segunda clase | say-**goon**-dah **klah**-say |
| non-smoking | no fumadores | noh foo-mah-**doh**-rays |
| reduced fare | tarifa reducida | tah-**ree**-fah ray-doo-**thee**-dah |
| validate | válido | **vah**-lee-doh |
| schedule | horario | oh-**rah**-ree-oh |
| departure | salida | sah-**lee**-dah |
| direct | directo | dee-**rehk**-toh |
| transfer | transbordo | trahns-**bor**-doh |
| connection | enlace | ayn-**lah**-thay |
| express service | expreso | ayk-**spray**-soh |
| with supplement | con suplemento | kohn soo-play-**mehn**-toh |
| reservation | reserva | ray-**sehr**-bah |
| seat... | asiento... | ah-see-**ehn**-toh |
| ...by the window | ...con ventana | kohn bayn-**tah**-nah |
| ...on the aisle | ...cerca pasillo | **thehr**-kah pah-**see**-yoh |
| berth... | litera... | **lee**-tay-rah |
| ...upper | ...alta | **ahl**-tah |
| ...middle | ...media | **may**-thee-oh |
| ...lower | ...baja | **bah**-hah |

TRANSPORTATION

| | | |
|---|---|---|
| refund | **devolución** | day-voh-loo-thee-**ohn** |

## *At the train station:*

| | | |
|---|---|---|
| Spanish Railways | **R.E.N.F.E.** | **rehn**-fay |
| train station | **estación de tren** | ay-stah-thee-**ohn** day trayn |
| train information | **información de trenes** | een-for-mah-thee-**ohn** day **tray**-nays |
| train | **tren** | trayn |
| high-speed trains | **Talgo, AVE** | **tahl**-goh, **ah**-vay |
| arrival | **llegada** | yay-**gah**-dah |
| departure | **salida** | sah-**lee**-dah |
| delay | **retraso** | ray-**trah**-soh |
| toilets | **aseos** | ah-**say**-ohs |
| waiting room | **sala de espera** | **sah**-lah day ay-**spay**-rah |
| lockers | **casilleros** | kah-see-**yay**-rohs |
| baggage check room | **consigna** | kohn-**seen**-yah |
| lost and found office | **oficina de objetos perdidos** | oh-fee-**thee**-nah day ohb-**hay**-tohs pehr-**dee**-dohs |
| tourist information office | **Oficina de Turismo** | oh-fee-**thee**-nah day too-**rees**-moh |
| to the platforms | **a los andenes** | ah lohs **ahn**-deh-nays |
| platform | **andén** | ahn-**dayn** |
| track | **vía** | **bee**-ah |
| train car | **vagón, coche** | bah-**gohn**, **koh**-chay |
| dining car | **coche comedor** | **koh**-chay koh-may-**dor** |
| sleeper car | **coche cama** | **koh**-chay **kah**-mah |
| conductor | **conductor** | kohn-dook-**tor** |

*Reading Spanish train schedules and tickets:*

| | |
|---|---|
| a | to |
| aviso | advisory (listing changes) |
| con retraso | late |
| clase | class |
| coche | car |
| de | from |
| destino | destination |
| diario | daily |
| días | days |
| días de semana | weekdays |
| días laborales | workdays (Monday-Saturday) |
| domingo | Sunday |
| domingos y festivos | Sunday and holidays |
| excepto | except |
| fecha | date |
| festivos | holiday |
| hasta | until |
| hora salida | departure time |
| llegadas | arrivals |
| no | not |
| plaza | seat, place |
| sábado | Saturday |
| salidas | departures |
| salidas immediatas | immediate departures |
| solo | only |
| también | too |
| tipo de tren | type of train |
| todos | every |
| via | track (or via) |
| 1-5, 6, 7 | Monday-Friday, Saturday, Sunday |

Spanish schedules use the 24-hour clock. It's like American time until noon. After that, subtract twelve and add p.m. So 13:00 is 1 p.m., 19:00 is 7 p.m., and midnight is 24:00. If your train is scheduled to depart at 00:01, it'll leave one minute after midnight.

Spanish trains require reservations for longer trips (even if you have a Eurailpass and the train is empty). When you arrive in a town, make your out-bound reservation right away. In bigger cities, the downtown RENFE (Spanish Railways) office is sometimes more efficient at making reservations than the train station.

Trains in Spain range in speed from glacial to gunshot. The *regional* and *correo* are milk runs—you'll curdle. The *cercania* is a commuter train for big-city workers. The *rapido, tranvia, semi-directo,* and *expreso* are not as rapido as they sound. The *Intercity* and *Electro* are faster. The comfortable *Talgo* is even speedier, but can't beat the *AVE* (**ah**-vay) Spain's bullet train, connecting Madrid and Sevilla in just 3 hours (85% covered by Eurailpass).

## Buses and subways:

| | | |
|---|---|---|
| How do I get to...? | ¿Cómo llego a...? | koh-moh yay-goh ah |
| Which bus to...? | ¿Qué autocar para...? | kay ow-toh-kar pah-rah |
| Does it stop at...? | ¿Tiene parada en....? | tee-ehn-ay pah-rah-dah ayn |
| Which metro stop for...? | ¿Qué parada de metro para...? | kay pah-rah-dah day may-troh pah-rah |
| Which direction for...? | ¿Qué dirección para...? | kay kee-rehk-thee-ohn pah-rah |
| Must I transfer? | ¿Tengo que cambiar? | tayn-goh kay kahm-bee-ar |
| How much is a ticket? | ¿Cuánto cuesta el billete? | kwahn-toh kway-stah ehl bee-yeh-tay |
| Where can I buy a ticket? | ¿Dónde puedo comprar un billete? | dohn-day pway-doh kohm-prar oon bee-yeh-tay |

| When is the...? | ¿Cuando sale...? | kwahn-doh sah-lay |
| ...first | ...primero | pree-may-roh |
| ...next | ...siguiente | seeg-ee-ehn-tay |
| ...last | ...último | ool-tee-moh |
| ...bus / subway | ...autobús / metro | ow-toh-boos / may-troh |
| What's the frequency per hour / day? | ¿Qué frecuencia tiene por hora / día? | kay fray-kwayn-thee-ah tee-ehn-ay por oh-rah / dee-ah |
| I'm going to... | Voy a... | boy ah |
| Tell me when to get off? | ¿Digame cuándo tengo que bajarme? | dee-gah-may kwahn-doh tayn-goh kay bah-har-may |
| Is there a bus to the airport? | ¿Hay un autobús que va hacia el aeropuerto? | ī oon ow-toh-boos kay bah ah-thee-ah ehl ah-ay-roh-pwehr-toh |
| Is there a bus from the airport to...? | ¿Hay un autobús que va desde el aeropuerto a...? | ī oon ow-toh-boos kay bah dehs-day ehl ah-ay-roh-pwehr-toh ah |

**TRANSPORTATION**

## Key bus and subway words:

| ticket | billete | bee-yeh-tay |
| city bus | autobús | ow-toh-boos |
| long-distance bus | autocar | ow-toh-kar |
| bus stop | parada de autobus | pah-rah-dah day ow-toh-boos |
| bus station | estación de autobuses | ay-stah-thee-ohn day ow-toh-boo-says |
| subway | metro | may-troh |
| entrance / exit | entrada / salida | ayn-trah-dah / sah-lee-dah |
| stop | parada | pah-rah-dah |
| map | mapa | mah-pah |
| schedule | horario | oh-rah-ree-oh |
| daily | diario | dee-ah-ree-oh |
| direct | directo | dee-rehk-toh |
| pick-pocket | carterista | kar-tay-ree-stah |

Buses (*autocars*) connect many smaller towns better and cheaper than trains. *Autopistas* are fast buses that take freeway routes. Tourist information offices have bus schedules. Subways are handy in Madrid and Barcelona.

## Taxis:

| | | |
|---|---|---|
| Taxi! | ¡Taxi! | **tahk**-see |
| Can you call a taxi? | ¿Puede llamarme a un taxi? | **pway**-day yah-**mar**-may ah oon **tahk**-see |
| Where is a taxi stand? | ¿Dónde está la parada de taxi? | **dohn**-day ay-**stah** lah pah-**rah**-dah day **tahk**-see |
| Are you free? | ¿Está libre? | ay-**stah** lee-bray |
| Occupied. | Ocupado. | oh-koo-**pah**-doh |
| How much will it cost to go to...? | ¿Cuánto me costará...? | **kwahn**-toh may koh-stah-**rah** |
| ...the airport | ...al aeropuerto | ahl ah-ay-roh-**pwehr**-toh |
| ...the train station | ...a la estación de trenes | ah lah ay-stah-thee-**ohn** day **tray**-nays |
| ...this address | ...a esta dirección | ah **ay**-stah dee-rehk-thee-**ohn** |
| Too much. | Demasiado. | day-mah-see-**ah**-doh |
| This is all I have. | Esto es todo lo que tengo. | **ay**-stoh ays **toh**-doh loh kay **tayn**-goh |
| Can you take ___ people? | ¿Puede llevar a ___ personas? | **pway**-day yay-**bar** ah ___ pehr-**soh**-nahs |
| Any extra fee? | ¿Tiene cuota extra? | tee-**ehn**-ay **kwoh**-tah **ayk**-strah |
| The meter, please. | El taxímetro, por favor. | ehl tahk-**see**-may-troh por fah-**bor** |
| Where is the meter? | ¿Dónde está el taxímetro? | **dohn**-day ay-**stah** ehl tahk-**see**-may-troh |

|  |  |  |
|---|---|---|
| The most direct route. | **La ruta más directa.** | lah **roo**-tah mahs dee-**rehk**-tah |
| I'm in a hurry. | **Tengo prisa.** | **tayn**-goh **pree**-sah |
| Slow down. | **Más despacio.** | mahs day-**spah**-thee-oh |
| If you don't slow down, I'll throw up. | **Si no va más despacio, voy a vomitar.** | see noh bah mahs day-**spah**-thee-oh boy ah boh-mee-**tar** |
| Stop here. | **Pare aquí.** | **pah**-ray ah-**kee** |
| Can you wait? | **¿Puede esperar?** | **pway**-day ay-spay-**rar** |
| I'll never forget this ride. | **Nunca me voy a olvidar de este recorrido.** | **noon**-kah may boy ah ohl-bee-**dar** day **ay**-stay ray-koh-**ree**-doh |
| Where did you learn to drive? | **¿Dónde aprendió a conducir?** | **dohn**-day ah-prehn-dee-**oh** ah kohn-doo-**theer** |
| I'll only pay what's on the meter. | **Solo voy a pagar lo que dice el taxímetro.** | **soh**-loh boy ah pah-**gar** loh kay **dee**-thay ehl tahk-**see**-may-troh |
| My change, please. | **Mí cambio, por favor.** | mee **kahm**-bee-oh por fah-**bor** |
| Keep the change. | **Quédese con el cambio.** | **kay**-day-say kohn ehl **kahm**-bee-oh |

**TRANSPORTATION**

Taxis in Spain are cheap, except for going to and from airports (use local buses for these trips). Taxis usually take up to four people. If you have trouble flagging down a taxi, ask for directions to a *parada de taxi* (taxi stand). In Madrid and Barcelona, subways are cheap and efficient.

## Rental wheels:

| | | |
|---|---|---|
| car rental office | **alquiler de coches** | ahl-**kee**-ler day **koh**-chays |
| I want to rent... | **Quiero alquilar...** | kee-**ehr**-oh ahl-kee-**lar** |
| ...a car. | **...un coche.** | oon **koh**-chay |
| ...a station wagon. | **...un coche familiar.** | oon **koh**-chay fah-mee-lee-**ar** |
| ...a van. | **...una frugoneta.** | **oo**-nah froo-goh-**nay**-tah |
| ...a motorcycle. | **...una moto.** | **oo**-nah **moh**-toh |
| ...a motor scooter. | **...una motocicleta.** | **oo**-nah moh-toh-thee-**klay**-tah |
| ...a bicycle. | **...una bicicleta.** | **oo**-nah bee-thee-**klay**-tah |
| How much per...? | **¿Cuánto es por...?** | **kwahn**-toh ays por |
| ...hour | **...hora** | **oh**-rah |
| ...day | **...día** | **dee**-ah |
| ...week | **...semana** | say-**mah**-nah |
| Unlimited mileage? | **¿Sin límite de kilómetros?** | seen **lee**-mee-tay day kee-**loh**-may-trohs |
| I brake for bakeries. | **Paro en cada panadería.** | **pah**-roh ayn **kah**-dah pah-nah-deh-**ree**-ah |
| Is there...? | **¿Hay...?** | ī |
| ...a helmet | **...un casco** | oon **kah**-skoh |
| ...a discount | **...un descuento** | oon days-**kwehn**-toh |
| ...a deposit | **...un depósito** | oon day-**poh**-see-toh |
| ...insurance | **...seguro** | say-**goo**-roh |
| When do I bring it back? | **¿Cuándo lo traigo de vuelta?** | **kwahn**-doh loh **trī**-goh day boo-**ayl**-tah |

Rather than dollars and gallons, gas pumps in Spain read pesetas and liters. Gas costs roughly $1 per liter (about 4 liters in a gallon). In parts of Spain, diesel is called *gasoleo*.

# Driving:

| gas station | gasolinera | gah-soh-lee-**nay**-rah |
|---|---|---|
| The nearest gas station? | ¿La gasolinera más cercana? | lah gah-soh-lee-**nay**-rah mahs thehr-**kah**-nah |
| Self-service? | ¿Auto-servicio? | ow-toh-sehr-**bee**-thee-oh |
| Fill the tank. | Llene el depósito. | **yay**-nay ehl day-**poh**-see-toh |
| I need... | Necesito... | nay-thay-**see**-toh |
| ...gas. | ...gasolina. | gah-soh-**lee**-nah |
| ...unleaded. | ...sin plomo. | seen **ploh**-moh |
| ...regular. | ...normal. | nor-**mahl** |
| ...super. | ...super. | soo-**pehr** |
| ...diesel. | ...diesel, gasoleo. | **dee**-sehl, gah-**soh**-lee-oh |
| Check... | Cheque... | **chay**-kay |
| ...the oil. | ...el aceite. | ehl ah-**thay**-tay |
| ...the air in the tires. | ...el aire en las ruedas. | ehl **ah**-ray ayn lahs roo-**ay**-dahs |
| ...the radiator. | ...el radiador. | ehl rah-dee-ah-**dor** |
| ...the battery. | ...la batería. | lah bah-tay-**ree**-ah |
| ...the fuses. | ...los fusibles. | lohs foo-**see**-blays |
| ...the sparkplugs. | ...las bujías. | lahs boo-**hee**-ahs |
| ...the headlights. | ...los faros. | lohs **fah**-rohs |
| ...the tail lights. | ...las luces de atrás. | lahs **loo**-thays day ah-**trahs** |
| ...the directional signal. | ...el intermitente. | ehl een-tehr-mee-**tehn**-tay |
| ...the car mirror. | ...el retrovisor. | ehl reh-troh-vee-**sor** |
| ...the fanbelt. | ...la correa del ventilador. | lah koh-**ray**-ah dayl bayn-tee-lah-**dor** |
| ...the brakes. | ...los frenos. | lohs **fray**-nohs |
| ...my pulse. | ...mi pulso. | mee **pool**-soh |

## *Car trouble:*

| | | |
|---|---|---|
| accident | **accidente** | ahk-thee-**dehn**-tay |
| breakdown | **averiado** | ah-bay-ree-**ah**-doh |
| funny noise | **ruido extraño** | roo-**ee**-doh ayk-**strahn**-yoh |
| electrical problem | **problema eléctrico** | proh-**blay**-mah ay-**lehk**-tree-koh |
| shop with parts | **repuestos** | ray-**pway**-stohs |
| flat tire | **rueda pinchada** | roo-**ay**-dah peen-**chah**-dah |
| dead battery | **batería descargada** | bah-tay-**ree**-ah dehs-kar-**gah**-dah |
| My car won't start. | **Mi coche no enciende.** | mee **koh**-chay noh ayn-thee-**ehn**-day |
| This doesn't work. | **Esto no funciona.** | **ay**-stoh noh foonk-thee-**oh**-nah |
| It's overheating. | **Está caliente.** | ay-**stah** kahl-**yehn**-tay |
| It's a lemon (swindle). | **Es un timo.** | ehs oon **tee**-moh |
| I need... | **Necesito...** | nay-thay-**see**-toh |
| ...a tow truck. | **...una grúa.** | **oo**-nah **groo**-ah |
| ...a mechanic. | **...un mecánico.** | oon may-**kah**-nee-koh |
| ...a stiff drink. | **...un trago.** | oon **trah**-goh |

For help with repair, look up "Repair" under Shopping.

## *Parking:*

| | | |
|---|---|---|
| parking garage | **parking, garage** | **par**-keeng, gah-**rah**-hay |
| parking lot | **aparcamiento** | ah-par-kah-mee-**ehn**-toh |
| Where can I park? | **¿Dónde puedo aparcar?** | **dohn**-day **pway**-doh ah-par-**kar** |
| Is parking nearby? | **¿Hay un parking cercano?** | ī oon **par**-keeng thehr-**kahn**-noh |

| Can I park here? | ¿Puedo aparcar aquí? | pway-doh ah-par-kar ah-kee |
| How long can I park here? | ¿Por cuánto tiempo puedo aparcar aquí? | por kwahn-toh tee-ehm-poh pway-doh ah-par-kar ah-kee |
| Must I pay to park here? | ¿Tengo que pagar por aparcar aquí? | tayn-goh kay pah-gar por ah-par-kar ah-kee |
| Is this a safe place to park? | ¿Es este un sitio seguro para aparcar? | ays ay-stay oon see-tee-oh say-goo-roh pah-rah ah-par-kar |

TRANSPORTATION

Parking in Spain can be hazardous. Park legally. Many towns require parking permits, sold at tobacco shops. To give your car a local profile, cover the rental decal and put a local newspaper inside the back window. Leave the car empty and, some would advise, unlocked overnight. If it's a hatchback, remove the shelf behind the back seat to show thieves you have *nada* in the trunk. Get safe parking tips from your hotel.

## Finding your way:

| I'm going to... | Voy a... | boy ah |
| How do I get to...? | ¿Cómo llego a...? | koh-moh yay-goh ah |
| Is there a map? | ¿Hay un mapa? | ī oon mah-pah |
| How many minutes...? | ¿Cuántos minutos...? | kwahn-tohs mee-noo-tohs |
| How many hours...? | ¿Cuántos horas...? | kwahn-tohs oh-rahs |
| ...on foot | ...a pié | ah pee-ay |
| ...by bicycle | ...en bicicleta | ayn bee-thee-klay-tah |
| ...by car | ...en coche | ayn koh-chay |
| How many kilometers to...? | ¿Cuántos kilómetros a...? | kwahn-tohs kee-loh-may-trohs ah |

| What's the... | ¿Cuál es el... | kwahl ays ehl... kah-**mee**-noh |
| route to Madrid? | camino para Madrid? | **pah**-rah mah-**dreed** |
| ...best | ...mejor | may-**hor** |
| ...fastest | ...más rápido | mahs **rah**-pee-doh |
| ...most interesting | ...más interesante | mahs een-tay-ray-**sahn**-tay |
| Point it out? | ¿Señálelo? | sayn-**yah**-lay-loh |
| I'm lost. | Estoy perdido[a]. | ay-**stoy** pehr-**dee**-doh |
| Where am I? | ¿Dónde estoy? | **dohn**-day ay-**stoy** |
| Who am I? | ¿Quién soy? | kee-**ehn** soy |
| Where is...? | ¿Dónde está...? | **dohn**-day ay-**stah** |
| The nearest ...? | ¿El más cercano...? | ehl mahs thehr-**kah**-noh |
| Where is this address? | ¿Dónde se encuentra esta dirección? | **dohn**-day say ayn-**kwehn**-trah ay-**stah** dee-rehk-thee-**ohn** |

## Key route-finding words:

| city map | mapa de la ciudad | **mah**-pah day lah thee-oo-**dahd** |
| road map | mapa de carretera | **mah**-pah day kah-ray-**tay**-rah |
| downtown | centro ciudad | **thayn**-troh **thee**-oo-dahd |
| straight | derecho | day-**ray**-choh |
| left | izquierda | eeth-kee-**ehr**-dah |
| right | derecha | day-**ray**-chah |
| first | primero | pree-**may**-roh |
| next | siguiente | seeg-ee-**ehn**-tay |
| intersection | intersección | een-tehr-sehk-thee-**ohn** |
| stoplight | semáforo | say-**mah**-foh-roh |
| traffic circle | glorieta | gloh-ree-**eh**-tah |
| (main) square | plaza (principal) | **plah**-thah (preen-thee-**pahl**) |

| street | calle | **kah**-yay |
| bridge | puente | **pwehn**-tay |
| tunnel | túnel | **too**-nehl |
| highway | carretera | kah-ray-**tay**-rah |
| freeway | autopista | ow-toh-**pee**-stah |
| north | norte | **nor**-tay |
| south | sur | soor |
| east | este | **ay**-stay |
| west | oeste | oh-**ay**-stay |

## *Reading road signs:*

| | |
| --- | --- |
| **ceda el paso** | yield |
| **centro de la ciudad** | to the center of town |
| **contrucción** | construction |
| **cuidado** | caution |
| **despacio** | slow |
| **desvío** | detour |
| **dirección única** | one-way street |
| **entrada** | entrance |
| **estacionamiento prohibido** | no parking |
| **obras** | workers ahead |
| **próxima salida** | next exit |
| **peage** | toll road |
| **peatones** | pedestrians |
| **salida** | exit |
| **stop** | stop |
| **todas direcciones** | out of town (all directions) |

Here are the standard symbols you'll see:

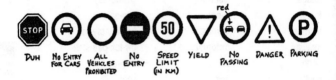

DUH    NO ENTRY FOR CARS    ALL VEHICLES PROHIBITED    NO ENTRY    SPEED LIMIT (IN KM)    YIELD    NO PASSING    DANGER    PARKING

In any country, the flashing lights of a patrol car are a sure sign that someone's in trouble. If it's you, say, *"Lo siento, soy un turista."* (Sorry, I'm a tourist.) Or, for the adventurous: *"Si no le gusta como conduzco, sácate de la acera."* (If you don't like how I drive, stay off the sidewalk.)

## *Other signs you may bump into:*

| | |
|---|---|
| abierto | open |
| abierto de... a... | open from... to... |
| agua no potable | undrinkable water |
| alquilo | for rent |
| averiado | out of service |
| caballeros | men |
| camas | vacancy |
| cerrado | closed |
| cerrado por vacaciones | closed for vacation |
| cerrado por obras | closed for restoration |
| completo | no vacancy |
| empujar / tirar | push / pull |
| entrada libre | free admission |
| habitaciones | vacancy |
| hay... | we have... |
| no fumar | no smoking |
| no tocar | do not touch |
| ocupado | occupied |
| paso prohibido | no entry |
| peligro | danger |
| perro molesto | mean dog |
| prohibido | forbidden |
| salida de emergencia | emergency exit |
| señoras | women |
| servicios | toilets |
| tirar / empujar | pull / push |
| Turismo | tourist information office |
| vendo | for sale |

TRANSPORTATION

# Sleeping

## Places to stay:

| | | |
|---|---|---|
| hotel | **hotel** | oh-**tehl** |
| small, family-run hotel | **pensión** | payn-see-**ohn** |
| room in private home | **habitación** | ah-bee-tah-thee-**ohn** |
| youth hostel | **albergue de juventud** | ahl-**behr**-gay day hoo-behn-**tood** |
| vacancy sign (literally "rooms," "beds") | **habitaciones, camas** | ah-bee-tah-thee-**oh**-nays, **kah**-mahs |
| no vacancy | **completo** | kohm-**play**-toh |

Spanish hotels come with a handy government-regulated classification system. Look for a blue and white plaque by the hotel door indicating the category.

**Hotel (H) and Hostales (Hs):** The most comfortable and expensive (rated with stars).
**Hotel-Residencia (HR) and Hostal-Residencia (HsR):** Basically hotels without restaurants. Don't confuse hostales with youth hostels.
**Pensión (P), Casa de Huéspedes (CH), & Fonda (F):** Cheaper, usually family-run places. If you're on a tight budget, these can be a good value.
**Parador:** Government-run hotels, often in refurbished castles or palaces. They can be a good value, but most feature snooty staff, snooty clientele, and rooms costing well over $100 per double.

## Reserving a room:

A good time to call to reserve a room is the morning of the day you plan to arrive. If you want to reserve by fax from the U.S.A, use the nifty form in the appendix.

| | | |
|---|---|---|
| Hello. | **Hola.** | **oh**-lah |
| Do you speak English? | **¿Habla usted inglés?** | ah-blah oo-**stehd** een-**glays** |
| Do you have a room...? | **¿Tiene una habitación libre...?** | tee-**ehn**-ay oo-**nah** ah-bee-tah-thee-**ohn** lee-bray |
| ...for one person | **...para una persona** | **pah**-rah oo-nah pehr-**soh**-nah |
| ...for two people | **...para dos personas** | **pah**-rah dohs pehr-**soh**-nahs |
| ...for today | **...para hoy** | **pah**-rah oy |
| ...for two nights | **...para dos noches** | **pah**-rah dohs **noh**-chays |
| ...for this Friday | **...para este viernes** | **pah**-rah ay-stay bee-**ehr**-nays |
| ...for June 21 | **...para 21 de Junio** | **pah**-rah bayn-tee-**oo**-noh day *hoon*-yoh |
| Yes or no? | **¿Sí o no?** | see oh noh |
| I want... | **Quiero...** | kee-**ehr**-oh |
| ...a private bathroom. | **...un baño privado.** | **bahn**-yoh pree-**vah**-doh |
| ...your cheapest room. | **...su habitación más barata.** | soo ah-bee-tah-thee-**ohn** mahs bah-**rah**-tah |
| ...___ bed(s) for ___ people in ___ room(s). | **...___ cama(s) para ___ personas en ___ habitación(es).** | **kah**-mah(s) **pah**-rah ___ pehr-**soh**-nahs ayn ___ ah-bee-tah-thee-**ohn**(ays) |
| How much is it? | **¿Cuánto cuesta?** | **kwahn**-toh **kway**-stah |
| Anything cheaper? | **¿Nada más barato?** | **nah**-dah mahs bah-**rah**-toh |
| I'll take it. | **La quiero.** | lah kee-**ehr**-oh |
| My name is... | **Me llamo...** | may **yah**-moh |

| | | |
|---|---|---|
| I'll stay... | Quedaré... | kay-dah-**ray** |
| We'll stay... | Quedaremos... | kay-dah-**ray**-mohs |
| ...for ___ night(s). | ...para ___ noche(s). | pah-rah ___ **noh**-chay(s) |
| I'll come... | Vendré... | bayn-**dray** |
| We'll come... | Vendremos... | bayn-**dray**-mohs |
| ...in one hour. | ...en una hora. | ayn **oo**-nah **oh**-rah |
| ...before 4:00 in the afternoon. | ...antes de las cuatro de la tarde. | **ahn**-tays day lahs **kwah**-troh day lah **tar**-day |
| ...Friday before 6 p.m. | ...viernes antes de las 6:00 de la tarde. | bee-**ehr**-nays **ahn**-tays day lahs says day lah **tar**-day |
| Thank you. | Gracias. | **grah**-thee-ahs |

## Getting specific:

| | | |
|---|---|---|
| I want a room... | Quiero una habitación... | kee-**ehr**-oh **oo**-nah ah-bee-tah-thee-**ohn** |
| ...with / without / and | ...con / sin / y | kohn / seen / ee |
| ...toilet | ...aseo | ah-**say**-oh |
| ...shower | ...ducha | **doo**-chah |
| ...shower down the hall | ...ducha al fondo del pasillo | **doo**-chah ahl **fohn**-doh dayl pah-**see**-yoh |
| ...bathtub | ...bañera | bahn-**yay**-rah |
| ...double bed | ...cama de matrimonio | **kah**-mah day mah-tree-**moh**-nee-oh |
| ...twin beds | ...dos camas | dohs **kah**-mahs |
| ...balcony | ...balcón | bahl-**kohn** |
| ...view | ...vista | **bee**-stah |
| ...with only a sink | ...solo con lavabo | **soh**-loh kohn lah-**bah**-boh |
| ...on the ground floor | ...en el piso bajo | ayn ehl **pee**-soh **bah**-hoh |
| ...television | ...televisión | tay-lay-bee-see-**ohn** |

| ...telephone | ...teléfono | tay-**lay**-foh-noh |
| Is there an elevator? | ¿Hay un ascensor? | ī oon ahs-thehn-**sor** |
| We arrive Monday, depart Wednesday. | Llegamos el lunes, salimos el miércoles. | yay-**gah**-mohs ehl **loo**-nays, sah-**lee**-mohs ehl mee-**ehr**-koh-lays |
| I'll sleep anywhere. I'm desperate. | Puedo dormir en cualquier sitio. Estoy desesperado[a]. | **pway**-doh **dor**-meer ayn kwahl-kee-**ehr** see-tee-oh. ay-**stoy** day-say-spay-**rah**-doh |
| I have a sleeping bag. | Tengo un saco de dormir. | **tayn**-goh oon **sah**-koh day dor-**meer** |
| Will you call another hotel? | ¿Llamaría a otro hotel? | yah-mah-**ree**-ah ah **oh**-troh oh-**tehl** |

## Confirming, changing, and canceling reservations:

You can use this template for your telephone call.

| I have a reservation. | Tengo la reserva hecha. | **tayn**-goh lah ray-**sehr**-bah **ay**-chah |
| My name is... | Me llamo... | may **yah**-moh |
| I'd like to... my reservation. | Me gustaría... mi reserva. | may goo-stah-**ree**-ah mee ray-**sehr**-bah |
| ...confirm | ...confirmar | kohn-feer-**mar** |
| ...reconfirm | ...reconfirmar | ray-kohn-feer-**mar** |
| ...cancel | ...cancelar | kahn-thay-**lar** |
| ...change | ...cambiar | kahm-bee-**ar** |
| The reservation is / was for... | La reserva es / era para... | lah ray-**sehr**-bah ehs / **eh**-rah **pah**-rah |
| ...one person / two people | ...una persona / dos personas | **oo**-nah pehr-**soh**-nah / dohs pehr-**soh**-nahs |
| ...today / tomorrow | ...oy / mañana | oy / mahn-**yah**-nah |

| ...August 13 | ...el trece de agosto | ehl **tray**-thay day ah-**goh**-stoh |
| ...one night / two nights | ...una noche / dos noches | **oo**-nah **noh**-chay / dohs **noh**-chays |
| Did you find my reservation? | ¿Encontró mi reserva? | ayn-kohn-**troh** mee ray-**sehr**-bah |
| I'd like to arrive instead on... | En lugar, me gustaría llegar... | ayn loo-**gar** may goo-stah-**ree**-ah yay-**gar** |
| Is everything O.K.? | ¿Está todo bien? | ay-**stah** toh-doh bee-**yehn** |
| Thank you. I'll see you then. | Gracias. Hasta entonces. | **grah**-thee-ahs ah-**stah** ayn-**tohn**-thays |
| I'm sorry I need to cancel. | Lo siento pero necesito cancelar. | loh see-**ehn**-toh **peh**-roh nay-thay-**see**-toh kahn-thay-**lar** |

## Nailing down the price:

| How much is...? | ¿Cuánto cuesta...? | **kwahn**-toh **kway**-stah |
| ...a room for ___ people | ...una habitación para ___ personas | **oo**-nah ah-bee-tah-thee-**ohn** **pah**-rah ___ pehr-**soh**-nahs |
| ...your cheapest room | ...su habitación más barata | soo ah-bee-tah-thee-**ohn** mahs bah-**rah**-tah |
| Is breakfast included? | ¿El desayuno está incluido? | ehl day-sah-**yoo**-noh ay-**stah** een-kloo-**ee**-doh |
| Is breakfast required? | ¿Se requiere desayuno? | say ray-kee-**ay**-ray day-sah-**yoo**-noh |
| How much without breakfast? | ¿Cuánto cuesta sin el desayuno? | **kwahn**-toh **kway**-stah seen ehl day-sah-**yoo**-noh |
| Complete price? | ¿El precio completo? | ehl **pray**-thee-oh kohm-**play**-toh |

| | | |
|---|---|---|
| Is it cheaper if I stay ___ nights? | ¿Es más barato si quedo ___ noches? | ays mahs bah-**rah**-toh see **kay**-doh ___ **noh**-chays |
| I will stay ___ nights. | Me quedaré ___ noches. | may kay-dah-**ray** ___ **noh**-chays |

## Choosing a room:

| | | |
|---|---|---|
| Can I see the room? | ¿Puedo ver la habitación? | **pway**-doh behr lah ah-bee-tah-thee-**ohn** |
| Show me another room? | ¿Enséñeme otra habitación? | ayn-**sayn**-yay-may oh-trah ah-bee-tah-thee-**ohn** |
| Do you have something...? | ¿Tiene algo...? | tee-**ehn**-ay **ahl**-goh |
| ...larger / smaller | ...más grande / más pequeño | mahs **grahn**-day / mahs pay-**kayn**-yoh |
| ...better / cheaper | ...mejor / más barato | may-**hor** / mahs bah-**rah**-toh |
| ...brighter | ...con más claridad | kohn mahs klah-ree-**dahd** |
| ...in the back | ...en la parte de atrás | ayn lah **par**-tay day ah-**trahs** |
| ...quieter | ...más tranquillo | mahs trahn-**kee**-yoh |
| I'll take it. | La quiero. | lah kee-**ehr**-oh |
| My key, please. | Mi llave, por favor. | mee **yah**-bay por fah-**bor** |
| Sleep well. | Que duerma bien. | kay **dwehr**-mah bee-**yehn** |
| Good night. | Buenas noches. | **bway**-nahs **noh**-chays |

In Spain, views often come with street noise (a Spanish specialty). You can ask for a room *"con vista"* or *"tranquillo."* If sleep is a priority, go with the latter.

If the management treats you like a *cucaracha* (cockroach), ask to see the hotel's *libro de reclamaciones* (the government-required complaint book). Your problems will generally get solved in a jiffy.

## Hotel help:

| I want... | Quiero... | kee-**ehr**-oh |
|---|---|---|
| ...a / another | ...un / otro | oon / **oh**-troh |
| ...towel. | ...toalla. | toh-**ah**-yah |
| ...pillow. | ...almohada. | ahl-moh-**ah**-dah |
| ...clean sheets. | ...sábanas limpias. | **sah**-bah-nahs **leem**-pee-ahs |
| ...blanket. | ...manta. | **mahn**-tah |
| ...glass. | ...vaso. | **bah**-soh |
| ...sink stopper. | ...tapon. | tah-**pohn** |
| ...soap. | ...jabón. | *h*ah-**bohn** |
| ...toilet paper. | ...papel higiénico. | pah-**pehl** ee-*h*ee-ay-nee-koh |
| ...crib. | ...cuna. | **koo**-nah |
| ...extra roll-away bed. | ...cama plegable extra. | **kah**-mah play-**gah**-blay **ayk**-strah |
| ...different room. | ...habitación diferente | ah-bee-tah-thee-**ohn** dee-fay-**rehn**-tay |
| ...silence. | ...silencio. | see-**lehn**-thee-oh |
| Where can I wash / hang my laundry? | ¿Dónde puedo lavar / tender mi ropa? | **dohn**-day **pway**-doh lah-**bar** / tehn-**dehr** mee **roh**-pah |
| I want to stay another night. | Quiero quedarme otra noche. | kee-**ehr**-oh kay-**dar**-may **oh**-trah **noh**-chay |
| Where can I park? | ¿Dónde puedo aparcar? | **dohn**-day **pway**-doh ah-par-**kar** |
| What time do you lock up? | ¿A qué hora cierran la puerta? | ah kay **oh**-rah thee-**ay**-rahn lah **pwehr**-tah |
| What time is breakfast? | ¿A qué hora es el desayuno? | ah kay **oh**-rah ays ehl day-sah-**yoo**-noh |
| Please wake me at 7:00. | Despiérteme a las 7:00, por favor. | days-pee-**ehr**-tay-may ah lahs see-**eh**-tay por fah-**bor** |

## Hotel hassles:

| | | |
|---|---|---|
| Come with me. | **Venga conmigo.** | **vayn**-gah kohn-**mee**-goh |
| I have a problem in my room. | **Tengo un problema en mi habitación.** | **tayn**-goh oon proh-**blay**-mah ayn mee ah-bee-tah-thee-**ohn** |
| It smells bad. | **Huele mal.** | **way**-lay mahl |
| bugs | **moscas** | **moh**-skahs |
| cockroaches | **cucarachas** | koo-kah-**rah**-chahs |
| mice | **ratones** | rah-**toh**-nays |
| prostitutes | **prostitutas** | proh-stee-**too**-tahs |
| The bed is too soft / hard. | **La cama es muy blanda / dura.** | lah **kah**-mah ays **moo**-ee **blahn**-dah / **doo**-rah |
| Lamp... | **Lámpara...** | **lahm**-pah-rah |
| Lightbulb... | **Bombilla...** | bohm-**bee**-yah |
| Electrical outlet... | **Enchufe...** | ayn-**choo**-fay |
| Key... | **Llave...** | **yah**-bay |
| Lock... | **Cerradura...** | thehr-rah-**doo**-rah |
| Window... | **Ventana...** | bayn-**tah**-nah |
| Faucet... | **Grifo...** | **gree**-foh |
| Sink... | **Lavabo...** | lah-**bah**-boh |
| Toilet... | **Aseo...** | ah-**say**-oh |
| Shower... | **Ducha...** | **doo**-chah |
| ...doesn't work. | **...no funciona.** | noh foonk-thee-**oh**-nah |
| There is no hot water. | **No hay agua caliente.** | noh ī ah-gwah kahl-**yehn**-tay |
| When is the water hot? | **¿Cuándo hay agua caliente?** | **kwahn**-doh ī ah-gwah kahl-**yehn**-tay |

SLEEPING

## Checking out:

| | | |
|---|---|---|
| I'll leave... | **Me iré...** | may ee-**ray** |
| We'll leave... | **Nos iremos...** | nohs ee-**ray**-mohs |
| ...today / tomorrow. | **...hoy / mañana.** | oy / mahn-**yah**-nah |
| ...very early. | **...muy temprano.** | moo-ee tehm-**prah**-noh |
| When is check-out time? | **¿Cuándo es la hora de salida?** | **kwahn**-doh ays lah **oh**-rah day sah-**lee**-dah |
| Can I pay now? | **¿Le pago ahora?** | lay **pah**-goh ah-**oh**-rah |
| The bill, please. | **La cuenta, por favor.** | lah **kwayn**-tah por fah-**bor** |
| Credit card O.K.? | **¿Tarjeta de crédito O.K.?** | tar-**hay**-tah day **kray**-dee-toh "O.K." |
| I slept like a log. (Sleep grabbed me.) | **Dormí de un tirón.** | dor-**mee** day oon tee-**rohn** |
| Everything was great. | **Todo estuvo muy bien.** | **toh**-doh ay-**stoo**-boh **moo**-ee bee-**yehn** |
| Will you call my next hotel for me? | **Puede llamar a mí próximo hotel?** | **pway**-day yah-**mar** ah mee **prohk**-see-moh oh-**tehl** |
| Can I...? | **¿Puedo...?** | **pway**-doh |
| Can we...? | **¿Podemos...?** | poh-**day**-mohs |
| ...leave baggage here until ___ | **...guardar aquí las maletas hasta ___** | gwar-**dar** ah-**kee** lahs mah-**lay**-tahs **ah**-stah |

## Camping:

| | | |
|---|---|---|
| tent | **tienda** | tee-**ayn**-dah |
| camping | **camping** | **kahm**-peeng |
| The nearest campground? | **¿El camping más cercano?** | ehl **kahm**-peeng mahs thehr-**kah**-noh |
| Can I...? | **¿Puedo...?** | **pway**-doh |
| Can we...? | **¿Podemos...?** | poh-**day**-mohs |

| ...camp here for one night | ...acampar aquí por una noche | ah-kahm-**par** ah-**kee** por **oo**-nah **noh**-chay |
| Do showers cost extra? | ¿Cuestan extra las duchas? | **kway**-stahn **ayk**-strah lahs **doo**-chahs |

## Laundry:

| self-service laundry | launderama | lahn-deh-**rah**-mah |
| wash / dry | lavar / secar | lah-**var** / say-**kar** |
| washer / dryer | lavadora / secadora | lah-vah-**doh**-rah / say-kah-**doh**-rah |
| detergent | detergente | day-tehr-**hayn**-tay |
| token | ficha | **fee**-chah |
| whites / colors | blanca / de color | **blahn**-kah / day koh-**lor** |
| How does this work? | ¿Cómo funciona? | **koh**-moh foonk-thee-**oh**-nah |
| Where is the soap? | ¿Dónde está el jabón? | **dohn**-day ay-**stah** ehl hah-**bohn** |
| I need change. | Necesito cambio. | nay-thay-**see**-toh **kahm**-bee-oh |
| full-service laundry | lavandería | lah-vahn-deh-**ree**-ah |
| Same-day service? | ¿Sirven en el mismo día? | **seer**-vehn ayn ehl **mees**-moh **dee**-ah |
| By when do I need to drop off my clothes? | ¿Cuándo tengo que traer mi ropa? | **kwahn**-doh **tayn**-goh kay trah-**ehr** mee **roh**-pah |
| When will my clothes be ready? | ¿Cuándo estará lista la ropa? | **kwahn**-doh ay-stah-**rah** **lee**-stah lah **roh**-pah |

SLEEPING

# Eating

## Finding a restaurant:

| | | |
|---|---|---|
| Where's a good... restaurant? | ¿Dónde hay un buen restaurante...? | **dohn**-day ī oon bwayn ray-stoh-**rahn**-tay |
| ...cheap | ...barato | bah-**rah**-toh |
| ...local-style | ...regional | ray-hee-oh-**nahl** |
| ...untouristy | ...que no sea un sitio de turistas | kay noh **say**-ah oon **see**-tee-oh day too-**ree**-stahs |
| ...Chinese | ...chino | **chee**-noh |
| ...fast food | ...comida rápida | koh-**mee**-dah **rah**-pee-dah |
| ...cafeteria | ...cafetería | kah-fay-**tay**-ree-ah |
| with a salad bar | con ensaladas | kohn ayn-sah-**lah**-dahs |
| with terrace | con terraza | kohn tehr-**rah**-thah |
| with candles | con velas | kohn **bay**-lahs |
| romantic | romántico | roh-**mahn**-tee-koh |
| moderate price | precio moderado | **pray**-thee-oh moh-day-**rah**-doh |
| a splurge | una extravagancia | **oo**-nah ehk-strah-bah-**gahn**-thee-ah |

## Getting a table and menu:

| | | |
|---|---|---|
| Waiter. | Camarero. | kah-mah-**ray**-roh |
| Waitress. | Camarera. | kah-mah-**ray**-rah |
| I want... | Quiero... | kee-**ehr**-oh |
| ...a table for one / two. | ...una mesa para uno / dos. | **oo**-nah **may**-sah **pah**-rah **oo**-noh / dohs |
| ...non-smoking. | ...no fumadores. | noh foo-mah-**doh**-rays |
| ...just a drink. | ...solo para una bebida. | **soh**-loh **pah**-rah **oo**-nah bay-**bee**-dah |

| ...a snack. | ...un pincho. | oon **peen**-choh |
| ...just a salad. | ...sólo una ensalada. | **soh**-loh oo-nah ayn-sah-**lah**-dah |
| ...to see the menu. | ...ver el menú. | behr ehl may-**noo** |
| ...to order a meal. | ...ordenar la comida. | or-day-**nar** lah koh-**mee**-dah |
| ...to eat. | ...comer. | koh-**mehr** |
| ...to pay. | ...pagar. | pah-**gar** |
| ...to throw up. | ...vomitar. | boh-mee-**tar** |
| What do you recommend? | ¿Qué es lo que me recomienda? | kay ays loh kay may ray-kohm-**yehn**-dah |
| What's your favorite dish? | ¿Cuál es su plato favorito? | kwahl ays soo **plah**-toh fah-boh-**ree**-toh |
| Is it...? | ¿Es esto...? | ays **ay**-stoh |
| ...tasty | ...sabroso | sah-**broh**-soh |
| ...expensive | ...caro | **kah**-roh |
| ...light | ...ligero | lee-**hay**-roh |
| Is it filling? | ¿Esto le llena? | **ay**-stoh lay **yay**-nah |
| What is...? | ¿Qué es...? | kay ays |
| ...that | ...esto | **ay**-stoh |
| ...local | ...típico | **tee**-pee-koh |
| ...fast | ...lo más rápido | loh mahs **rah**-pee-doh |
| ...cheap and filling | ...lo que llena y es barato | loh kay **yay**-nah ee ays bah-**rah**-toh |
| Do you have...? | ¿Tiene...? | tee-**ehn**-ay |
| ...an English menu | ...un menú en inglés | oon may-**noo** ayn een-**glays** |
| ...children's portions | ...raciónes para niños | rah-thee-**oh**-nays **pah**-rah **neen**-yohs |

The Spanish eat late, and so will you if you'll be dining in restaurants. No self-respecting restaurant serves dinner before 8 p.m. To eat early, well, and within even the tightest budget, duck into a bar, where you can stab toothpicks into local munchies (see *Tapas* below).

## The menu:

| menu | menú | may-**noo** |
|---|---|---|
| menu of the day | menú del día | may-**noo** dayl **dee**-ah |
| tourist menu | menú de turista | meh-**noo** day too-**ree**-stah |
| combination plate | plato combinado | **plah**-toh kohm-bee-**nah**-doh |
| special of the day | especial del día | ay-spay-thee-**ahl** dayl **dee**-ah |
| specialty of the house | especialidad de la casa | ay-spay-thee-ah-lee-**dahd** day lah **kah**-sah |
| breakfast | desayuno | day-sah-**yoo**-noh |
| lunch | almuerzo | ahlm-**wehr**-thoh |
| dinner | cena | **thay**-nah |
| appetizers | aperitivos | ah-pay-ree-**tee**-bohs |
| bread | pan | pahn |
| salad | ensalada | ayn-sah-**lah**-dah |
| soup | sopa | **soh**-pah |
| first course | primer plato | pree-**mehr plah**-toh |
| main course | segundo plato | say-**goon**-doh **plah**-toh |
| meat | carne | **kar**-nay |
| poultry | aves | **ah**-bays |
| seafood | marisco | mah-**ree**-skoh |
| egg dishes | tortillas | tor-**tee**-yahs |
| side dishes | a parte | ah **par**-tay |
| vegetables | verduras | behr-**doo**-rahs |
| cheese | queso | **kay**-soh |
| dessert | postres | **poh**-strays |

EATING

| beverages | **bebidas** | bay-**bee**-dahs |
| beer | **cerveza** | thehr-**bay**-thah |
| wine | **vino** | **bee**-noh |
| cover charge | **precio de entrada** | **pray**-thee-oh day ayn-**trah**-dah |
| service (not) included | **servicio (no) incluido** | sehr-**bee**-thee-oh (noh) een-kloo-**ee**-doh |
| with / without | **con / sin** | kohn / seen |
| and / or | **y / o** | ee / oh |

## Dietary restrictions:

| I'm allergic to... | **Soy alérgico[a] a...** | soy ah-**lehr**-*h*ee-koh ah |
| I cannot eat... | **No puedo comer...** | noh **pway**-doh koh-**mehr** |
| ...dairy products. | **...productos lácteos.** | proh-**dook**-tohs **lahk**-tay-ohs |
| ...meat / pork. | **...carne / cerdo.** | **kar**-nay / **thehr**-doh |
| ...salt / sugar. | **...sal / azúcar.** | sahl / ah-**thoo**-kar |
| I'm diabetic. | **Soy diabético[a].** | soy dee-ah-**bay**-tee-koh |
| Low cholesterol. | **Bajo en colesterol.** | **bah**-*h*oh ayn koh-lay-stay-**rohl** |
| No / Minimal fat. | **Sin / Poca grasa.** | seen / **poh**-kah **grah**-sah |
| No caffeine. | **No cafeina.** | noh kah-**fay**-nah |
| No alcohol. | **No alcohol.** | noh ahl-**kohl** |
| I'm a... | **Soy...** | soy |
| ...vegetarian. | **...vegetariano[a].** | bay-*h*ay-tah-ree-**ah**-noh |
| ...strict vegetarian. | **...estricto[a] vegetariano[a].** | ay-**streek**-toh bay-*h*ay-tah-ree-**ah**-noh |
| ...carnivore. | **...carnívoro[a].** | kar-**nee**-boh-roh |
| ...big eater. | **...glotón.** | gloh-**tohn** |

## Tableware and condiments:

| | | |
|---|---|---|
| plate | **plato** | **plah**-toh |
| extra plate | **otro plato** | **oh**-troh **plah**-toh |
| napkin | **servilleta** | sehr-vee-**yay**-tah |
| silverware | **cubiertos** | koo-bee-**yehr**-tohs |
| knife | **cuchillo** | koo-**chee**-yoh |
| fork | **tenedor** | tay-nay-**dor** |
| spoon | **cuchara** | koo-**chah**-rah |
| cup | **taza** | **tah**-thah |
| glass | **vaso** | **bah**-soh |
| carafe | **garrafa** | gah-**rah**-fah |
| water | **agua** | **ah**-gwah |
| bread | **pan** | pahn |
| butter | **mantequilla** | mahn-tay-**kee**-yah |
| margarine | **margarina** | mar-gah-**ree**-nah |
| salt / pepper | **sal / pimienta** | sahl / pee-mee-**ehn**-tah |
| sugar | **azúcar** | ah-**thoo**-kar |
| artifical sweetener | **edulcorante** | ay-dool-koh-**rahn**-tay |
| honey | **miel** | mee-**ehl** |
| mustard | **mostaza** | moh-**stah**-thah |
| mayonnaise | **mayonesa** | mah-yoh-**nay**-sah |

## Restaurant requests and regrets:

| | | |
|---|---|---|
| A little. / More. | **Un poco. / Más.** | oon **poh**-koh / mahs |
| Another. | **Otro.** | **oh**-troh |
| The same. | **El mismo.** | ehl **mees**-moh |
| I did not order this. | **No ordené esto.** | noh or-day-**nay ay**-stoh |
| Is this included with the meal? | **¿Está esto incluido con la comida?** | ay-**stah ay**-stoh een-kloo-**ee**-doh kohn lah koh-**mee**-dah |
| I'm in a hurry. | **Tengo prisa.** | **tayn**-goh **pree**-sah |

EATING

| | | |
|---|---|---|
| I must leave by... | **Tengo que salir a...** | **tayn**-goh kay sah-**leer** ah |
| When will the food be ready? | **¿Cuando estará la comida lista?** | **kwahn**-doh ay-stah-**rah** lah koh-**mee**-dah **lee**-stah |
| I've changed my mind. | **Cambié de idea.** | kahm-bee-**ay** day ee-**day**-ah |
| Can I get it "to go"? | **¿Me lo empaqueta para llevar?** | may loh aym-pah-**kay**-tah **pah**-rah yay-**bar** |
| This is... | **Esto es...** | **ay**-stoh ays |
| ...dirty. | **...sucio.** | **soo**-thee-oh |
| ...greasy. | **...grasiento.** | grah-see-**ehn**-toh |
| ...salty. | **...salado.** | sah-**lah**-doh |
| ...undercooked. | **...crudo.** | **kroo**-doh |
| ...overcooked. | **...muy hecho.** | **moo**-ee ay-choh |
| ...inedible. | **...asqueroso.** | ahs-kway-**roh**-soh |
| ...cold. | **...frío.** | **free**-oh |
| Can you heat this up? | **¿Me puede calentar esto?** | may **pway**-day kah-lehn-**tar** **ay**-stoh |
| Enjoy your meal! | **¡Qué aproveche!** | kay ah-proh-**vay**-chay |
| Enough. | **Suficiente.** | soo-fee-thee-**ehn**-tay |
| Finished. | **Terminado.** | tehr-mee-**nah**-doh |
| Yuck! | **¡Que asco!** | kay **ah**-skoh |
| Delicious! | **¡Delicioso!** | day-lee-thee-**oh**-soh |
| I'm stuffed! (I put on my boots!) | **¡Me he puesto las botas!** | may ay **pway**-stoh lahs **boh**-tahs |

## Paying for your meal:

| | | |
|---|---|---|
| Waiter. | **Camarero.** | kah-mah-**ray**-roh |
| Waitress. | **Camarera.** | kah-mah-**ray**-rah |
| The bill, please. | **La cuenta, por favor.** | lah **kwayn**-tah por fah-**bor** |

| Together. | **Junto.** | *h*oon-toh |
| Separate checks. | **En cheques separados.** | ayn **chay**-kays say-pah-**rah**-dohs |
| Credit card O.K.? | **¿Tarjeta de crédito O.K.?** | tar-*h*ay-tah day **kray**-dee-toh "O.K." |
| Service included? | **¿Servicio incluido?** | sehr-**bee**-thee-oh een-kloo-**ee**-doh |
| This is not correct. | **Esto no es correcto.** | ay-stoh noh ays koh-**rehk**-toh |
| Can you explain this? | **¿Me puede expliqar esto?** | may **pway**-day ayk-splee-**kar** ay-stoh |
| What if I wash the dishes? | **¿Qué le parece si lavo los platos?** | kay lay pah-**ray**-thay see **lah**-boh lohs **plah**-tohs |
| Keep the change. | **Quédese con el cambio.** | **kay**-day-say kohn ehl **kahm**-bee-oh |
| This is for you. | **Esto es para usted.** | ay-stoh ays **pah**-rah oo-**stehd** |

If the menu says *servicio incluido*, it means just that. While it's good style to leave the coins, there's no need to tip beyond what's already been tacked on to your bill. If the menu says *servicio no incluido*, leave about 10 to 15 percent for a tip.

## Breakfast:

| breakfast | **desayuno** | day-sah-**yoo**-noh |
| bread | **pan** | pahn |
| roll | **panecillo** | pah-nay-**thee**-yoh |
| toast | **tostadas** | toh-**stah**-dahs |
| butter | **mantequilla** | mahn-tay-**kee**-yah |
| jelly | **mermelada** | mehr-may-**lah**-dah |
| pastry | **pasteles** | pah-**stay**-lays |

| | | |
|---|---|---|
| fritters | **churros** | **choo**-rohs |
| omelet | **omelet** | **ohm**-let |
| potato omelet | **tortilla española** | tor-**tee**-yah ay-spahn-**yoh**-lah |
| eggs... | **huevos...** | **way**-bohs |
| ...fried | **...fritos** | **free**-tohs |
| ...scrambled | **...revueltos** | ray-**bwehl**-tohs |
| boiled egg... | **huevo cocido...** | **way**-boh koh-**thee**-doh |
| ...hard | **...duro** | **doo**-roh |
| ...soft | **...pasado por agua** | pah-**sah**-doh por **ah**-gwah |
| ham | **jamón** | *hah-***mohn** |
| cheese | **queso** | **kay**-soh |
| yogurt | **yogur** | yoh-**goor** |
| cereal | **cereales** | thay-ray-**ah**-lays |
| milk | **leche** | **lay**-chay |
| hot cocoa | **chocolate caliente** | choh-koh-**lah**-tay kahl-**yehn**-tay |
| fruit juice | **zumo de fruta** | **thoo**-moh day **froo**-tah |
| orange juice | **zumo de naranja** | **thoo**-moh day nah-**rahn**-*hah* |
| coffee / tea (see Drinking) | **café / té** | kah-**fay** / tay |
| Is breakfast included (in the room cost)? | **¿El desayuno está incluido?** | ehl day-sah-**yoo**-noh ay-**stah** een-kloo-**ee**-doh |

The traditional Spanish breakfast is *churros con chocolate*—greasy, cigar-shaped fritters or doughnuts that you dip in pudding-like chocolate. Try these at least once. For a more solid breakfast I prefer a slice of *tortilla española,* the hearty potato omelet that most cafés serve every morning. Add a little bread and *café con leche,* and you've got a cheap, filling meal.

## Tapas:

Bars called *tascas* or *tabernas* offer delicious appetizers called *tapas* during "normal" American-style eating hours when Spanish restaurants are still closed. If you want a cheap, quick, tasty meal before the sun sets, do the "Tapa Tango." Just point to the food you want and say, *"un pincho"* for a bite-sized serving, *"una tapa"* for a larger serving, *"una ración"* for a generous serving, or *"un bocadillo"* for an appetizer sandwich. Be careful. While veggies are cheap, seafood can be very expensive. If you see a sign, usually handwritten, that reads, *"Hay...,"* it means, "Today we have..." (as in *"Hay caracoles,"* which means "We have snails").

To quench your thirst, ask for *una caña* (small draft beer), *un vinito tinto/blanco* (small glass of red or white wine), *una sangria* (mix of fruit juice and wine), or *un vaso de agua del grifo* (free glass of tap water).

| | |
|---|---|
| aceitunas | olives |
| albóndigas | spiced meatballs with sauce |
| almejas a la marinera | clams in paprika sauce |
| bocadillo chiquito | tiny sandwich |
| bacalao | cod |
| brocheta | meat shishkebabs |
| calamares a la Romana | rings of deep-fried squid |
| callos | chickpeas with tripe and sauce |
| caña | small draft beer |
| caracoles | tree snails |
| chorizo | spicy Spanish sausage |
| con alioli | with a sauce of garlic and olive oil |

| | |
|---|---|
| **croquetas** | fried meatballs |
| **empanadillas** | pastries stuffed with meat or seafood |
| **ensalada Rusa** | Russian salad of peas and carrots |
| **gambas a la plancha** | grilled prawns |
| **gambas al ajillo** | prawns cooked in garlic and olive oil |
| **gazpacho** | cold tomato soup |
| **jamón serrano** | cured ham |
| **judías verdes** | green beans |
| **mejillon** | mussels |
| **merluza** | hake fish |
| **morcilla** | blood sausage |
| **morros** | pig snout |
| **queso** | cheese |
| **patatas bravas** | fried potatoes with hot sauce |
| **pinchos de queso** | pieces of cheese |
| **pan** | bread |
| **pescaditos fritos** | assortment of little fried fish |
| **pinchos morunos** | skewer of spicy lamb or pork |
| **pollo ali-oli** | chicken with garlic and olive oil sauce |
| **pulpo** | octopus |
| **queso manchego** | sheep cheese |
| **sardines** | sardines |
| **seso** | lamb brains |
| **setas** | mushrooms |
| **tortilla** | omelet (usually made with potatoes) |

## Sandwiches:

| | | |
|---|---|---|
| I want a sandwich. | **Quiero un bocadillo.** | kee-**ehr**-oh oon boh-kah-**dee**-yoh |
| cheese | **queso** | **kay**-soh |

| tuna | atún | ah-**toon** |
|------|------|-------------|
| chicken | **pollo** | **poh**-yoh |
| turkey | **pavo** | **pah**-boh |
| ham | **jamón** | *h*ah-**mohn** |
| salami | **salami** | sah-**lah**-mee |
| egg salad | **ensalada de huevo** | ayn-sah-**lah**-dah day **way**-boh |
| lettuce | **lechuga** | lay-**choo**-gah |
| tomatoes | **tomates** | toh-**mah**-tays |
| onions | **cebollas** | thay-**boh**-yahs |
| mustard | **mostaza** | moh-**stah**-thah |
| mayonnaise | **mayonesa** | mah-yoh-**nay**-sah |

**EATING**

## Soups and salads:

| soup | **sopa** | **soh**-pah |
|------|----------|-------------|
| soup of the day | **sopa del día** | **soh**-pah dayl **dee**-ah |
| broth... | **caldo...** | **kahl**-doh |
| ...chicken | **...de pollo** | day **poh**-yoh |
| ...meat | **...de carne** | day **kar**-nay |
| ...fish | **...de pescado** | day pay-**skah**-doh |
| ...with noodles | **...con tallarines** | kohn tah-yah-**ree**-nays |
| ...with rice | **...con arroz** | kohn ah-**rohth** |
| thick vegetable soup | **puré de vegetales** | poo-**ray** day bay-*h*ay-**tah**-lays |
| seafood soup | **sopa de mariscos** | **soh**-pah day mah-**ree**-skohs |
| chilled soup | **gazpacho** | gahth-**pah**-choh |
| green salad | **ensalada verde** | ayn-sah-lah-dah **behr**-day |
| chef's salad... | **ensalada de la casa...** | ayn-sah-**lah**-dah day lah **kah**-sah |
| ...with ham and cheese | **...con queso y jamón** | kohn **kay**-soh ee *h*ah-mohn |
| ...with egg | **...con huevo** | kohn **way**-boh |
| lettuce | **lechuga** | lay-**choo**-gah |

| tomatoes | **tomates** | toh-**mah**-tays |
| cucumbers | **pepinos** | pay-**pee**-nohs |
| oil / vinegar | **aceite / vinagre** | ah-**thay**-tay / bee-**nah**-gray |
| What is in this salad? | **¿Que tiene esta ensalada?** | kay tee-**ehn**-ay **ay**-stah ayn-sah-**lah**-dah |

In Spanish restaurants, salad dressing is normally just the oil and vinegar at the table. The bread (*pan*) is usually white, not whole wheat (*integral*). Rolls are *bollos*.

## Seafood:

| seafood | **marisco** | mah-**ree**-skoh |
| assorted seafood | **marisco variado** | mah-**ree**-skoh bah-ree-**ah**-doh |
| fish | **pescado** | pay-**skah**-doh |
| cod | **bacalao** | bah-kahl-**ow** |
| salmon | **salmón** | sahl-**mohn** |
| trout | **trucha** | **troo**-chah |
| tuna | **atún** | ah-**toon** |
| herring | **arenque** | ah-**rayn**-kay |
| sardines | **sardinas** | sar-**dee**-nahs |
| anchovies | **anchoas** | ahn-**choh**-ahs |
| clams | **almejas** | ahl-**may**-hahs |
| mussels | **mejillones** | may-hee-**yoh**-nays |
| oysters | **ostras** | **oh**-strahs |
| prawns | **gambas** | **gahm**-bahs |
| large prawns | **langostinos** | lahn-goh-**stee**-nohs |
| crab | **cangrejo** | kahn-**greh**-hoh |
| lobster | **langosta** | lahn-**goh**-stah |
| octopus | **pulpo** | **pool**-poh |
| squid | **calamares** | kah-lah-**mah**-rays |

| Where did this live? | ¿Dónde vivía este? | dohn-day bee-bee-ah ay-stay |
| Just the head, please. | Solo la cabeza, por favor. | soh-loh lah kah-bay-thah por fah-bor |

## Poultry and meat:

| poultry | aves | ah-bays |
| chicken | pollo | poh-yoh |
| turkey | pavo | pah-boh |
| duck | pato | pah-toh |
| meat | carne | kar-nay |
| beef | carne de vaca | kar-nay day bah-kah |
| roast beef | carne asada | kar-nay ah-sah-dah |
| beef steak | biftec | beef-tayk |
| hamburger | hamburguesa | ahm-boor-gay-sah |
| sausage | chorizo, salchichon | choh-ree-thoh, sahl-chee-chon |
| veal | ternera | tehr-nay-rah |
| cutlet | chuleta | choo-lay-tah |
| pork | cerdo | thehr-doh |
| ham | jamón | hah-mohn |
| lamb | carnero | kar-nay-roh |
| a wee goat | cabrito | kah-bree-toh |
| bunny | conejo | koh-nay-hoh |
| brains | sesos | say-sohs |
| tongue | lengua | lehn-gwah |
| liver | hígado | ee-gah-doh |
| kidney | riñones | reen-yoh-nays |
| tripe | tripa | tree-pah |
| horse | caballo | kah-bah-yoh |
| How long has this been dead? | ¿Cuánto tiempo hace que lo mataron? | kwahn-toh tee-ehm-poh ah-thay kay loh mah-tah-rohn |

EATING

## How it's prepared:

| | | |
|---|---|---|
| hot | **caliente** | kahl-**yehn**-tay |
| cold | **frío** | **free**-oh |
| raw | **crudo** | **kroo**-doh |
| cooked | **cocinado** | koh-thee-**nah**-doh |
| baked | **asado** | ah-**sah**-doh |
| boiled | **cocido** | koh-**thee**-doh |
| fillet | **filete** | fee-**lay**-tay |
| fresh | **fresco** | **fray**-skoh |
| fried | **frito** | **free**-toh |
| grilled | **a la plancha** | ah lah **plahn**-chah |
| homemade | **casera** | kah-**sehr**-ah |
| medium | **medio** | **may**-dee-oh |
| microwave | **microondas** | mee-kroh-**ohn**-dahs |
| mild | **templado** | tehm-**plah**-doh |
| poached | **escalfado** | ay-skahl-**fah**-doh |
| rare | **poco hecho** | **poh**-koh ay-**choh** |
| roasted | **asado** | ah-**sah**-doh |
| smoked | **ahumado** | ah-oo-**mah**-doh |
| spicy hot | **picante** | pee-**kahn**-tay |
| steamed | **hervido** | ehr-**bee**-doh |
| stuffed | **relleno** | ray-**yay**-noh |
| sweet | **dulce** | **dool**-thay |
| well-done | **muy hecho** | **moo**-ee ay-**choh** |

## Spanish specialties:

| | |
|---|---|
| **cochinillo asado** | roasted suckling pig marinated in herbs, oil, and white wine (Segovia & Toledo) |
| **empanada gallega** | a pizza-like pie of beef, pork or seafood with onions, tomatoes, and bell peppers |
| **fabada asturiana** | beans, pork, and paprika stew |

| | | |
|---|---|---|
| gazpacho | | chilled soup of tomatoes, garlic, and vinegar |
| horchata | | refreshing almond-flavored drink served at outdoor food and drink stalls |
| paella | | saffron-flavored rice dish with seafood or rabbit |
| pimientos a la riojana | | sweet peppers stuffed with minced meat |
| pisto | | vegetarian stew of zucchini, tomatoes, and bell peppers |
| riñones al jerez | | kidneys in a sherry sauce |
| sopa castellana | | soup with egg, garlic, and bread |
| tortilla española | | thick potato omelet |

EATING

## Veggies, pasta, beans, and rice:

| | | |
|---|---|---|
| vegetables | verduras | behr-**doo**-rahs |
| artichoke | alcachofa | ahl-kah-**choh**-fah |
| asparagus | espárragos | ay-**spah**-rah-gohs |
| beans | frijoles | free-**hoh**-lays |
| beets | remolachas | ray-moh-**lah**-chahs |
| broccoli | brécol | **bray**-kohl |
| cabbage | col | kohl |
| carrots | zanahorias | thah-nah-oh-**ree**-ahs |
| cauliflower | coliflor | koh-lee-**flor** |
| corn | maíz | mah-**eeth** |
| cucumber | pepino | pay-**pee**-noh |
| eggplant | berenjena | bay-rehn-**hay**-nah |
| French fries | patatas fritas | pah-**tah**-tahs **free**-tahs |
| garlic | ajo | **ah**-hoh |
| green beans | judías verdes | hoo-**dee**-ahs **behr**-days |
| lentils | lentejas | layn-**tay**-hahs |
| mushrooms | setas | **say**-tahs |

| olives | **aceitunas** | ah-thay-**too**-nahs |
| onions | **cebollas** | thay-**boh**-yahs |
| pasta | **pasta** | **pah**-stah |
| peas | **guisantes** | gee-**sahn**-tays |
| pepper... | **pimiento...** | pee-mee-**ehn**-toh |
| ...green / red | **...verde / rojo** | **behr**-day / **roh**-hoh |
| ...hot | **...picante** | pee-**kahn**-tay |
| pickles | **pepinillos** | pay-pee-**nee**-yohs |
| potatoes | **patatas** | pah-**tah**-tahs |
| rice | **arroz** | ah-**rohth** |
| spaghetti | **espaguetis** | ay-spah-**geh**-tees |
| spinach | **espinacas** | ay-spee-**nah**-kahs |
| tomatoes | **tomates** | toh-**mah**-tays |
| zucchini | **calabacín** | kah-lah-bah-**theen** |

## Fruits and nuts:

| almond | **almendra** | ahl-**mayn**-drah |
| apple | **manzana** | mahn-**thah**-nah |
| apricot | **albaricoque** | ahl-bah-ree-**koh**-kay |
| banana | **plátano** | **plah**-tah-noh |
| canteloupe | **melón** | may-**lohn** |
| cherry | **cereza** | thay-**ray**-thah |
| chestnut | **castaña** | kah-**stahn**-yah |
| coconut | **coco** | **koh**-koh |
| date | **dátile** | **dah**-tee-lay |
| fig | **higo** | **ee**-goh |
| fruit | **fruta** | **froo**-tah |
| grapefruit | **pomelo** | poh-**may**-loh |
| grapes | **uvas** | **oo**-bahs |
| hazelnut | **avellana** | ah-bay-**yah**-nah |
| lemon | **limón** | lee-**mohn** |
| orange | **naranja** | nah-**rahn**-hah |

| | | |
|---|---|---|
| big, mean peach | **melocotón** | may-loh-koh-**tohn** |
| peanut | **cacahuete** | kah-kah-**way**-tay |
| pear | **pera** | **pay**-rah |
| pineapple | **piña** | **peen**-yah |
| pistachio | **pistacho** | pee-**stah**-choh |
| plum | **ciruela** | theer-**way**-lah |
| prune | **ciruela seca** | theer-**way**-lah **say**-kah |
| raspberry | **frambuesa** | frahm-**bway**-sah |
| strawberry | **fresa** | **fray**-sah |
| tangerine | **mandarina** | mahn-dah-**ree**-nah |
| walnut | **nuez** | noo-**ayth** |
| watermelon | **sandía** | sahn-**dee**-ah |

## Just desserts:

| | | |
|---|---|---|
| dessert | **postres** | **poh**-strays |
| little tarts and cakes | **pastas** | **pah**-stahs |
| caramel custard | **flan** | flahn |
| cake | **bizcocho** | beeth-**koh**-choh |
| cupcakes | **magdalenas** | mahg-dah-**lay**-nahs |
| ice cream cake | **tarta helada** | **tar**-tah ay-**lah**-dah |
| fruit cup | **macedonia** | mah-theh-**doh**-nee-ah |
| tart | **tarta** | **tar**-tah |
| whipped cream | **nata montada** | **nah**-tah mohn-**tah**-dah |
| chocolate mousse | **mousse** | moos |
| pudding | **pudín** | poo-**deen** |
| pastry | **pasteles** | pah-**stay**-lays |
| cookies | **galletas** | gah-**yay**-tahs |
| candy | **caramelo** | kah-rah-**may**-loh |
| low calorie | **bajo en calorías** | **bah**-hoh ayn kah-loh-**ree**-ahs |
| homemade | **hecho en casa** | **ay**-choh ayn **kah**-sah |
| Superb! | **¡Riquísimo!** | ree-**kee**-see-moh |
| Exquisite! | **¡Exquisito!** | ayk-see-**see**-toh |

### Ice cream:

| | | |
|---|---|---|
| ice cream | **helado** | ay-**lah**-doh |
| sherbet | **sorbete** | sor-**bay**-tay |
| cone | **cucurucho** | koo-koo-**roo**-choh |
| cup | **tarrina** | tah-**ree**-nah |
| vanilla | **vainilla** | bī-**nee**-yah |
| chocolate | **chocolate** | choh-koh-**lah**-tay |
| strawberry | **fresa** | **fray**-sah |
| lemon | **limón** | lee-**mohn** |

# Drinking

### Water, milk, and juice:

| | | |
|---|---|---|
| mineral water | **agua mineral** | ah-gwah mee-nay-**rahl** |
| with / without... | **con / sin...** | kohn / seen |
| ...carbonation | **...gas** | gahs |
| tap water | **agua del grifo** | ah-gwah dayl **gree**-foh |
| milk... | **leche...** | **lay**-chay |
| ...skim | **...desnatada** | days-nah-**tah**-dah |
| ...fresh | **...fresca** | **fray**-skah |
| ...hot | **...caliente** | kahl-**yehn**-tay |
| hot chocolate | **chocolate caliente** | choh-koh-**lah**-tay kahl-**yehn**-tay |
| juice... | **zumo...** | **thoo**-moh |
| ...fruit | **...de fruta** | day **froo**-tah |
| ...orange | **...de naranja** | day nah-**rahn**-hah |
| ...apple | **...de manzana** | day mahn-**thah**-nah |
| with / without... | **con / sin...** | kohn / seen |
| ...ice / sugar | **...hielo / azúcar** | **yay**-loh / ah-**thoo**-kar |
| glass / cup | **vaso / taza** | **bah**-soh / **tah**-thah |

| bottle | botella | boh-**tay**-yah |
| small / large | pequeña / grande | pay-**kayn**-yah / **grahn**-day |
| Is the water | ¿Es el agua | ays ehl ah-gwah |
| safe to drink? | potable? | poh-**tah**-blay |

A *horchata* (or-**chah**-tah) is a refreshing drink made of almonds.

## Coffee and tea:

| coffee... | café... | kah-**feh** |
| ...espresso | ...espreso | ay-**spreh**-soh |
| ...black | ...solo | **soh**-loh |
| ...with a little milk | ...cortado | kor-**tah**-doh |
| ...with a lot of milk | ...con leche | kohn **lay**-chay |
| ...with sugar | ...con azúcar | kohn ah-**thoo**-kar |
| ...decaffeinated | ...descafeinado | day-skah-fay-**nah**-doh |
| ...instant | ...Nescafe | **nehs**-kah-fay |
| ...iced | ...con hielo | kohn **yay**-loh |
| ...American-syle | ...americano | ah-may-ree-**kah**-noh |
| hot water | agua caliente | **ah**-gwah kahl-**yehn**-tay |
| tea / lemon | té / limón | tay / lee-**mohn** |
| tea bag | infusion de té | een-foo-see-**ohn** day tay |
| iced tea | té con hielo | tay kohn **yay**-loh |
| small / large | corto / largo | **kor**-toh / **lar**-goh |
| small cup | taza mediana | **tah**-thah may-dee-**ah**-nah |
| large cup | taza grande | **tah**-thah **grahn**-day |
| Another cup. | Otra taza. | **oh**-trah **tah**-thah |
| Same price at the bar or the table? | ¿Es el mismo precio de barra o mesa? | ehs ehl **mees**-moh **pray**-thee-oh day **bah**-rah oh **may**-sah |

In bigger cities, bars have menu boards that clearly list three price levels: prices are cheapest at the *barra* (counter), higher at the *mesa* (table), and highest on the *terraza* (terrace).

## Wine:

| | | |
|---|---|---|
| I want... | **Quiero...** | kee-**ehr**-oh |
| We want... | **Queremos...** | kehr-**ay**-mohs |
| ...a glass | **...un vaso** | oon **bah**-soh |
| ...a carafe | **...una jarra** | **oo**-nah *hah*-rah |
| ...a bottle | **...una botella** | **oo**-nah boh-**tay**-yah |
| ...of red wine | **...de vino tinto** | day **bee**-noh **teen**-toh |
| ...of white wine | **...de vino blanco** | day **bee**-noh **blahn**-koh |
| ...of the region | **...de la región** | day lah ray-*hee*-**ohn** |
| ...the wine list | **...la carta de vinos** | lah **kar**-tah day **bee**-nohs |

## Wine words:

| | | |
|---|---|---|
| wine | **vino** | **bee**-noh |
| table wine | **vino de mesa** | **bee**-noh day **may**-sah |
| cheap house wine | **vino de la casa** | **bee**-noh day lah **kah**-sah |
| local | **de la región** | day lah ray-*hee*-**ohn** |
| red | **tinto** | **teen**-toh |
| white | **blanco** | **blahn**-koh |
| rosé | **rosado** | roh-**sah**-doh |
| sparkling | **cava** | **kah**-vah |
| sweet | **dulce** | **dool**-thay |
| medium | **semi-seco** | say-mee-**say**-koh |
| dry | **seco** | **say**-koh |
| very dry | **muy seco** | **moo**-ee **say**-koh |
| cork | **corcho** | **kor**-choh |

In Spain, wine lovers will find delicious wines at reasonable prices. *Rioja* wines are excellent. The words *Reserva* and *Gran Reserva* on the label are signs of a better quality. Whites and reds from the *Penedés* region near Barcelona are a good value. *Valdepeñas* wines are usually cheap and forgettable. A carafe of house wine with your meal is often very cheap.

*Jerez* (sherry), a fortified wine from the Jerez region, is an acquired taste. Types of sherry range from dry to sweet: *fino, manzanilla, amontillado, olovoso, cream.*

For a refreshing blend of red wine, seltzer, fruit, and fruit juice, try *Sangria. Chinchon* is an anise-flavored liqueur, and *cava* is Spanish champagne. *¡Salud!*

**EATING**

## Beer:

| | | |
|---|---|---|
| beer | **cerveza** | thehr-**bay**-thah |
| glass of draft beer | **caña** | **kahn**-yah |
| big glass of draft beer | **tubo** | **too**-boh |
| bottle | **botella** | boh-**tay**-yah |
| light / dark | **rubia / negra** | **roo**-bee-ah / **nay**-grah |
| local / imported | **local / importada** | loh-**kahl** / eem-por-**tah**-dah |
| small / large | **pequeña / grande** | pay-**kayn**-yah / **grahn**-day |
| alcohol-free | **sin-alcohol** | seen-ahl-**kohl** |
| low calorie | **light** | "light" |
| cold / colder | **fría / más fría** | **free**-ah / mahs **free**-ah |

## Bar talk:

| | | |
|---|---|---|
| What would you like? | ¿Qué quiere? | kay kee-**ay**-ray |
| What is the local specialty? | ¿Cuál es la especialidad regional? | kwahl ays lah ay-spay-thee-ah-lee-**dahd** ray-*hee*-oh-**nahl** |
| Straight. | Solo. | **soh**-loh |
| With / Without... | Con / Sin... | kohn / seen |
| ...alcohol. | ...alcohol. | ahl-**kohl** |
| ...ice. | ...hielo. | **yay**-loh |
| One more. | Otro. | **oh**-troh |
| Cheers! | ¡Salud! | sah-**lood** |
| Let's make a toast to...! | ¡Vamos a brindar por...! | **bah**-mohs ah breen-**dar** por |
| ...you | ...usted | oo-**stehd** |
| ...Spain | ...España | ay-**spahn**-yah |
| I'm feeling... | Me siento... | may see-**ehn**-toh |
| ...a little drunk. | ...un poco borracho[a]. | oon **poh**-koh boh-**rah**-choh |
| ...blitzed. | ...borracho[a]. | boh-**rah**-choh |

# Picnicking

## At the market:

| | | |
|---|---|---|
| Self-service? | ¿Auto-servicio? | ow-toh-sehr-bee-thee-oh |
| Ripe for today? | ¿Maduro para hoy? | mah-doo-roh pah-rah oy |
| Does it need to be cooked? | ¿Esto necesita cocinarse? | ay-stoh nay-thay-see-tah koh-thee-nar-say |
| May I taste a little? | ¿Podría probarlo? | poh-dree-ah proh-bar-loh |
| Fifty grams. | Cincuenta gramos. | theen-kwehn-tah grah-mohs |
| One hundred grams. | Cien gramos. | thee-ehn grah-mohs |
| More. / Less. | Más. / Menos. | mahs / may-nohs |
| A piece. | Un trozo. | oon troh-thoh |
| A slice. | Una rodaja. | oo-nah roh-dah-hah |
| Sliced. | En rodajas. | ayn roh-dah-hahs |
| A small bag. | Una bolsita. | oo-nah bohl-see-tah |
| A bag, please. | Una bolsa, por favor. | oo-nah bohl-sah por fah-bor |
| Will you make me a sandwich? | ¿Me puede hacer un bocadillo? | may pway-day ah-thehr oon boh-kah-dee-yoh |
| To take out. | Para llevar. | pah-rah yay-bar |
| Is there a park nearby? | ¿Hay un parque cerca de aquí? | ī oon par-kay thehr-kah day ah-kee |
| Okay to picnic here? | ¿Se puede hacer picnic aquí? | say pway-day hah-thehr peek-neek ah-kee |
| Enjoy your meal! | ¡Qué aproveche! | kay ah-proh-vay-chay |

EATING

While you can opt for the one-stop *supermercado,* it's more fun to assemble your picnic and practice your Spanish visiting the small shops. A hundred grams of meat or cheese is about ¼ pound, enough for two sandwiches.

## Picnic prose:

| | | |
|---|---|---|
| open air market | **mercado municipal** | mehr-**kah**-doh moo-nee-thee-**pahl** |
| supermarket | **supermercado** | soo-pehr-mehr-**kah**-doh |
| picnic | **picnic** | peek-**neek** |
| sandwich | **bocadillo** | boh-kah-**dee**-yoh |
| bread | **pan** | pahn |
| whole wheat bread | **pan de trigo** | pahn day **tree**-goh |
| roll | **panecillo** | pah-nay-**thee**-yoh |
| ham | **jamón** | *h*ah-**mohn** |
| smoked ham | **jamón serrano** | *h*ah-**mohn** say-**rah**-noh |
| sausage | **salchichón** | sahl-chee-**chohn** |
| cheese | **queso** | **kay**-soh |
| mild / sharp | **suave / fuerte** | **swah**-bay / **fwehr**-tay |
| mustard... | **mostaza...** | mohs-**tah**-thah |
| mayonnaise... | **mayonesa...** | mah-yoh-**nay**-sah |
| ...in a tube | **...en tubo** | ayn **too**-boh |
| yogurt | **yogur** | yoh-**goor** |
| fruit | **fruta** | **froo**-tah |
| box of juice | **lata de zumo** | **lah**-tah day **thoo**-moh |
| cold drinks | **bebidas frías** | bay-**bee**-dahs **free**-ahs |
| spoon / fork... | **cuchara / tenedor...** | koo-**chah**-rah / tay-nay-**dor** |
| ...made of plastic | **...de plástico** | day **plah**-stee-koh |
| cup / plate... | **vaso / plato...** | **bah**-soh / **plah**-toh |
| ...made of paper | **...de papel** | day **pah**-pehl |

# Spanish-English Menu Decoder

This decoder won't unlock every word on the menu, but it'll get you *ostras* (oysters) instead of *orejas* (pigs' ears).

**a parte**  side dish
**aceite**  oil
**aceitunas**  olives
**agua**  water
**ahumado**  smoked
**ajo**  garlic
**albaricoque**  apricot
**albóndigas**  meatballs
**alcachofa**  artichoke
**almejas**  clams
**almendra**  almond
**almuerzo**  lunch
**anchoas**  anchovies
**aperitivos**  appetizers
**arenque**  herring
**arroz**  rice
**asado**  baked
**atún**  tuna
**avellana**  hazelnut
**aves**  poultry
**azúcar**  sugar
**bacalao**  cod
**bebida**  beverage
**berenjena**  eggplant
**biftec**  beef steak
**bizcocho**  cake
**blanco**  white
**bocadillo**  sandwich
**bocadillo chiquito**  tiny sandwich
**botella**  bottle
**brocheta**  meat shish kebabs

**brécol**  broccoli
**burbujas**  carbonation
**caballo**  horse
**cabrito**  a wee goat
**cacahuete**  peanut
**café**  coffee
**calabacín**  zucchini
**calamares**  squid
**caldo**  broth
**caliente**  hot (not cold)
**cangrejo**  crab
**caña**  draft beer
**caracoles**  tree snails
**caramelo**  candy
**carne**  meat
**carne de vaca**  beef
**carnero**  lamb
**carta de vinos**  wine list
**casa**  house
**casera**  homemade
**castaña**  chestnut
**cebollas**  onions
**cena**  dinner
**cerdo**  pork
**cereales**  cereal
**cereza**  cherry
**cerveza**  beer
**chino**  chinese
**chorizo**  sausage
**chuleta**  cutlet
**churros**  fritters

MENU DECODER

**ciruela** plum
**cochinillo** suckling pig
**cocido** broiled
**cocinado** cooked
**coco** coconut
**col** cabbage
**coliflor** cauliflower
**combinado** combination
**comida** food
**con** with
**con alioli** with garlic & olive oil
**conejo** rabbit
**cono** cone
**corto** small
**croquetas** fried meatballs
**crudo** raw
**cuchara** scoop, spoon
**dátile** date
**delicioso** delicious
**del día** of the day
**desayuno** breakfast
**dulce** sweet
**duro** hard
**empanada** meat pie
**ensalada** salad
**escalfado** poached
**espaguetis** spaghetti
**espárragos** asparagus
**especial** special
**espinacas** spinach
**espumoso** sparkling
**filete** fillet
**flan** caramel custard
**frambuesa** raspberry
**fresa** strawberry
**fresco** fresh

**frijoles** beans
**frío** cold
**fritos** fried
**fruta** fruit
**galletas** cookies
**gambas** prawns
**garrafa** carafe
**gas** carbonation
**gazpacho** chilled tomato soup
**gelatina** jelly
**grande** large
**guisantes** peas
**hamburguesa** hamburger
**hay...** we have
**hecho en casa** homemade
**helado** ice cream
**hervido** steamed
**hielo** ice
**hígado** liver
**higo** fig
**horchata** almond drink
**huevos** eggs
**importada** imported
**incluido** included
**jamón** ham
**jarra** carafe
**judías verdes** green beans
**langosta** lobster
**langostinos** large prawns
**leche** milk
**lechuga** lettuce
**lengua** tongue
**lentejas** lentils
**ligero** light
**limón** limon
**macedonia** fruit cup

**magdalenas** cupcakes
**maíz** corn
**mandarina** tangerine
**mantequilla** butter
**manzana** apple
**margarina** margarine
**marisco** seafood
**mayonesa** mayonnaise
**medio** medium
**mejillones** mussels
**melocotón** big, harsh peach
**melón** canteloupe
**merluze** hake fish
**mermelada** jam
**mesa** table
**microondas** microwave
**miel** honey
**morcilla** blood sausage
**mostaza** mustard
**naranja** orange
**negra** dark
**no** not
**no incluido** not included
**nuez** walnut
**o** or
**orejas** pigs' ears
**ostras** oysters
**paella** saffron rice dish
**pan** bread
**panecillo** roll
**para llevar** to go
**pastas** tarts & cakes
**pasteles** pastries
**patatas** potatoes
**patatas fritas** French fries
**pato** duck

**pavo** turkey
**pepinillos** pickles
**pepinos** cucumber
**pequeño** small
**pera** pear
**pescado** fish
**picante** spicy hot
**pimiento** bell pepper
**pincho** snack
**piña** pineapple
**pistacho** pistachio
**plancha** grilled
**plátano** banana
**plato** plate
**pollo** chicken
**pomelo** grapefruit
**postres** desserts
**primer** first
**pudín** pudding
**pulpo** octopus
**queso** cheese
**ración** portion
**rápido** fast
**relleno** stuffed
**remolachas** beets
**revueltos** scrambled
**riñones** kidney
**rodaja** slice
**rojo** red
**rosado** rosé
**rubia** light
**sabroso** tasty
**sal** salt
**salchichón** sausage
**salmón** salmon
**sandía** watermelon

**sardinas** sardines
**seco** dry
**segundo** second
**servicio** service
**sesos** brains
**setas** mushrooms
**sin** without
**solo** only
**sopa** soup
**sorbete** sherbet
**tallarines** noodles
**tapas** appetizers
**tarrina** cup
**tarta** tart
**taza** cup
**té** tea
**templado** mild
**ternera** veal
**tinto** red
**típico** typical
**tomates** tomatoes
**tortilla** omelet
**tortilla español** potato omelet
**tostadas** toast
**tripa** tripe
**trozo** piece
**trucha** trout
**tubo** draft beer
**turista** tourist
**uvas** grapes
**vainilla** vanilla
**variado** assorted
**vaso** glass
**vegetales** vegetables
**vegetariano** vegetarian
**verde** green

**verdura** vegetable
**vinagre** vinegar
**vino** wine
**y** and
**yogur** yoghurt
**zanahorias** carrots
**zumo** juice

# Sightseeing

| Where is...? | ¿Dónde está...? | dohn-day ay-**stah** |
|---|---|---|
| ...the best view | ...la mejor vista | lah may-**hor** bee-stah |
| ...the main square | ...la plaza mayor | lah **plah**-thah **may**-yor |
| ...the old town center | ...el viejo centro | ehl bee-**ay**-hoh **thayn**-troh |
| ...the museum | ...el museo | ehl moo-**say**-oh |
| ...the castle | ...el castillo | ehl kah-**stee**-yoh |
| ...the palace | ...el palacio | ehl pah-**lah**-thee-oh |
| ...the ruins | ...las ruinas | lahs **rwee**-nahs |
| ...the tourist information office | ...la Oficina de Turismo | lah oh-fee-**thee**-nah day too-**rees**-moh |
| ...the toilet | ...los aseos | lohs ah-**say**-ohs |
| ...the entrance / exit | ...la entrada / salida | lah ayn-**trah**-dah / sah-**lee**-dah |
| Is there a festival nearby? | ¿Hay una fiesta cerca? | ī **oo**-nah fee-**eh**-stah **thehr**-kah |
| Do you have...? | ¿Tiene...? | tee-**ehn**-ay |
| ...a map | ...un mapa | oon **mah**-pah |
| ...information | ...información | een-for-mah-thee-**ohn** |
| ...a guidebook | ...una guía | **oo**-nah **gee**-ah |
| ...a guided tour | ...una visita con guía | **oo**-nah bee-**see**-tah kohn **gee**-ah |
| ...in English | ...en inglés | ayn een-**glays** |
| When is the next tour in English? | ¿Cuándo es la siguiente visita en inglés? | **kwahn**-doh ays lah seeg-ee-**ehn**-tay bee-**see**-tah ayn een-**glays** |
| Is it free? | ¿Es gratis? | ays grah-**tees** |
| How much is it? | ¿Cuánto cuesta? | **kwahn**-toh **kway**-stah |

| Is (the ticket) good all day? | ¿Es válido para todo el día? | ays **bah**-lee-doh **pah**-rah **toh**-doh ehl **dee**-ah |
| Can I get back in? | ¿Puedo volver a entrar? | **pway**-doh bohl-**behr** ah ayn-**trar** |
| What time does this open / close? | ¿A qué hora abren / cierran? | ah kay **oh**-rah **ah**-brehn / thee-**ay**-rahn |
| What time is the last entry? | ¿A qué hora es la última entrada? | ah kay **oh**-rah ays lah **ool**-tee-mah ayn-**trah**-dah |
| PLEASE let me in. | POR FAVOR, déjeme entrar. | por fah-**bor** **day**-hay-may ayn-**trar** |
| I've traveled all the way from... | He viajado desde... | ay bee-ah-**hah**-doh **dehs**-day |
| I must leave tomorrow. | Tengo que irme mañana. | **tayn**-goh kay **eer**-may mahn-**yah**-nah |
| I promise I'll be fast. | Le prometo que vendré rápido. | lay proh-**may**-toh kay bayn-**dray rah**-pee-doh |

To help you decipher entrance signs, an *exposición* is an exhibit, a *bono* is a combo ticket, and the words *"Está aquí"* on a map mean "You are here."

## Discounts:

You may be eligible for a discount at tourist sites, hotels, or on buses and trains—ask.

| Are there discounts for...? | ¿Tienen descuentos para...? | tee-**ehn**-en days-**kwehn**-tohs **pah**-rah |
| ...youths | ...jovenes | *h*oh-bay-nays |
| ...students | ...estudiantes | ay-stoo-dee-**ahn**-tays |
| ...families | ...familias | fah-**meel**-yahs |
| ...seniors | ...jubilados | *h*oo-bee-**lah**-dohs |

| I am... | Tengo... | **tayn**-goh |
| He / She is... | Él / Ella tiene... | ehl / **ay**-yah tee-**ehn**-ay |
| ..._____ years old. | ..._____ años. | **ahn**-yohs |

## At the bullring:

| bullfight | corrida de toros | koh-**ree**-dah day **toh**-rohs |
| bullring | plaza del toros | **plah**-thah dayl **toh**-rohs |
| the bull | el toro | ehl **toh**-roh |
| kill | matar | mah-**tar** |
| sunny / shady side | sol / sombra | sohl / **sohm**-brah |
| bull run | encierro | ayn-thee-**ay**-roh |

The bulls run through Pamplona (and some people) every July. Bullfights occur throughout April-October, usually on Sundays. In a Spanish bullfight, *el toro* (the bull) is killed by the *matador* (literally killer) and his assistants: *picadores* (guys on horseback) and *banderilleros* (acrobatic helpers). If you're squeamish, go to Portugal, where the bull is killed after the fight.

## In the museum:

| Where is...? | ¿Dónde está...? | **dohn**-day ay-**stah** |
| I want to see... | Quiero ver... | kee-**ehr**-oh behr |
| Photo / Video O.K.? | ¿Foto / Vídeo O.K.? | **foh**-toh / **bee**-day-oh "O.K." |
| No flash / tripod. | No flash / trípode. | noh flahsh / **tree**-poh-day |
| I like it. | Me gusta. | may **goo**-stah |
| It's so... | Es tan... | ays tahn |
| ...beautiful. | ...bonito. | boh-**nee**-toh |
| ...ugly. | ...feo. | **fay**-oh |

| | | |
|---|---|---|
| ...strange. | ...extraño. | ayk-**strahn**-yoh |
| ...boring. | ...aburrido. | ah-boo-**ree**-doh |
| ...interesting. | ...interesante. | een-tay-ray-**sahn**-tay |
| Wow! | ¡Caray! | kah-**rī** |
| My feet hurt! | ¡Me duelen los pies! | may **dway**-lehn lohs pee-**ays** |
| I'm exhausted! | ¡Estoy muy cansado[a]! | ay-**stoy** moo-ee kahn-**sah**-doh |

## Art and architecture:

| | | |
|---|---|---|
| art | arte | **ar**-tay |
| artist | artista | ar-**tee**-stah |
| painting | cuadro | **kwah**-droh |
| self portrait | autorretrato | ow-toh-ray-**trah**-toh |
| sculptor | escultor | ay-skool-**tor** |
| sculpture | escultura | ay-skool-**too**-rah |
| architect | arquitecto | ar-kee-**tehk**-toh |
| architecture | arquitectura | ar-kee-tehk-**too**-rah |
| original | original | oh-ree-*hee*-**nahl** |
| restored | restaurado | ray-stow-**rah**-doh |
| B.C. | A.C. | ah thay |
| A.D. | D.C. | day thay |
| century | siglo | **see**-gloh |
| style | estilo | ay-**stee**-loh |
| Abstract | Abstracto | ahb-**strahk**-toh |
| Ancient | Antiguo | ahn-**tee**-gwoh |
| Art Nouveau | Modernista | moh-dehr-**nee**-stah |
| Baroque | Barroco | bah-**roh**-koh |
| Classical | Clásico | **klah**-see-koh |
| Gothic | Gótico | **goh**-tee-koh |
| Impressionist | Impresionismo | eem-pray-see-oh-**nees**-moh |
| Medieval | Medieval | may-dee-ay-**vahl** |

| Modern | **Moderno** | moh-**dehr**-noh |
| Moorish | **Moros** | moh-rohs |
| Renaissance | **Renacimiento** | ray-nah-thee-mee-**ehn**-toh |
| Romanesque | **Románico** | roh-**mah**-nee-koh |
| Romantic | **Romanticismo** | roh-mahn-tee-**thees**-moh |

## Art terms unique to Spain:

**Alcazaba**: A Moorish castle.

**Alcázar**: A Moorish fortress or palace.

**Azulejo**: Blue tile.

**Churrigueresque**: Super-thick Spanish Baroque, named after a local artist.

**Moriscos**: The Islamic Arabs (Moors) who ruled much of Spain and Portugal from 711 to 1492. The Moorish culture left a deep mark on Iberia. An understanding of the Moorish occupation will help you better understand your sightseeing.

**Mozarabs**: Christians in Spain under Moorish rule.

**Mudejar**: The Gothic-Islamic style of the Moors in Spain after the Christian conquest.

**Plateresque**: The frilly late Gothic style of Spain.

## Castles and palaces:

| castle | **castillo** | kah-**stee**-yoh |
| palace | **palacio** | pah-**lah**-thee-oh |
| kitchen | **cocina** | koh-**thee**-nah |
| cellar | **bodega** | boh-**day**-gah |
| dungeon | **calabozo** | kah-lah-**boh**-thoh |
| moat | **foso** | **foh**-soh |
| fortified walls | **paredes fortificadas** | pah-**ray**-days for-tee-fee-**kah**-dahs |

SIGHTSEEING

| tower | torre | **toh**-ray |
| fountain | fuente | **fwehn**-tay |
| garden | jardín | *h*ar-**deen** |
| king | rey | ray |
| queen | reina | ray-**ee**-nah |
| knights | caballería | kah-bah-yay-**ree**-ah |

## Religious words:

| cathedral | catedral | kah-tay-**drahl** |
| church | iglesia | ee-**glay**-see-ah |
| synagogue | sinagoga | see-nah-**goh**-gah |
| chapel | capilla | kah-**pee**-yah |
| cross | cruz | krooth |
| treasury | tesoro | tay-**soh**-roh |
| crypt | cripta | **kreep**-tah |
| dome | cúpula | **koo**-poo-lah |
| bells | campanas | kahm-**pah**-nahs |
| organ | órgano | **or**-gah-noh |
| choir | coro | **koh**-roh |
| relic | reliquia | ray-**lee**-kee-ah |
| saint | santo[a] | **sahn**-toh |
| God | Dios | **dee**-ohs |
| Jewish | judío | *h*oo-**dee**-oh |
| Moslem | musulmán | moo-sool-**mahn** |
| Protestant | protestante | proh-tay-**stahn**-tay |
| Catholic | católico | kah-**toh**-lee-koh |
| agnostic | agnóstico | ahg-**noh**-stee-koh |
| atheist | ateo | ah-**tay**-oh |
| When is the mass / service? | ¿A qué hora es la misa / servicio? | ah kay **oh**-rah ays lah **mee**-sah / sehr-**bee**-thee-oh |
| Are there concerts in the church? | ¿Hay conciertos en la iglesia? | ī kohn-thee-**ehr**-tohs ayn lah ee-**glay**-see-ah |

# Shopping

## Names of shops:

| Where is a...? | Dónde está un...? | dohn-day ay-stah oon |
|---|---|---|
| antique shop | anticuarios | ahn-tee-kwah-ree-ohs |
| art gallery | galería de arte | gah-lay-ree-ah day ar-tay |
| bakery | panadería | pah-nah-deh-ree-ah |
| barber shop | barbería | bar-beh-ree-ah |
| beauty salon | peluquería | pay-loo-keh-ree-ah |
| book shop | librería | lee-bray-ree-ah |
| camera shop | tienda de fotos | tee-ehn-dah day foh-tohs |
| coffee shop | cafetería | kah-fay-tay-ree-ah |
| department store | grandes almacenes | grahn-days ahl-mah-thay-nays |
| flea market | rastro | rahs-troh |
| flower market | floristería | floh-ree-steh-ree-ah |
| grocery store | supermercado | soo-pehr-mehr-kah-doh |
| hardware store | ferretería | fehr-ray-tay-ree-ah |
| jewelry shop | joyería | hoy-eh-ree-ah |
| laundromat | lavandería | lah-bahn-deh-ree-ah |
| newsstand | kiosco | kee-oh-skoh |
| open air market | mercado municipal | mehr-kah-doh moo-nee-thee-pahl |
| office supplies | material de oficina | mah-tay-ree-ahl day oh-fee-thee-nah |
| optician | óptico[a] | ohp-tee-koh |
| pastry shop | pastelería | pah-stay-lay-ree-ah |
| pharmacy | farmacia | far-mah-thee-ah |

SHOPPING

| | | |
|---|---|---|
| photocopy shop | **fotocopias** | foh-toh-**koh**-pee-ahs |
| shopping mall | **centro comercial** | **thehn**-troh koh-mehr-thee-**ahl** |
| souvenir shop | **tienda de souvenirs** | tee-**ehn**-dah day soo-bay-**neers** |
| supermarket | **supermercado** | soo-pehr-mehr-**kah**-doh |
| toy store | **juguetería** | *h*oo-gay-teh-**ree**-ah |
| travel agency | **agencia de viajes** | ah-**hayn**-thee-ah day bee-**ah**-*h*ays |
| used bookstore | **tienda de libros usados** | tee-**ehn**-dah day lee-brohs oo-**sah**-dohs |
| wine shop | **tienda de vinos** | tee-**ehn**-dah day bee-nohs |

## Shop till you drop:

| | | |
|---|---|---|
| opening hours | **horas de apertura** | **oh**-rahs day ah-pay-**too**-rah |
| sale | **rebajas** | ray-**bah**-*h*ahs |
| gifts | **regalos** | ray-**hah**-lohs |
| How much is it? | **¿Cuánto cuesta?** | **kwahn**-toh **kway**-stah |
| I'm / We're... | **Estoy / Estamos...** | ay-**stoy** / ay-**stah**-mohs |
| ...browsing. | **...mirando.** | mee-**rahn**-doh |
| Where can I buy...? | **¿Dónde puedo comprar...?** | **dohn**-day **pway**-doh kohm-**prar** |
| I want... | **Quiero...** | kee-**ehr**-oh |
| Do you have...? | **¿Tiene usted...?** | tee-**ehn**-ay oo-**stehd** |
| ...something cheaper | **...algo más barato** | **ahl**-goh mahs bah-**rah**-toh |
| ...more | **...más** | mahs |
| Better quality, please. | **Mejor calidad, por favor.** | may-*h*or kah-lee-**dahd** por fah-**bor** |
| Can I see...? | **¿Puedo ver...?** | **pway**-doh behr |
| This one. | **Este.** | **ay**-stay |
| Can I try it on? | **¿Puedo probarlo?** | **pway**-doh proh-**bar**-loh |

| Do you have a mirror? | ¿Tiene un espejo? | tee-**ehn**-ay oon ay-**spay**-hoh |
| Too... | Muy... | moo-ee |
| ...big. | ...grande. | grahn-day |
| ...small. | ...pequeño. | pay-**kayn**-yoh |
| ...expensive. | ...caro. | **kah**-roh |
| Did you make this? | ¿Hizo usted esto? | ee-thoh oo-**stehd** ay-stoh |
| What is this made of? | ¿De qué está hecho esto? | day kay ay-**stah** ay-choh ay-stoh |
| Is it machine washable? | ¿Se puede lavar en la lavadora? | say **pway**-day lah-**bar** ayn lah lah-bah-**doh**-rah |
| Will it shrink? | ¿Esto se encoge? | **ay**-stoh say ayn-**koh**-hay |
| Credit card O.K.? | ¿Tarjeta de crédito O.K.? | tar-**hay**-tah day **kray**-dee-toh "O.K." |
| Can you ship this? | ¿Puede enviar esto? | **pway**-day ayn-bee-**ar ay**-stoh |
| Tax-free? | ¿Libre de impuestos? | **lee**-bray day eem-**pway**-stohs |
| I'll think about it. | Voy a pensármelo. | boy ah payn-**sar**-may-loh |
| What time do you close? | ¿A qué hora cierran? | ah kay **oh**-rah thee-**ay**-rahn |
| What time do you open tomorrow? | ¿A qué hora abren mañana? | ah kay **oh**-rah **ah**-brehn mahn-**yah**-nah |
| Is that your best price? | ¿Es éste su mejor precio? | ays **ay**-stay soo may-**hor pray**-thee-oh |
| My last offer. | Mi última oferta. | mee **ool**-tee-mah oh-**fehr**-tah |
| Good price. | Buen precio. | bwayn **pray**-thee-oh |
| I'll take it. | Lo quiero. | loh kee-**ehr**-oh |
| I don't have a nickel. | No tengo un duro. | no **tayn**-goh oon **doo**-roh |
| My friend... | Mi amigo[a]... | mee ah-**mee**-goh |
| My husband... | Mi marido... | mee mah-**ree**-doh |
| My wife... | Mi mujer... | mee moo-**hehr** |
| ...has the money. | ...tiene el dinero. | tee-**ehn**-ay ehl dee-**nay**-roh |

In Spain, shops are closed for a long lunch from 13:30 until about 16:30, and all day on Sundays.

Local souvenirs and postcards are cheapest in the big department stores. *El Corte Inglés* is Spain's ultimate department store, offering everything from cheap souvenirs, train and theater tickets, a money exchange office, to haircuts on Sundays. Madrid's is a block uphill from the *Puerta del Sol*. If you brake for garage sales, you'll pull a U-turn for Madrid's *El Rastro* flea market. Europe's biggest flea market sprawls for miles each Sunday.

You can find colors and types of fabrics listed in the dictionary near the end of this book.

## Repair:

These handy lines can apply to any repair, whether it's a stuck zipper, broken leg, or dying car.

| | | |
|---|---|---|
| This is broken. | **Esto está roto.** | ay-stoh ay-**stah roh**-toh |
| Can you fix it? | **¿Lo puede arreglar?** | loh **pway**-day ah-ray-**glar** |
| Just do the essentials. | **Haga solo lo esencial.** | ah-gah **soh**-loh loh ay-sehn-thee-**ahl** |
| How much will it cost? | **¿Cuánto costará?** | **kwahn**-toh koh-stah-**rah** |
| When will it be ready? | **¿Cuándo estará listo?** | **kwahn**-doh ay-stah-**rah lee**-stoh |
| I need it by ___. | **Lo necesito para ___.** | loh nay-thay-**thee**-toh **pah**-rah |

# Entertainment

| | | |
|---|---|---|
| What's happening tonight? | **¿Qué hay esta noche?** | kay ī **ay**-stah **noh**-chay |
| Can you recommend something? | **¿Me recomienda algo?** | may ray-kohm-**yehn**-dah **ahl**-goh |
| Is it free? | **¿Es gratis?** | ays grah-**tees** |
| Where can I buy a ticket? | **¿Dónde puedo comprar un billete?** | **dohn**-day pway-doh kohm-**prar** oon bee-**yeh**-tay |
| When does it start? | **¿Cuándo empieza esto?** | **kwahn**-doh aym-pee-**ay**-thah **ay**-stoh |
| When does it end? | **¿Cuándo acaba esto?** | **kwahn**-doh ah-**kah**-bah **ay**-stoh |
| Will you go out with me? | **¿Vendría conmigo?** | bayn-**dree**-ah kohn-**mee**-goh |
| Where's the best place to dance nearby? | **¿Dónde está el más cercano y mejor sitio para bailar?** | **dohn**-day ay-**stah** ehl mahs thehr-**kah**-noh ee may-**hor** **see**-tee-oh pah-rah bī-**lar** |
| Do you want to dance? | **¿Quiere bailar conmigo?** | kee-**ay**-ray bī-**lar** kohn-**mee**-goh |
| Again? | **¿Otra más?** | **oh**-trah mahs |
| Where is the best place to stroll? | **¿Dónde está el mejor paseo?** | **dohn**-day ay-**stah** ehl may-**hor** pah-**say**-oh |
| It's been a wonderful night. | **Ha sido una noche encantadora.** | ah **see**-doh oo-nah **noh**-chay ayn-kahn-tah-**doh**-rah |

## Entertaining words:

| | | |
|---|---|---|
| movie... | **película...** | pay-**lee**-koo-lah |
| ...original version | **...versión original** | behr-see-**ohn** oh-ree-**hee**-**nahl** |
| ...in English | **...en Inglés** | ayn een-**glays** |

ENTERTAINMENT

| | | |
|---|---|---|
| ...with subtitles | ...con subtítulos | kohn soob-**tee**-too-lohs |
| ...dubbed | ...doblada | doh-**blah**-dah |
| music... | música... | **moo**-see-kah |
| ...live | ...en vivo | ayn **bee**-boh |
| ...classical | ...clásica | **klah**-see-kah |
| ...folk | ...folklórica | fohk-**loh**-ree-kah |
| rock | rock | rohk |
| jazz | jazz | "jazz" |
| blues | blues | "blues" |
| singer | cantante | kahn-**tahn**-tay |
| concert | concierto | kohn-thee-**ehr**-toh |
| show | espectáculo | ay-spehk-**tah**-koo-loh |
| dancing | baile | **bī**-lay |
| flamenco | flamenco | flah-**mayn**-koh |
| folk dancing | baile folklórico | **bī**-lay fohk-**loh**-ree-koh |
| disco | disco | **dee**-skoh |
| cover charge | entrada | ayn-**trah**-dah |

For free, enjoyable entertainment, join the locals for a *paseo*, an evening stroll through town.

# Phoning

|  |  |  |
|---|---|---|
| Where is the nearest phone? | ¿Dónde está el teléfono más cercano? | **dohn**-day ay-**stah** ehl tay-**lay**-foh-noh mahs thehr-**kah**-noh |
| Where is the telephone office? | ¿Dónde está la Telefónica? | **dohn**-day ay-**stah** lah tay-lay-**foh**-nee-kah |
| I want to telephone... | Quiero llamar... | kee-**ehr**-oh yah-**mar** |
| ...the United States. | ...a los Estados Unidos. | ah lohs ay-**stah**-dohs oo-**nee**-dohs |
| How much per minute? | ¿Cuánto es por minuto? | **kwahn**-toh ays por mee-**noo**-toh |
| I want to make a... call. | Quiero hacer una llamada... | kee-**ehr**-oh ah-**thehr oo**-nah yah-**mah**-dah |
| ...local | ...local. | loh-**kahl** |
| ...collect | ...a cobro revertido. | ah **koh**-broh ray-behr-**tee**-doh |
| ...credit card | ...con tarjeta de crédito. | kohn tar-**hay**-tah day **kray**-dee-toh |
| ...long distance (within Spain) | ...nacional. | nah-thee-oh-**nahl** |
| ...international | ...internacional. | een-tehr-nah-thee-oh-**nahl** |
| It doesn't work. | No funciona. | noh foonk-thee-**oh**-nah |
| May I use your phone? | ¿Puedo usar su teléfono? | **pway**-doh oo-**sar** soo tay-**lay**-foh-noh |
| Can you dial for me? | ¿Puede marcarme el número? | **pway**-day mar-**kar**-may ehl **noo**-may-roh |
| Can you talk for me? | ¿Puede hablar usted por mi? | **pway**-day ah-**blar** oo-**stehd** por mee |
| It's busy. | Está occupado. | ay-**stah** oh-koo-**pah**-doh |
| Will you try again? | ¿Llamará otra vez? | yay-mah-**rah oh**-trah bayth |
| Hello. (on phone) | Diga. | **dee**-gah |

| My name is... | **Me llamo...** | may **yah**-moh |
| My number is... | **Mi número es...** | mee **noo**-may-roh ays |
| Speak slowly and clearly. | **Hable despacio y claro.** | **ah**-blay day-**spah**-thee-oh ee **klah**-roh |
| Wait a moment. | **Un momento.** | oon moh-**mehn**-toh |
| Don't hang up. | **No cuelgue.** | noh **kwayl**-gay |

## Key telephone words:

| telephone | **teléfono** | tay-**lay**-foh-noh |
| telephone card | **tarjeta telefónica** | tar-**hay**-tah tay-lay-**foh**-nee-kah |
| telephone office | **Telefónica** | tay-lay-**foh**-nee-kah |
| operator | **telefonista** | tay-lay-foh-**nee**-stah |
| international assistance | **asistencia internacional** | ah-see-**stehn**-thee-ah een-tehr-nah-thee-oh-**nahl** |
| country code | **prefijo del país** | pray-**fee**-hoh dayl pah-**ees** |
| area code | **prefijo** | pray-**fee**-hoh |
| telephone book | **guía de teléfonos** | **gee**-ah day tay-**lay**-foh-nohs |
| toll-free call | **llamada gratuita** | yah-**mah**-dah grah-**twee**-tah |
| out of service | **averiado** | ah-bay-ree-**ah**-doh |

Buy a handy *tarjeta telefónica* (phone card) for 1,000 or 2,000 pesetas at a *tabacos* (tobacco) shop. Insert the card into a phone and dial away. If you get a wrong number, you'll hear the dreaded recording, *"Se ha equivocado de número."* See "Let's Talk Telephones" near the end of this book for tips on making calls.

You can often also buy postage stamps at the corner *tabacos* shop. As long as you know which stamps you need, this is a great convenience.

# E-mail

| | | |
|---|---|---|
| e-mail | **correo electrónico** | koh-**ray**-oh ay-lehk-**troh**-nee-koh |
| internet | **internet** | **een**-tehr-neht |
| May I check my e-mail? | **¿Puedo buscar mi correo electrónico?** | **pway**-day boos-**kar** mee koh-**ray**-oh ay-lehk-**troh**-nee-koh |
| Where can I get access to the internet? | **¿Dónde puedo acceder a internet?** | **dohn**-day **pway**-day ahk-thay-**dehr** ah **een**-tehr-neht |
| Where is the nearest cybercafé? | **¿Dónde está el café cibernético más próximo?** | dohn-day ay-stah ehl kah-fay thee-behr-nay-tee-koh mahs **prohk**-see-moh |

## On the computer screen:

| | |
|---|---|
| **abrir** | open |
| **borrar** | delete |
| **enviar** | send |
| **escribir** | write |
| **fichero** | file |
| **guardar** | save |
| **imprimir** | print |
| **mensaje** | message |
| **responder** | reply |

# Post Office

| | | |
|---|---|---|
| Where is the post office? | **¿Dónde está la oficina de correos?** | **dohn**-day ay-**stah** lah oh-fee-**thee**-nah day koh-**ray**-ohs |
| Which window for...? | **¿Cuál es la ventana para...?** | kwahl ays lah bayn-**tah**-nah **pah**-rah |
| Is this the line for...? | **¿Es esta la fila para...?** | ays **ay**-stah lah **fee**-lah **pah**-rah |

POST OFFICE

| | | |
|---|---|---|
| ...stamps | **...sellos** | **say**-yohs |
| ...packages | **...paquetes** | pah-**kay**-tays |
| To the United States... | **Para los Estados Unidos...** | **pah**-rah lohs ay-**stah**-dohs oo-**nee**-dohs |
| ...by air mail. | **...por avión.** | por ah-bee-**ohn** |
| ...slow and cheap. | **...por barco.** | por **bar**-koh |
| How much is it? | **¿Cuánto cuesta?** | **kwahn**-toh **kway**-stah |
| How many days will it take? | **¿Cuántos días tardará?** | **kwahn**-tohs **dee**-ahs tar-dah-**rah** |

## Handy postal words:

| | | |
|---|---|---|
| post office | **oficina de correos** | oh-fee-**thee**-nah day koh-**ray**-ohs |
| stamp | **sello** | **say**-yoh |
| postcard | **postal** | poh-**stahl** |
| letter | **carta** | **kar**-tah |
| aerogram | **aerograma** | ah-ay-roh-**grah**-mah |
| envelope | **sobre** | **soh**-bray |
| package | **paquete** | pah-**kay**-tay |
| box | **caja** | **kah**-*h*ah |
| string | **cordón** | kor-**dohn** |
| tape | **cinta adhesiva** | **theen**-tah ah-day-**see**-bah |
| mailbox | **buzón** | boo-**thohn** |
| air mail | **por avión** | por ah-bee-**ohn** |
| express | **rápido** | **rah**-pee-doh |
| surface mail (slow and cheap) | **por barco** | por **bar**-koh |
| book rate | **tarifa** | tah-**ree**-fah |
| weight limit | **peso máximo** | **pay**-soh **mahk**-see-moh |

| registered | **certificada** | thehr-tee-fee-**kah**-dah |
| insured | **asegurada** | ah-say-goo-**rah**-dah |
| fragile | **frágil** | **frah**-_heel_ |
| contents | **contenido** | kohn-teh-**nee**-doh |
| customs | **aduana** | ah-**dwah**-nah |
| to / from | **a / desde** | ah / **dehs**-day |
| address | **dirección** | dee-rehk-thee-**ohn** |
| zip code | **código postal** | **koh**-dee-goh poh-**stahl** |
| general delivery | **Lista de Correos** | **lee**-stah day koh-**ray**-ohs |

# Red Tape & Profanity

## Filling out forms:

| | |
| --- | --- |
| **Sr. / Sra. / Srta.** | Mr. / Mrs. / Miss |
| **nombre** | first name |
| **apellido** | last name |
| **dirección** | address |
| **domicilio** | address |
| **calle** | street |
| **ciudad** | city |
| **estado** | state |
| **país** | country |
| **nacionalidad** | nationality |
| **origen / destino** | origin / destination |
| **edad** | age |
| **fecha de nacimiento** | date of birth |
| **lugar de nacimiento** | place of birth |
| **sexo** | sex |
| **masculino** | male |
| **femenino** | female |
| **casado / casada** | married man / married woman |

| | |
|---|---|
| **soltero / soltera** | single man / single woman |
| **profesión** | profession |
| **adulto** | adult |
| **niño / niña** | boy / girl |
| **niños** | children |
| **familia** | family |
| **firma** | signature |
| **fecha** | date |

When filling out dates, use this order: day/month/year (Christmas is 25/12/01).

## Spanish profanity:

In any country, red tape inspires profanity. In case you're wondering what the more colorful locals are saying...

| Go to shit! | ¡Andar a la mierda! | **ahn**-dar ah lah mee-**ehr**-dah |
|---|---|---|
| Kiss my ass. | **Bésame culo.** | bay-sah-may **koo**-loh |
| bastard | **bastardo** | bah-**star**-doh |
| bitch | **perra** | **pehr**-rah |
| child of a whore | **hijo[a] de puta** | ee-hoh day **poo**-tah |
| breasts (colloq.) | **tetas** | **tay**-tahs |
| penis (colloq.) | **polla, minga** | **poh**-yah, **meen**-gah |
| shit | **mierda** | mee-**ehr**-dah |
| drunk | **borracho[a]** | boh-**rah**-choh |
| idiot | **idiota** | ee-dee-**oh**-tah |
| imbecile | **imbécil** | eem-**bay**-theel |
| jerk (horned sheep) | **cabrón[a]** | kah-**brohn** |
| stupid | **estúpido[a]** | ay-**stoo**-pee-doh |

Like most Mediterranean people, the Spanish employ some colorful gestures. For a run-down on these, see "Gestures" near the end of this book.

# Help!

| | | |
|---|---|---|
| Help! | **¡Ayuda!** | ah-**yoo**-dah |
| Help me! | **!Ayúdenme!** | ah-**yoo**-dehn-may |
| Call a doctor! | **¡Llamen a un médico!** | **yah**-mehn ah oon **may**-dee-koh |
| ambulance | **ambulancia** | ahm-boo-**lahn**-thee-ah |
| accident | **accidente** | ahk-thee-**dehn**-tay |
| injured | **herido** | ay-**ree**-doh |
| emergency | **emergencia** | ay-mehr-*hayn*-thee-ah |
| fire | **fuego** | **fway**-goh |
| police | **policía** | poh-lee-**thee**-ah |
| thief | **ladrón** | lah-**drohn** |
| pick-pocket | **carterista** | kar-tay-**ree**-stah |
| I've been ripped off. | **Me han robado.** | may ahn roh-**bah**-doh |
| I've lost my... | **He perdido mi...** | ay pehr-**dee**-doh mee |
| ...passport. | **...pasaporte.** | pah-sah-**por**-tay |
| ...ticket. | **...billete.** | bee-**yeh**-tay |
| ...baggage. | **...equipaje.** | ay-kee-**pah**-*h*ay |
| ...purse. | **...bolso.** | **bohl**-soh |
| ...wallet. | **...cartera.** | kar-**tay**-rah |
| ...faith in humankind. | **...fe en los seres humanos.** | fay ayn lohs **say**-rays oo-**mah**-nohs |
| I'm lost. | **Estoy perdido[a].** | ay-**stoy** pehr-**dee**-doh |

HELP!

## Help for women:

| | | |
|---|---|---|
| Leave me alone. | **Déjame sola.** | **day-**hah-may **soh-**lah |
| I *vant* to be alone. | **Me gustaría estar sola.** | may goo-stah-**ree-**ah ay-**star soh-**lah |
| I'm not interested. | **No estoy interesada.** | noh ay-**stoy** een-tay-ray-**sah-**dah |
| I'm married. | **Estoy casada.** | ay-**stoy** kah-**sah-**dah |
| I'm a lesbian. | **Soy lesbiana.** | soy lehs-bee-**ah-**nah |
| I have a contagious disease. | **Tengo una enfermedad contagiosa.** | **tayn-**goh **oo-**nah ayn-fehr-may-**dahd** kohn-tah-**hee-oh-**sah |
| You are bothering me. | **Me está molestando.** | may ay-**stah** moh-lay-**stahn-**doh |
| This man is bothering me. | **Este señor me está molestando.** | **ay-**stay **sayn-**yor may ay-**stah** moh-lay-**stahn-**doh |
| Don't touch me. | **No me toque.** | noh may **toh-**kay |
| You're disgusting. | **Es asqueroso.** | ays ah-skay-**roh-**soh |
| Stop following me. | **No me siga.** | noh may **see-**gah |
| Enough! | **¡Basta!** | **bah-**stah |
| Go away. | **Déjeme.** | **day-**heh-may |
| Get lost! | **¡Vete!** | **bay-**tay |
| I'll call the police! | **¡Voy a llamar a la policía!** | boy ah yah-**mar** ah lah poh-lee-**thee-**ah |

Whenever macho males threaten to turn leering into a contact sport, local women stroll holding hands or arm-in-arm. Wearing conservative clothes and avoiding smiley eye contact also convey a "No way, José" message.

# Health

| | | |
|---|---|---|
| I feel sick. | **Estoy enfermo[a].** | ay-**stoy** ayn-**fehr**-moh |
| I need a doctor... | **Necesito un doctor...** | nay-thay-**see**-toh oon dohk-**tor** |
| ...who speaks English. | **...que hable inglés.** | kay ah-**blay** een-**glays** |
| It hurts here. | **Me duele aquí.** | may dway-lay ah-**kee** |
| I'm allergic to... | **Soy alérgico[a] a...** | soy ah-**lehr**-*h*ee-koh ah |
| ...penicillin. | **...penicilina.** | pay-nee-thee-**lee**-nah |
| I am diabetic. | **Soy diabético[a].** | soy dee-ah-**bay**-tee-koh |
| I've missed a period. | **No me vino el periodo.** | noh may **bee**-noh ehl pay-ree-**oh**-doh |
| My friend has.. | **Mi amigo[a] tiene...** | mee ah-**mee**-goh tee-**ehn**-ay |
| I have... | **Tengo...** | **tayn**-goh |
| ...asthma. | **...asma.** | **ahz**-mah |
| ...athlete's foot. | **...hongos en los pies.** | **ohn**-gohs ayn lohs pee-**ays** |
| ...a broken heart. | **...una corazón roto.** | oo-nah kor-ah-**thohn** roh-toh |
| ...bug bites. | **...picaduras.** | pee-kah-**doo**-rahs |
| ...a burn. | **...una quemadura.** | **oo**-nah kay-mah-**doo**-rah |
| ...chest pains. | **...dolor de pecho.** | doh-**lor** day **pay**-choh |
| ...a cold. | **...un resfriado.** | oon rays-free-**ah**-doh |
| ...constipation. | **...estreñimiento.** | ay-strayn-yee-mee-**ehn**-toh |
| ...a cough. | **...tos.** | tohs |
| ...diarrhea. | **...diarrea.** | dee-ah-**ray**-ah |
| ...dizziness. | **...vértigo.** | **behr**-tee-goh |
| ...a fever. | **...fiebre.** | fee-**ay**-bray |
| ...the flu. | **...gripe.** | **gree**-pay |
| ...a headache. | **...dolor de cabeza.** | doh-**lor** day kah-**bay**-thah |
| ...hemorrhoids. | **...hemorroides.** | ay-moh-**roy**-days |

| | | |
|---|---|---|
| ...high blood pressure. | ...tensión alta. | tayn-thee-**ohn** ahl-tah |
| ...indigestion. | ...indigestión. | een-dee-*h*ay-stee-**ohn** |
| ...an infection. | ...una infección. | **oo**-nah een-fehk-thee-**ohn** |
| ...a migraine. | ...una jaqueca. | **oo**-nah *h*ah-**kay**-kah |
| ...nausea. | ...náuseas. | **now**-see-ahs |
| ...a rash. | ...erupción. | ay-roop-thee-**ohn** |
| ...a sore throat. | ...dolor de garganta. | doh-**lor** day gar-**gahn**-tah |
| ...a stomach ache. | ...dolor de estómago. | doh-**lor** day ay-**stoh**-mah-goh |
| ...a swelling. | ...un hinchazón. | oon een-chah-**thohn** |
| ...terrible breath. | ...mal haliento. | mahl ah-lee-**ehn**-toh |
| ...a toothache. | ...dolor de muelas. | doh-**lor** day moo-**ay**-lahs |
| ...a urinary infection. | ...una infección urinaria. | **oo**-nah een-fehk-thee-**ohn** oo-ree-**nah**-ree-ah |
| ...a venereal disease. | ...una enfermedad venérea. | **oo**-nah ayn-fehr-may-**dahd** vay-**nay**-ray-ah |
| ...worms. | ...lombrices. | lohm-**bree**-thays |
| I have body odor. | Huelo a sudor. | **way**-loh ah soo-**dor** |
| Is it serious? | ¿Es esto serio? | ays ay-stoh **say**-ree-oh |

## Handy Spanish health words:

| | | |
|---|---|---|
| pain | dolor | doh-**lor** |
| dentist | dentista | dayn-**tee**-stah |
| doctor | doctor[a] | dohk-**tor** |
| nurse | enfermera | ayn-fehr-**may**-rah |
| health insurance | seguro médico | say-**goo**-roh may-dee-koh |
| hospital | hospital | oh-spee-**tahl** |
| blood | sangre | sahn-**gray** |
| bandage | venda | **bayn**-dah |

| medicine | **medicina** | may-dee-**thee**-nah |
| pharmacy | **farmacia** | far-mah-**thee**-ah |
| prescription | **receta** | ray-**thay**-tah |
| pill | **pastilla** | pah-**stee**-yah |
| aspirin | **aspirina** | ah-spee-**ree**-nah |
| non-aspirin substitute | **Nolotil** | **noh**-loh-teel |
| antibiotic | **antibiótico** | ahn-tee-bee-**oh**-tee-koh |
| cold medicine | **medicina para el resfriado** | may-dee-**thee**-nah **pah**-rah ehl rays-free-**ah**-doh |
| cough drops | **pastilles de tós** | pah-**stee**-yahs day tohs |
| antacid | **antiácido** | ahn-tee-**ah**-thee-doh |
| pain killer | **analgésico** | ah-nahl-**hay**-see-koh |
| Preparation H | **Hemoal** | **ay**-moh-al |
| vitamins | **vitaminas** | bee-tah-**mee**-nahs |

## Contacts and glasses:

| glasses | **gafas** | **gah**-fahs |
| sunglasses | **gafas de sol** | **gah**-fahs day sohl |
| prescription | **prescripción** | pray-skreep-thee-**ohn** |
| contact lenses... | **lentillas...** | layn-**tee**-yahs |
| ...soft / hard | **...blandas / de cristal** | **blahn**-dahs / day kree-**stahl** |
| solution... | **solución...** | soh-loo-thee-**ohn** |
| ...cleaning | **...limpiadora** | leemp-yah-**doh**-rah |
| ...soaking | **...de jabón** | day *hah*-bohn |
| I've lost / swallowed a contact lens. | **Tengo perder / tragar una lentilla.** | tayn-goh pehr-**dehr** / trah-**gar** oo-nah layn-**tee**-yah |

HEALTH

## Toiletries:

| comb | peine | **pay**-nay |
|---|---|---|
| conditioner | **acondicionador** | ah-kohn-dee-thee-oh-nah-**dor** |
| condoms | **preservativos** | pray-sehr-bah-**tee**-bohs |
| dental floss | **seda dental** | **say**-dah dayn-**tahl** |
| deodorant | **desodorante** | day-soh-doh-**rahn**-tay |
| hairbrush | **cepillo del pelo** | thay-**pee**-yoh dayl **pay**-loh |
| hand lotion | **crema de manos** | **kray**-mah day **mah**-nohs |
| lip salve | **cacao de labios** | kah-**kah**-oh day **lah**-bee-ohs |
| nail clipper | **corta uñas** | **kor**-tah **oon**-yahs |
| razor | **maquinilla de afeitar** | mah-kee-**nee**-yah day ah-fay-**tar** |
| sanitary napkins | **compresas** | kohm-**pray**-sahs |
| shampoo | **champú** | **chahm**-poo |
| shaving cream | **espuma de afeitar** | **ay**-spoo-mah day ah-fay-**tar** |
| soap | **jabón** | *h*ah-bohn |
| sunscreen | **protección de sol** | proh-tehk-thee-**ohn** day sohl |
| tampons | **tampones** | tahm-**poh**-nays |
| tissues | **pañuelos de papel** | pahn-yoo-**ay**-lohs day pah-**pehl** |
| toilet paper | **papel higiénico** | pah-**pehl** ee-*h*ee-**ay**-nee-koh |
| toothbrush | **cepillo de dientes** | thay-**pee**-yoh day dee-**ehn**-tays |
| toothpaste | **pasta de dientes** | **pah**-stah day dee-**ehn**-tays |
| tweezers | **pinzas** | **peen**-thahs |

# Chatting

| My name is... | **Me llamo...** | may **yah**-moh |
|---|---|---|
| What's your name? | **¿Cómo se llama?** | **koh**-moh say **yah**-mah |
| How are you? | **¿Cómo está?** | **koh**-moh ay-**stah** |
| Fine, thanks. | **Bien, gracias.** | bee-**yehn grah**-thee-ahs |
| Where are you from? | **¿De dónde es?** | day **dohn**-day ays |
| What city? | **¿Qué ciudad?** | kay thee-oo-**dahd** |
| What country? | **¿Qué país?** | kay pah-**ees** |
| What planet? | **¿Qué planeta?** | kay plah-**nay**-tah |
| I'm... | **Soy...** | soy |
| ...American. | **...americano[a].** | ah-may-ree-**kah**-noh |
| ...Canadian. | **...canadiense.** | kah-nah-dee-**ehn**-say |

## Nothing more than feelings:

| I am / You are... | **Estoy / Está...** | ay-**stoy** / ay-**stah** |
|---|---|---|
| ...happy. | **...feliz.** | fay-**leeth** |
| ...sad. | **...triste.** | **tree**-stay |
| ...tired. | **...cansado[a].** | kahn-**sah**-doh |
| ...thirsty. | **...sediento[a].** | say-dee-**ehn**-toh |
| I am / You are... | **Tengo / Tiene...** | **tayn**-goh / tee-**ehn**-ay |
| ...hungry. | **...hambre.** | **ahm**-bray |
| ...cold / hot. | **...frío / calor.** | **free**-oh / kah-**lor** |
| ...homesick. | **...morriña.** | moh-**reen**-yah |
| ...lucky. | **...suerte.** | **swehr**-tay |

CHATTING

## Who's who:

| My... | Mi... | mee |
|---|---|---|
| ...male friend / female friend. | ...amigo / amiga. | ah-**mee**-goh / ah-**mee**-gah |
| ...boyfriend / girlfriend. | ...**novio / novia.** | **noh**-bee-oh / **noh**-bee-ah |
| ...husband / wife. | ...**marido / esposa.** | mah-**ree**-doh / ay-**spoh**-sah |
| ...son / daughter. | ...**hijo / hija.** | ee-*h*oh / ee-*h*ah |
| ...brother / sister. | ...**hermano / hermana.** | ehr-**mah**-noh / ehr-**mah**-nah |
| ...father / mother. | ...**padre / madre.** | **pah**-dray / **mah**-dray |
| ...uncle / aunt. | ...**tío / tía.** | **tee**-oh / **tee**-ah |
| ...nephew / niece. | ...**sobrino / sobrina.** | soh-**bree**-noh / soh-**bree**-nah |
| ...male / female cousin. | ...**primo / prima.** | **pree**-moh / **pree**-mah |
| ...grandpa / grandma. | ...**abuelo / abuela.** | ah-**bway**-loh / ah-**bway**-lah |
| ...grandson / granddaughter. | ...**nieto / nieta.** | nee-**ay**-toh / nee-**ay**-tah |

## Family and work:

| Are you married? (asked of a man) | ¿**Está casado?** | ay-**stah** kah-**sah**-doh |
|---|---|---|
| Are you married? (asked of a woman) | ¿**Está casada?** | ay-**stah** kah-**sah**-dah |
| Do you have children? | ¿**Tiene hijos?** | tee-**ehn**-ay ee-*h*ohs |
| How many boys / girls? | ¿**Cuántos niños / niñas?** | **kwahn**-tohs neen-yohs / neen-yahs |
| Do you have photos? | ¿**Tiene fotos?** | tee-**ehn**-ay **foh**-tohs |
| How old is your child? | ¿**Cuántos años tiene su hijo[a]?** | **kwahn**-tohs **ahn**-yohs tee-**ehn**-ay soo ee-*h*oh |
| Beautiful child! | ¡**Qué niño[a] más guapo[a]!** | kay **neen**-yoh mahs **gwah**-poh |

| Beautiful children! | ¡Qué niños[as] más guapos[as]! | kay **neen**-yohs mahs **gwah**-pohs |
| What is your job? | ¿En qué trabaja? | ayn kay trah-**bah**-hah |
| Do you like your work? | ¿Le gusta su trabajo? | lay **goo**-stah soo trah-**bah**-hoh |
| I'm a... | Soy... | soy |
| ...student. | ...estudiante. | ay-stoo-dee-**ahn**-tay |
| ...teacher. | ...profesor[a]. | proh-fay-**sor** |
| ...worker. | ...trabajador[a]. | trah-bah-hah-**dor** |
| ...bureaucrat. | ...burocrático[a]. | boo-roo-**krah**-tee-koh |
| ...professional traveler. | ...viajante de profesión. | bee-ah-**hahn**-tay day proh-fay-see-**ohn** |
| Can I take a photo of you? | ¿Puedo hacerle una foto? | **pway**-doh ah-**thehr**-lay **oo**-nah **foh**-toh |

## Chatting with children:

| What's your name? | ¿Cómo te llama? | **koh**-moh tay **yah**-mah |
| My name is... | Me llamo... | may **yah**-moh |
| How old are you? | ¿Cuántos años tienes? | **kwahn**-tohs **ahn**-yohs tee-**ehn**-ays |
| Do you have brothers and sisters? | ¿Tienes hermanos y hermanas? | tee-**ehn**-ays ehr-**mah**-nohs ee ehr-**mah**-nahs |
| Do you like school? | ¿Te gustas la escuela? | tay goo-stahs lah ays-**kway**-lah |
| What are you studying? | ¿Qué estás estudiando? | kay ay-**stahs** ay-stoo-dee-**ahn**-doh |
| I'm studying... | Estoy estudiando... | ay-**stoy** ay-stoo-dee-**ahn**-doh |
| What's your favorite subject? | ¿Cúal es tu asignatura favorita? | kwahl ehs too ah-seeg-nah-**too**-rah fah-boh-**ree**-tah |
| Do you have pets? | ¿Tienes mascotas? | tee-**eh**-nays mah-**skoh**-tahs |

| | | |
|---|---|---|
| ...cat / dog / fish | ...gato / perro / peces | gah-toh / pehr-roh / pay-thays |
| Will you teach me some Spanish words? | ¿Me enseñas algunas palabras en español? | may ayn-**sayn**-yahs ahl-**goo**-nahs pah-**lah**-brahs ayn ay-spahn-**yohl** |
| What is this? | ¿Qué es esto? | kay ays **ay**-stoh |
| Will you teach me a simple Spanish song? | ¿Me enseñarias una canción simple en español? | may ayn-sayn-yah-**ree**-ahs **oo**-nah kahn-thee-**ohn** seem-play ayn ay-spahn-**yohl** |
| Guess which country I live in. | Adivinas en que país vivo. | ah-dee-**bee**-nahs ayn kay pah-**ees bee**-boh |
| How old am I? | ¿Cuántos años tengo? | **kwahn**-tohs **ahn**-yohs **tayn**-goh |
| I'm ___ years old. | Tengo ___ años. | **tayn**-goh ___ **ahn**-yohs |
| Want to thumb-wrestle? | ¿Quieres hacer un pulso gitano? | kee-**ehr**-ehs ah-**thehr** oon **pool**-soh gee-**tah**-noh |
| Want to hear me burp? | ¿Quieres oírme eructar? | kee-**ehr**-ehs oh-**eer**-may ay-**rook**-tar |
| Teach me a fun game. | Enséñame un juego divirtido. | ayn-**sayn**-yah-may oon hway-goh dee-vir-**tee**-doh |
| Got any candy? | ¿Tienes caramelos? | tee-**eh**-nays kah-rah-**may**-lohs |

## Travel talk:

| | | |
|---|---|---|
| I am / Are you...? | Estoy / ¿Está...? | ay-**stoy** / ay-**stah** |
| ...on vacation | ...de vacaciones | day bah-kah-thee-**oh**-nays |
| ...on business | ...de negocios | day nay-**goh**-thee-ohs |
| How long have you been traveling? | ¿Cuánto tiempo hace que están viajando? | **kwahn**-toh tee-**ehm**-poh **ah**-thay kay ay-**stahn** bee-ah-hahn-doh |
| day / week | día / semana | **dee**-ah / say-**mah**-nah |
| month / year | mes / año | mays / **ahn**-yoh |

| When are you going home? | ¿Cuándo va para casa? | **kwahn**-doh bah **pah**-rah **kah**-sah |
| This is my first time in... | Esta es mi primera vez en... | **ay**-stah ays mee pree-**may**-rah bayth ayn |
| It is (not) a tourist trap. | (No) es un timo turistica. | (noh) ays oon **tee**-moh too-**ree**-stee-kah |
| Today / Tomorrow I'll go to... | Hoy / Mañana iré a... | oy / mahn-**yah**-nah ee-**ray** ah |
| I'm happy here. | Estoy contento[a] aquí. | ay-**stoy** kohn-**tehn**-toh ah-**kee** |
| This is paradise. | Es un paraíso. | ehs oon pah-rah-**ee**-soh |
| The Spanish are friendly. | Los españoles son amables. | lohs ay-spahn-**yoh**-lays sohn ah-**mah**-blays |
| Spain is wonderful. | España es preciosa. | ay-**spahn**-yah ays pray-thee-**oh**-sah |
| To travel is to live. | Viajar es vivir. | bee-ah-**har** ays bee-**beer** |
| Have a good trip! | ¡Buen viaje! | bwayn bee-**ah**-hay |

## Map talk:

You can use these phrases, along with the maps of Iberia, Europe, and the U.S.A. near the end of this book, to delve into family history and explore travel dreams.

| I live here. | Vivo aquí. | **bee**-boh ah-**kee** |
| I was born here. | Nací aquí. | nah-**thee** ah-**kee** |
| My ancestors came from... | Mis familiares son de... | mee fah-mee-lee-**ah**-rays sohn day |
| I've traveled to... | He viajado a... | ay bee-ah-**hah**-doh ah |
| Next I'll go to... | Después iré a... | days-**pways** ee-**ray** ah |
| Where do you live? | ¿Dónde vive? | **dohn**-day **bee**-bay |
| Where were you born? | ¿Dónde ha nacido? | **dohn**-day ah nah-**thee**-doh |

CHATTING

| | | |
|---|---|---|
| Where did your ancestors come from? | ¿De dónde son sus familiares? | day **dohn**-day sohn soos fah-mee-lee-**ah**-rays |
| Where have you traveled? | ¿Adónde ha viajado? | ah-**dohn**-day ah bee-ah-*hah*-doh |
| Where are you going? | ¿Adónde va? | ah-**dohn**-day bah |
| Where would you like to go? | ¿Adónde le gustaría ir? | ah-**dohn**-day lay goo-stah-**ree**-ah eer |

## Favorite things:

| | | |
|---|---|---|
| What's your favorite...? | ¿Cuál es su... favorito? | kwahl ays soo... fah-voh-**ree**-toh |
| ...art | ...arte | **ar**-tay |
| ...book | ...libro | **lee**-broh |
| ...hobby | ...pasatiempo | pah-sah-tee-**ehm**-poh |
| ...ice cream | ...helado | ay-**lah**-doh |
| ...male singer | ...cantante | kahn-**tahn**-tay |
| ...male author | ...autor | ow-**tor** |
| ...male movie star | ...actor | ahk-**tor** |
| ...sport | ...deporte | day-**por**-tay |
| ...vice | ...vicio | **bee**-thee-oh |
| What's your favorite...? | ¿Cuál es su... favorita? | kwahl ays soo... fah-voh-**ree**-tah |
| ...food | ...comida | koh-**mee**-dah |
| ...music | ...música | **moo**-see-kah |
| ...female singer | ...cantante | kahn-**tahn**-tay |
| ...female author | ...autora | ow-**toh**-rah |
| ...female movie star | ...actriz | ahk-**treeth** |
| ...movie | ...película | pay-**lee**-koo-lah |

The Spanish say, *"La vida es corta. No corras."* (Life is short. Don't run.)

## Responses for all occasions:

| | | |
|---|---|---|
| I like that. | **Eso me gusta.** | **ay**-soh may **goo**-stah |
| I like you. | **Me cae bien.** | may kī bee-**yehn** |
| That's great! | **¡Qué bien!** | kay bee-**yehn** |
| Wow! | **¡Caray!** | kah-**rī** |
| What a nice place. | **Que sitio más bonito.** | kay **seet**-yoh mahs boh-**nee**-toh |
| Perfect. | **Perfecto.** | pehr-**fehk**-toh |
| Funny. | **Divertido.** | dee-behr-**tee**-doh |
| Interesting. | **Interesante.** | een-tay-ray-**sahn**-tay |
| I don't smoke. | **No fumo.** | noh **foo**-moh |
| I haven't any. | **No tengo nada.** | noh **tayn**-goh nah-dah |
| Really? | **¿De verdad?** | day behr-**dahd** |
| Congratulations! | **¡Felicidades!** | fay-lee-thee-**dah**-days |
| Well done! | **¡Bien hecho!** | bee-**ehn** ay-choh |
| You're welcome. | **De nada.** | day **nah**-dah |
| Bless you! (after sneeze) | **¡Salud!** | sah-**lood** |
| Excuse me. | **Perdóneme.** | pehr-**doh**-nay-may |
| What a pity! | **¡Qué lastima!** | kay lah-**stee**-mah |
| That's life. | **Así es la vida.** | ah-**see** ays lah bee-dah |
| No problem. | **No hay problema.** | noh ī proh-**blay**-mah |
| O.K. | **De acuerdo. / Vale.** | day ah-**kwehr**-doh / **vah**-lay |
| This is the good life! | **¡Esto si que es vida!** | ay-stoh see kay ays **bee**-dah |
| Good luck! | **¡Buena suerte!** | bway-nah **swehr**-tay |
| Let's go! | **¡Vamos!** | **bah**-mohs |

## Thanks a million:

| | | |
|---|---|---|
| Thank you very much. | **Muchas gracias.** | **moo**-chahs **grah**-thee-ahs |
| You are... | **Usted es...** | oo-**stehd** ays |
| ...kind. | **...amable.** | ah-**mah**-blay |
| ...generous. | **...generoso[a].** | *h*eh-nay-**roh**-soh |
| This is / You are... | **Esto es / Usted es...** | **ay**-stoh ays / oo-**stehd** ays |
| ...wonderful. | **...maravilloso[a].** | mah-rah-bee-**yoh**-soh |
| ...great fun. | **...muy divertido.** | **moo**-ee dee-behr-**tee**-doh |
| You've been a tremendous help. | **Me ha ayudado mucho.** | may ah ah-yoo-**dah**-doh **moo**-choh |
| You spoil me / us. | **Me / nos mima.** | may / nohs **mee**-mah |
| I will remember you... | **Le recordaré...** | lay ray-kor-dah-**ray** |
| ...always. | **...siempre.** | see-**aym**-pray |
| ...till Tuesday. | **...hasta el martes.** | **ah**-stah ehl **mar**-tays |

## Weather:

| | | |
|---|---|---|
| What will the weather be like tomorrow? | **¿Qué tiempo va a hacer mañana?** | kay tee-ehm-poh bah ah ah-**thehr** mahn-**yah**-nah |
| sunny / cloudy | **asoleado / nublado** | ah-soh-lay-**ah**-doh / noo-**blah**-doh |
| hot / cold | **caluroso / frío** | kah-loo-**roh**-soh / **free**-oh |
| muggy / windy | **húmedo / viento** | oo-may-doh / bee-**ehn**-toh |
| rain / snow | **lluvia / nieve** | **yoov**-yah / nee-**ay**-bay |

# Create Your Own Conversation

You can mix and match these words into a conversation.
Make it as deep or silly as you want.

## *Who:*

| | | |
|---|---|---|
| I / you | yo / usted | yoh / oo-**stehd** |
| he / she | él / ella | ehl / **ay**-yah |
| we / they | nosotros / ellos | noh-**soh**-trohs / **ay**-ohs |
| my / your... | mi / su... | mee / soo |
| ...parents / children | ...padres / niños | **pah**-drays / **neen**-yohs |
| men / women | hombres / mujeres | **ohm**-brays / moo-**heh**-rays |
| rich / poor | ricos / pobres | **ree**-kohs / **poh**-brays |
| politicians | políticos | poh-**lee**-tee-kohs |
| big business | gran negocio | grahn nay-**goh**-thee-oh |
| mafia | mafia | **mah**-fee-ah |
| military | militar | mee-lee-**tar** |
| Spanish | españoles | ay-spahn-**yoh**-lays |
| Portuguese | portugueses | por-too-**gay**-says |
| French | franceses | frahn-**thay**-says |
| Germans | alemanes | ah-lay-**mah**-nays |
| Americans | americanos | ah-may-ree-**kah**-nohs |
| liberals | liberales | lee-bay-**rah**-lays |
| conservatives | conservativos | kohn-sehr-bah-**tee**-bohs |
| radicals | radicales | rah-dee-**kah**-lays |
| travelers | viajantes | bee-ah-**hahn**-tays |
| everyone | todo la gente | **toh**-doh lah **hehn**-tay |
| God | Dios | **dee**-ohs |

CHATTING

## *What:*

| | | |
|---|---|---|
| want | **querer** | keh-**rehr** |
| need | **necesitar** | nay-thay-see-**tar** |
| take / give | **coger / dar** | koh-*h*ehr / dar |
| love / hate | **amar / odiar** | ah-**mar** / oh-dee-**ar** |
| work / play | **trabajar / jugar** | trah-bah-*h*ar / hoo-**gar** |
| have / lack | **tener / carecer de** | tay-**nehr** / kah-ray-**thehr** day |
| learn / fear | **aprender / temer** | ah-prehn-**dehr** / tay-**mehr** |
| help / abuse | **ayudar / abusar de** | ah-yoo-**dar** / ah-boo-**sar** day |
| prosper / suffer | **prosperar / sufrir** | proh-spay-**rar** / soof-**reer** |
| buy / sell | **comprar / vender** | kohm-**prar** / bayn-**dehr** |

## *Why:*

| | | |
|---|---|---|
| love / sex | **amor / sexo** | ah-**mor** / **sex**-oh |
| money / power | **dinero / poder** | dee-**nay**-roh / poh-**dehr** |
| work / food | **trabajo / comida** | trah-**bah**-*h*oh / koh-**mee**-dah |
| family | **familia** | fah-**meel**-yah |
| health | **salud** | sah-**lood** |
| hope | **esperanza** | ay-spay-**rahn**-thah |
| education | **educación** | ay-doo-kah-thee-**ohn** |
| guns | **pistolas** | pee-**stoh**-lahs |
| religion | **religión** | ray-lee-*h*ee-**ohn** |
| happiness | **alegría** | ah-lay-**gree**-ah |
| marijuana | **marijuana** | mah-ree-*h*wah-nah |
| democracy | **democracia** | day-moh-krah-**thee**-ah |
| taxes | **impuestos** | eem-**pway**-stohs |
| lies | **mentiras** | mayn-**tee**-rahs |
| corruption | **corrupción** | koh-roop-thee-**ohn** |
| pollution | **polución** | poh-loo-thee-**ohn** |
| television | **televisión** | tay-lay-bee-thee-**ohn** |
| relaxation | **relajación** | ray-lah-*h*ah-thee-**ohn** |

| violence | **violencia** | bee-oh-**layn**-thee-ah |
| respect | **respecto** | ray-**spehk**-toh |
| racism | **racismo** | rah-**thees**-moh |
| war / peace | **guerra / paz** | **gehr**-rah / pahth |
| global perspective | **perspectiva global** | pehr-spehk-**tee**-vah gloh-**bahl** |

## *You be the judge:*

| (no) problem | **(no hay) problema** | (noh ī) proh-**blay**-mah |
| (not) good | **(no es) bueno** | (noh ays) **bway**-noh |
| (not) dangerous | **(no es) peligroso** | (noh ays) pay-lee-**groh**-soh |
| (not) fair | **(no es) justo** | (noh ays) *hoo*-stoh |
| (not) guilty | **(no es) culpable** | (noh ays) kool-**pah**-blay |
| (not) powerful | **(no es) poderoso** | (noh ays) poh-day-**roh**-soh |
| (not) stupid | **(no es) estúpido** | (noh ays) ay-**stoo**-pee-doh |
| (not) happy | **(no es) feliz** | (noh ays) fay-**leeth** |
| because / for | **porque / para** | **por**-kay / **pah**-rah |
| and / or / from | **y / o / de** | ee / oh / day |
| too much | **demasiado** | day-mah-see-**ah**-doh |
| (never) enough | **(nunca) suficiente** | (**noon**-kah) soo-fee-thee-**ehn**-tay |
| same / better / worse | **igual / mejor / peor** | ee-**gwahl** / may-**hor** / pay-**or** |
| here | **aquí** | ah-**kee** |
| everywhere | **en todas partes** | ayn **toh**-dahs **par**-tays |

## *Assorted beginnings and endings:*

| I like... | **Me gusta...** | may **goo**-stah |
| I don't like... | **No me gusta...** | noh may **goo**-stah |
| Do you like...? | **¿Le gusta...?** | lay **goo**-stah |
| When I was young... | **Cuando era más joven...** | **kwahn**-doh **ay**-rah mahs *hoh*-behn |

| I am / Are you...? | Estoy / ¿Está...? | ay-**stoy** / ay-**stah** |
|---|---|---|
| ...optimistic / pessimistic | ...**optimista /** **pesimista** | ohp-tee-**mee**-stah / pay-see-**mee**-stah |
| I (don't) believe... | Yo (no) creo... | yoh (noh) **kray**-oh |
| Do you believe in...? | ¿Cree usted en...? | **kray**-yay oo-**stehd** ayn |
| ...God | ...Dios | dee-ohs |
| ...life after death | ...la vida después de la muerte | lah **bee**-dah days-**pways** day lah **mwehr**-tay |
| ...extraterrestrial life | ...la vida extraterreste | lah **bee**-dah ayk-strah-tay-**rehs**-tay |
| ...Santa Claus | ...Papá Noel | pah-**pah** noh-**ehl** |
| Yes. / No. | Sí. / No. | see / noh |
| Maybe. / I don't know. | Tal vez. / No sé. | tahl bayth / noh say |
| What is most important in life? | ¿Qué es lo más importante en la vida? | kay ays loh mahs eem-por-**tahn**-tay ayn lah **bee**-dah |
| The problem is... | El problema es... | ehl proh-**blay**-mah ays |
| The answer is... | La respuesta es... | lah rehs-**pway**-stah ays |
| We have solved the world's problems. | Nosotros hemos resuelto los problemas del mundo. | noh-**soh**-trohs **ay**-mohs ray-**swayl**-toh lohs proh-**blay**-mahs dayl **moon**-doh |

## Political words relevant to Spain:

**Basque ETA:** Separatist Basque terrorist group.
**Guerra Civil:** The 1936-1939 Civil War, which ended with Franco's Nationalists (fascists aided by Hitler) overthrowing the Spanish Republican government (aided by the USSR and Hemingway).
**Falange:** Franco's fascist party.
**Franco:** Spain's fascist dictator from 1939 to 1975.

**Guernica:** Basque town destroyed by Franco during the Civil War, immortalized by a Picasso painting (now in Madrid).

**Juan Carlos:** Democratic Bourbon king who succeeded the dictator Franco in 1975.

**OTAN:** NATO

**Republicanos:** Supporters of Spain's democratically elected government, overthrown by Franco's fascists.

**Nacionalistas:** Supporters of Franco during the Civil War.

# A Spanish Romance

## *Words of love:*

| | | |
|---|---|---|
| I / me / you | **yo / mi / tú** | yoh / mee / too |
| flirt | **coquetear** | koh-kay-tay-**ar** |
| kiss | **beso** | **bay**-soh |
| hug | **abrazo** | ah-**brah**-thoh |
| love | **amor** | ah-**mor** |
| make love | **hacer el amor** | ah-**thehr** ehl ah-**mor** |
| condom | **preservativo** | pray-sehr-bah-**tee**-boh |
| contraceptive | **contraceptivo** | kohn-trah-thehp-**tee**-boh |
| safe sex | **sexo sin peligro** | **sex**-oh seen pay-**lee**-groh |
| sexy | **sexy** | "sexy" |
| romantic | **romántico** | roh-**mahn**-tee-koh |
| honey | **cariño[a]** | kah-**reen**-yoh |
| my angel | **mi ángel** | mee **ahn**-hayl |
| my love | **mi amor** | mee ah-**mor** |
| my heaven | **mi cielo** | mee thee-**ay**-loh |

## *Ah, amor:*

|  |  |  |
|---|---|---|
| What's the matter? | ¿Qué le pasa? | kay lay **pah**-sah |
| Nothing. | Nada. | **nah**-dah |
| I am / Are you...? | Estoy / ¿Eres...? | ay-**stoy** / ay-rays |
| ...straight | ...heterosexual | ay-tay-roh-sehk-soo-**ahl** |
| ...gay | ...homosexual | oh-moh-sehk-soo-**ahl** |
| ...undecided | ...indeciso[a] | een-day-**thee**-soh |
| ...prudish | ...prudente | proo-**dehn**-tay |
| ...horny | ...caliente | kahl-**yehn**-tay |
| We are on our honeymoon. | Estamos de luna de miel. | ay-**stah**-mohs day **loo**-nah day mee-**ehl** |
| I have... | Tengo... | **tayn**-goh |
| ...a boyfriend. | ...un novio. | oon **noh**-bee-oh |
| ...a girlfriend. | ...una novia. | **oo**-nah **noh**-bee-ah |
| I'm married. | Estoy casado[a]. | ay-**stoy** kah-**sah**-doh |
| I'm not married. | No estoy casado[a]. | noh ay-**stoy** kah-**sah**-doh |
| I'm rich and single. | Soy rico[a] y soltero[a]. | soy **ree**-koh ee sohl-**tay**-roh |
| I'm lonely. | Estoy solo[a]. | ay-**stoy** **soh**-loh |
| I have no diseases. | No tengo enfermedades. | noh **tayn**-goh ayn-fehr-may-**dah**-days |
| I have many diseases. | Tengo muchas enfermedades. | **tayn**-goh **moo**-chahs ayn-fehr-may-**dah**-days |
| Can I see you again? | ¿Te puedo volver a ver? | tay **pway**-doh bohl-**behr** ah behr |
| You are my most beautiful souvenir. | Tú eres mi mejor recuerdo. | too ay-rays mee may-**hor** ray-**kwehr**-doh |
| Kiss me more. | Bésame más. | **bay**-sah-may mahs |
| Is this an aphrodisiac? | ¿Es esto un afrodisíaco? | ays **ay**-stoh oon ah-froh-dee-**see**-ah-koh |

| This is (not) my first time. | Esta (no) es mi primera vez. | ay-stah (noh) ays mee pree-**may**-rah bayth |
| Do you do this often? | ¿Haces esto muy a menudo? | **ah**-thays ay-stoh **moo**-ee ah may-**noo**-doh |
| How's my breath? | ¿Me huele el aliento? | may **way**-lay ehl ahl-**yehn**-toh |
| Let's just be friends. | Vamos a dejarlo como amigos. | bah-mohs ah day-**har**-loh **koh**-moh ah-**mee**-gohs |
| I'll pay for my share. | Pagaré mi parte. | pah-gah-**ray** mee **par**-tay |
| Would you like a massage...? | ¿Te gustaría un masaje...? | tay goo-stah-**ree**-ah oon mah-**sah**-hay |
| ...for your back | ...para tu espalda | **pah**-rah too ay-**spahl**-dah |
| ...for your feet | ...por tus pies | por toos pee-**ays** |
| Why not? | ¿Por qué no? | por kay noh |
| Try it. | Pruébalo. | proo-**ay**-bah-loh |
| It tickles. | Esto me hace cosquillas. | **ay**-stoh may **ah**-thay koh-**skee**-yahs |
| Oh my God! | ¡Dios mío! | **dee**-ohs **mee**-oh |
| I love you. | Te quiero. | tay kee-**ehr**-oh |
| Darling, will you marry me? | ¿Querida, te casarás conmigo? | kay-**ree**-dah tay kah-sah-**rahs** kohn-**mee**-goh |

## Conversing with Spanish animals:

| rooster / cock-a-doodle-doo | gallo / cacarea | **gah**-yoh / kah-kah-**ray**-ah |
| bird / tweet tweet | pajaro / pío pío | pah-**hah**-roh / **pee**-oh **pee**-oh |
| cat / meow | gato / miau | **gah**-toh / **mee**-ow |
| dog / woof woof | perro / guao guao | **pehr**-roh / gwow gwow |
| duck / quack quack | pato / cua cua | **pah**-toh / kwah kwah |
| cow / moo | vaca / muh | **bah**-kah / moo |
| pig / oink oink | cerdo / (just snort) | **thehr**-doh / (just snort) |

# PORTUGUESE

# Getting Started

## Portuguese

...is your passport to Europe's bargain basement. And for its wonderful pricetag, you'll enjoy piles of fresh seafood, brilliant sunshine, and local character that often feels decades behind the rest of Europe. With its old world charm comes a bigger language barrier than you'll find elsewhere in Europe. A phrase book is of greater value here than anywhere else in western Europe.

Here are a few tips on pronouncing Portuguese words:

*C* usually sounds like C in cat.
  But *C* followed by *E* or *I* sounds like S in sun.
*Ç* sounds like S in sun.
*CH* sounds like SH in shine.
*G* usually sounds like G in go.
  But *G* followed by *E* or *I* sounds like S in treasure.
*H* is silent.
*J* sounds like S in treasure.
*LH* sounds like LI in billion.
*NH* sounds like NI in onion.
*R* is trrrilled.
*S* can sound like S in sun (at the beginning of a word),
  Z in zoo (between vowels), or SH in shine.
*SS* sounds like S in sun.

Note: Barbaric as it may sound, you could cut this book in half at this page for your toting comfort.

Portuguese vowels:

*A* can sound like A in father or A in sang.
*E* can sound like E in get, AY in play, or I in wish.
*É* sounds like E in get.
*Ê* sounds like AY in play.
*I* sounds like EE in seed.
*O* can sound like O in note, AW in raw, or OO in
   moon.
*Ô* and *OU* sound like O in note.
*U* sounds like OO in moon.

As with any Romance language, sex is important. A man is *simpático* (friendly), a woman is *simpática*. In this book, we show bi-sexual words like this: *simpático[a]*. If you're speaking of a woman (which includes women speaking about themselves), use the *a* ending. It's always pronounced "ah." A word that ends in *r*, such as *cantor* (singer), will appear like this: *cantor[a]*. A *cantora* is a female singer. A word ending in *e*, such as *interessante* (interesting), applies to either sex.

Adjectives agree with the noun. A clean room is a *quarto limpo*, a clean towel is a *toalha limpa*. You'll be quizzed on this later.

If a word ends in a vowel, the Portuguese usually stress the second-to-last syllable. Words ending in a consonant are stressed on the last syllable. To override these rules, the Portuguese add an accent mark (such as ´, ˜, or ^) to the syllable that should be stressed, like this: *rápido* (fast) is pronounced **rah**-pee-doo.

Just like French, its linguistic buddy, Portuguese has

nasal sounds. A vowel followed by either *n* or *m* or topped
with a ~ (such as *ã* or *õ*) is usually nasalized. In the
phonetics, nasalized vowels are indicated by an underlined
<u>n</u> or <u>w</u>. As you say the vowel, let its sound come through
your nose as well as your mouth.

Here are the phonetics for nasal vowels:

| | |
|---|---|
| ay<u>n</u> | nasalize the AY in day. |
| oh<u>n</u> | nasalize the O in bone. |
| oo<u>n</u> | nazalize the O in moon. |
| o<u>w</u> | nasalize the OW in now. |

Some words have only a slight nasal sound. To help
you pronounce these words, I add an *ng* or *n* in the
phonetics: *sim* (yes) is pronounced seeng, and *muito* (very)
like **mween**-too.

Here's a quick guide to the rest of the phonetics used in
this book:

| | |
|---|---|
| a | like A in sang. |
| ah | like A in father. |
| aw | like AW in raw. |
| ay | like AY in play. |
| ee | like EE in seed. |
| eh | like E in get. |
| ehr | sounds like "air." |
| g | like G in go. |
| i | like I in hit. |
| ī | like I in light. |
| oh | like O in note. |
| oo | like OO in moon. |

| | |
|---|---|
| or | like OR in core. |
| ow | like OW in now. |
| oy | like OY in toy. |
| s | like S in sun. |
| zh | like S in treasure. |

Too often tourists insist on speaking Spanish to the Portuguese. Your attempts at Portuguese will endear you to the locals. And if you throw in *"por favor"* (please) whenever you can, you'll eat better, sleep easier, and make friends faster.

# Portuguese Basics

## Greeting and meeting the Portuguese:

| | | |
|---|---|---|
| Hello. | **Olá.** | oh-**lah** |
| Good morning. | **Bom-dia.** | boh<u>n</u>-**dee**-ah |
| Good afternoon. | **Boa-tarde.** | boh-ah-**tar**-deh |
| Good evening. | **Boa-noite.** | boh-ah-**noy**-teh |
| Good night. | **Boa-noite.** | boh-ah-**noy**-teh |
| Mr. / Mrs. | **Senhor / Senhora** | sin-**yor** / sin-**yoh**-rah |
| Miss | **Menina** | meh-**nee**-nah |
| How are you? | **Como está?** | **koh**-moo ish-**tah** |
| Very well. | **Muito bem.** | **mween**-too bay<u>n</u> |
| Thank you. (said by a male) | **Obrigado.** | oh-bree-**gah**-doo |
| Thank you. (said by a female) | **Obrigada.** | oh-bree-**gah**-dah |
| And you? | **E você?** | ee voh-**say** |
| My name is... | **Chamo-me...** | **shah**-moo-meh |
| What's your name? | **Como se chama?** | **koh**-moo seh **shah**-mah |
| Pleased to meet you. | **Prazer em conhecer.** | prah-**zehr** ay<u>n</u> kohn-yeh-**sehr** |
| Where are you from? | **De onde é que você é?** | deh **ohn**-deh eh keh voh-**say** eh |
| So long! | **Até logo!** | ah-**teh law**-goo |
| Goodbye. | **Adeus.** | ah-**deh**-oosh |
| Good luck! | **Boa sorte!** | **boh**-ah **sor**-teh |
| Have a good trip! | **Boa-viagem!** | boh-ah-vee-**ah**-zhay<u>n</u> |

The Portuguese say *"Bom-dia"* (Good morning) until noon, *"Boa-tarde"* (Good afternoon) until dark, and *"Boa-noite"* (Good evening) after dark.

## Survival phrases

In 1917, according to legend, the Virgin Mary visited Fatima using only these phrases. They're repeated on your tear-out cheat sheet near the end of this book.

### The essentials:

| | | |
|---|---|---|
| Hello. | Olá. | oh-**lah** |
| Do you speak English? | Fala inglês? | fah-lah een-**glaysh** |
| Yes. / No. | Sim. / Não. | seeng / no<u>w</u> |
| I don't speak Portuguese. | Não falo português. | no<u>w</u> fah-loo poor-too-**gaysh** |
| I'm sorry. | Desculpe. | dish-**kool**-peh |
| Please. | Por favor. | poor fah-**vor** |
| Thank you. | Obrigado[a]. | oh-bree-**gah**-doo |
| It's (not) a problem. | (Não) á problema. | (no<u>w</u>) ah proo-**blay**-mah |
| Very good. | Muito bem. | mween-too bay<u>n</u> |
| You are very kind. | É muito simpático[a]. | eh mween-too seeng-**pah**-tee-koo |
| Goodbye. | Adeus. | ah-**deh**-oosh |

### Where?

| | | |
|---|---|---|
| Where is...? | Onde é que é...? | oh<u>n</u>-deh eh keh eh |
| ...a hotel | ...um hotel | oo<u>n</u> oh-**tehl** |
| ...a youth hostel | ...uma pousada de juventude | oo-mah poh-**zah**-dah deh zhoo-vayn-**too**-deh |
| ...a restaurant | ...um restaurante | oo<u>n</u> rish-toh-**rahn**-teh |
| ...a supermarket | ...um supermercado | oo<u>n</u> soo-pehr-mehr-**kah**-doo |
| ...a pharmacy | ...uma farmácia | oo-mah far-**mah**-see-ah |
| ...a bank | ...um banco | oo<u>n</u> **bang**-koo |

| | | |
|---|---|---|
| ...the train station | ...a estação de comboio | ah ish-tah-**sow** deh koh**n**-**boy**-yoo |
| ...the tourist information office | ...a informação turística | ah een-for-mah-**sow** too-**reesh**-tee-kah |
| ...the toilet | ...a casa de banho | ah **kah**-zah deh **bahn**-yoo |
| men / women | homens / mulheres | **aw**-may**n**sh / mool-**yeh**-rish |

## How much?

| | | |
|---|---|---|
| How much is it? | Quanto custa? | **kwahn**-too **koosh**-tah |
| Write it? | Escreva? | ish-**kray**-vah |
| Cheap(er). | (Mais) barato. | (mīsh) bah-**rah**-too |
| Cheapest. | O mais barato. | oo mīsh bah-**rah**-too |
| Is it free? | É grátis? | eh **grah**-teesh |
| Is it included? | Está incluído? | ish-**tah** een-kloo-**ee**-doo |
| Do you have...? | Tem...? | tay**n** |
| Where can I buy...? | Onde posso comprar...? | **ohn**-deh **pos**-soh koh**n**-**prar** |
| I would like... | Gostaria... | goosh-tah-**ree**-ah |
| We would like... | Gostaríamos... | goosh-tah-**ree**-ah-moosh |
| ...this. | ...isto. | **eesh**-too |
| ...just a little. | ...só um bocadinho. | saw oo**n** boo-kah-**deen**-yoo |
| ...more. | ...mais. | mīsh |
| ...a ticket. | ...um bilhete. | oo**n** beel-**yeh**-teh |
| ...a room. | ...um quarto. | oo**n** **kwar**-too |
| ...the bill. | ...a conta. | ah **kohn**-tah |

## How many?

| | | |
|---|---|---|
| one | um | oo**n** |
| two | dois | doysh |
| three | três | traysh |

| four | **quatro** | **kwah**-troo |
| five | **cinco** | **seeng**-koo |
| six | **seis** | saysh |
| seven | **sete** | **seh**-teh |
| eight | **oito** | **oy**-too |
| nine | **nove** | **naw**-veh |
| ten | **dez** | dehsh |

You'll find more to count on in the Numbers chapter.

## When?

| At what time? | **A que horas?** | ah keh **aw**-rahsh |
| Just a moment. | **Um momento.** | oo<u>n</u> moo-**mayn**-too |
| Now. | **Agora.** | ah-**goh**-rah |
| Soon. | **Em breve.** | ay<u>n</u> **bray**-veh |
| Later. | **Mais tarde.** | mish **tar**-deh |
| Today. | **Hoje.** | **oh**-zheh |
| Tomorrow. | **Amanhã.** | ah-ming-**yah** |

Mix and match these survival phrases to say: "Two tickets," or "Yes, thanks," or "Where is a cheap restaurant?" or "The bill, please."

## Struggling with Portuguese:

| Do you speak English? | **Fala inglês?** | **fah**-lah een-**glaysh** |
| A teeny weeny bit? | **Um pouquinho?** | oo<u>n</u> poh-**keen**-yoo |
| Please speak English. | **Por favor fale inglês.** | poor fah-**vor fah**-leh een-**glaysh** |
| You speak English well. | **Fala bem inglês.** | **fah**-lah bay<u>n</u> een-**glaysh** |

| I don't speak Portuguese. | Não falo português. | no<u>w</u> fah-loo poor-too-gaysh |
| I speak a little Portuguese. | Falo um pouco em português. | fah-loo oo<u>n</u> poh-koo ay<u>n</u> poor-too-gaysh |
| What is this in Portuguese? | O que é isto em português? | oo keh eh eesh-too ay<u>n</u> poor-too-gaysh |
| Repeat? | Repita? | ray-pee-tah |
| Please speak slowly. | Por favor fale devegar. | poor fah-vor fah-leh deh-vah-gar |
| Slower. | Mais devagar. | mīsh deh-vah-gar |
| I understand. | Compreendo. | koh<u>n</u>-pree-ayn-doo |
| I don't understand. | Não compreendo. | no<u>w</u> koh<u>n</u>-pree-ayn-doo |
| Do you understand? | Compreende? | koh<u>n</u>-pree-ayn-deh |
| Write it? | Escreva? | ish-kray-vah |
| Is there someone who speaks English? | Alguem aí fala inglês? | ahl-gay<u>n</u> ī fah-lah een-glaysh |
| Who speaks English? | Quem fala inglês? | kay<u>n</u> fah-lah een-glaysh |

In Portugal, a woman who looks over 35 years old is addressed as *senhora*, younger than 35 as *menina*. Good luck.

## Common questions in Portuguese:

| How much? | Quanto custa? | kwahn-too koosh-tah |
| How many? | Quantos? | kwahn-toosh |
| How long...? | Quanto tempo...? | kwahn-too tay<u>n</u>-poo |
| ...is the trip | ...é a viagem | eh ah vee-ah-zhay<u>n</u> |
| How many minutes / hours? | Quantos minutos / horas? | kwahn-toosh mee-noo-toosh / aw-rahsh |
| How far? | A que distância? | ah keh deesh-tahn-see-ah |
| How? | Como? | koh-moo |

| Is it possible? | É possível? | eh poo-**see**-vehl |
| Is it necessary? | É necessário? | eh neh-seh-**sah**-ree-oo |
| Can you help me? | Pode me ajudar? | paw-deh meh ah-zhoo-**dar** |
| What? (didn't hear) | Diga? | **dee**-gah |
| What is that? | O que é isso? | oo keh eh **ee**-soo |
| What is better? | O que é melhor? | oo keh eh mil-**yor** |
| What's going on? | Que se passa? | keh seh **pah**-sah |
| When? | Quando? | **kwahn**-doo |
| What time is it? | Que horas são? | keh **aw**-rahsh sow |
| At what time? | A que horas? | ah keh **aw**-rahsh |
| On time? | Pontual? | pohn-too-**ahl** |
| Late? | Atrasado? | ah-trah-**zah**-doo |
| What time does this...? | A que horas é que...? | ah keh **aw**-rahsh eh keh |
| ...open | ...abre | **ah**-breh |
| ...close | ...fecha | **fay**-shah |
| Do you have...? | Tem...? | tayn |
| Where is...? | Onde é...? | **ohn**-deh eh |
| Where are...? | Onde estão...? | **ohn**-deh ish-**tow** |
| Where can I find...? | A onde posso encontrar...? | ah **ohn**-deh **paw**-soo ayn-kohn-**trar** |
| Where can I buy...? | Onde posso comprar...? | **ohn**-deh **pos**-soh kohn-**prar** |
| Who? | Quem? | kayn |
| Why? | Porquê? | poor-**kay** |
| Why not? | Porquê não? | poor-**kay** now |
| Yes or no? | Sim ou não? | seeng oh now |

You can turn a word or sentence into a question by asking it in a questioning tone. *"Isso é bom"* (It's good) becomes *"Isso é bom?"* (Is it good?).

## Yin and yang:

|  |  |  |
|---|---|---|
| cheap / expensive | **barato / caro** | bah-**rah**-too / **kah**-roo |
| big / small | **grande / pequeno** | **grahn**-deh / pay-**kay**-noo |
| hot / cold | **quente / frio** | **kayn**-teh / **free**-oo |
| open / closed | **aberto / fechado** | ah-**behr**-too / feh-**shah**-doo |
| entrance / exit | **entrada / saída** | ayn-**trah**-dah / sah-ee-dah |
| arrive / depart | **chegar / partir** | shay-**gar** / par-**teer** |
| early / late | **cedo / tarde** | **say**-doo / **tar**-deh |
| soon / later | **em breve / mais tarde** | ayn **bray**-veh / mīsh **tar**-deh |
| fast / slow | **rápido / lento** | **rah**-pee-doo / **layn**-too |
| here / there | **aqui / ali** | ah-**kee** / ah-**lee** |
| near / far | **perto / longe** | **pehr**-too / **lohn**-zheh |
| indoors / outdoors | **dentro / for a** | **dayn**-troo / for ah |
| good / bad | **bom / mau** | **bohn** / mow |
| best / worst | **melhor / pior** | mil-**yor** / pee-**yor** |
| a little / lots | **um pouco / muito** | oon **poh**-koo / **mween**-too |
| more / less | **mais / menos** | mīsh / **may**-noosh |
| mine / yours | **meu / vosso** | **meh**-oo / **vaw**-soo |
| everybody / nobody | **toda gente / ninguem** | **toh**-dah **zhayn**-teh / neeng-**gayn** |
| easy / difficult | **fácil / difícil** | **fah**-seel / dee-**fee**-seel |
| left / right | **esquerda / direita** | ish-**kehr**-dah / dee-**ray**-tah |
| up / down | **cima / baixo** | **see**-mah / **bī**-shoo |
| above / below | **em cima / em baixo** | ayn **see**-mah / ayn **bī**-shoo |
| young / old | **jovem / velho** | **zhaw**-vayn / **vehl**-yoo |
| new / old | **novo / velho** | **noh**-voo / **vehl**-yoo |
| heavy / light | **pesado / leve** | peh-**zah**-doo / **leh**-veh |
| dark / light | **escuro / claro** | ish-**koo**-roo / **klah**-roo |

| happy / sad | feliz / triste | feh-**leesh** / **treesh**-teh |
| beautiful / ugly | lindo / feio | **leen**-doo / **fay**-oo |
| nice / mean | simpático / mauzinho | seeng-**pah**-tee-koo / mow-**sheen**-yoo |
| smart / stupid | esperto / estúpido | ish-**pehr**-too / ish-**too**-pee-doo |
| vacant / occupied | livre / ocupado | **lee**-vreh / oo-koo-**pah**-doo |
| with / without | com / sem | koh<u>n</u> / say<u>n</u> |

## Big little words in Portugal:

| I | eu | **eh**-oo |
| you (formal) | você | voh-**say** |
| you (informal) | tu | too |
| we | nós | nawsh |
| he | ele | **eh**-leh |
| she | ela | **eh**-lah |
| they | eles | **eh**-lish |
| and | e | ee |
| at | á | ah |
| because | porque | **poor**-keh |
| but | mas | mahsh |
| by (via) | via | **vee**-ah |
| for | para | **pah**-rah |
| from | de | deh |
| here | aqui | ah-**kee** |
| if | se | seh |
| in | em | ay<u>n</u> |
| not | não | no<u>w</u> |
| now | agora | ah-**goh**-rah |
| only | só | saw |
| or | ou | oh |
| that | aquilo | ah-**kee**-loo |
| this | isto | **eesh**-too |

| to | para | pah-rah |
| very | muito | mween-too |

## Alphabet:
In case you want to spell your name out loud or participate in a spelling bee...

| | | | | | | | |
|---|---|---|---|---|---|---|---|
| A | ah | H | eh-**gah** | O | "o" | V | vay |
| B | bay | I | ee | P | pay | W | "w" |
| C | say | J | **zhot**-teh | Q | kay | X | sheesh |
| D | day | K | "k" | R | ehr | Y | "y" |
| E | eh | L | "l" | S | "s" | Z | zay |
| F | "f" | M | "m" | T | tay | | |
| G | zhay | N | "n" | U | oo | | |

## Portuguese names for places:

| | | |
|---|---|---|
| Portugal | **Portugal** | poor-too-**gahl** |
| Lisbon | **Lisboa** | leezh-**boh**-ah |
| Spain | **Espanha** | ish-**pahn**-yah |
| Morocco | **Marrocos** | mah-**raw**-koosh |
| France | **França** | **frahn**-sah |
| Germany | **Alemanha** | ah-leh-**mahn**-yah |
| Switzerland | **Suiça** | **swee**-sah |
| Italy | **Italia** | ee-**tahl**-yah |
| Great Britain | **Inglaterra** | eeng-glah-**tehr**-rah |
| Europe | **Europa** | eh-oo-**roh**-pah |
| United States | **Estados Unidos** | ish-**tah**-doosh oo-**nee**-doosh |
| Canada | **Canadá** | kah-nah-**dah** |
| world | **o mundo** | oo **moon**_-doo |

# Numbers

| 0 | zero | zeh-roo |
|---|---|---|
| 1 | um | oon |
| 2 | dois | doysh |
| 3 | três | traysh |
| 4 | quatro | kwah-troo |
| 5 | cinco | seeng-koo |
| 6 | seis | saysh |
| 7 | sete | seh-teh |
| 8 | oito | oy-too |
| 9 | nove | naw-veh |
| 10 | dez | dehsh |
| 11 | onze | ohn-zeh |
| 12 | doze | doh-zeh |
| 13 | treze | tray-zeh |
| 14 | catorze | kah-tor-zeh |
| 15 | quinze | keen-zeh |
| 16 | dezasseis | deh-zah-saysh |
| 17 | dezassete | deh-zah-seh-teh |
| 18 | dezoito | deh-zoy-too |
| 19 | dezanove | deh-zah-naw-veh |
| 20 | vinte | veen-teh |
| 21 | vinte e um | veen-teh ee oon |
| 22 | vinte e dois | veen-teh ee doysh |
| 23 | vinte e três | veen-teh ee traysh |
| 30 | trinta | treen-tah |
| 31 | trinta e um | treen-tah ee oon |
| 40 | quarenta | kwah-rayn-tah |
| 41 | quarenta e um | kwah-rayn-tah ee oon |

| 50 | cinquenta | seeng-**kwayn**-tah |
| 60 | sessenta | seh-**sayn**-tah |
| 70 | setenta | seh-**tayn**-tah |
| 80 | oitenta | oy-**tayn**-tah |
| 90 | noventa | noh-**vayn**-tah |
| 100 | cem | sayn |
| 101 | cento e um | **sayn**-too ee oon |
| 102 | cento e dois | **sayn**-too ee doysh |
| 200 | duzentos | doo-**zayn**-toosh |
| 1000 | mil | meel |
| 2000 | dois mil | doysh meel |
| 2001 | dois mil e um | doysh meel ee oon |
| million | milhão | mil-**yow** |
| billion | bilhão | bil-**yow** |
| first | primeiro | pree-**may**-roo |
| second | segundo | seh-**goon**-doo |
| third | terceiro | tehr-**say**-roo |
| half | metade | meh-**tah**-deh |
| 100% | cem per cento | sayn pehr **sayn**-too |
| number one | número um | **noo**-meh-roo oon |

# Money

| Can you change dollars? | Pode trocar dollares? | **paw**-deh troo-**kar** **daw**-lah-rish |
| What is your exchange rate for dollars...? | Qual é a taxa de câmbio para o dollar...? | kwahl eh ah **tah**-shah deh **kahm**-bee-oo **pah**-rah oo **daw**-lar |
| ...in traveler's checks | ...em cheque de viagem | ayn **sheh**-keh deh vee-**ah**-zhayn |

| What is the commission? | O que é a comissão? | oo keh eh ah koo-mee-**sow** |
| Any extra fee? | À taxa extra? | ah **tah**-shah **ish**-trah |
| I would like... | Gostaria... | goosh-teh-**ree**-ah |
| ...small bills. | ...notas pequenas. | **naw**-tahsh peh-**kay**-nahsh |
| ...large bills. | ...notas grandes. | **naw**-tahsh **grahn**-dish |
| ...coins. | ...moedas. | moo-**eh**-dahsh |
| Is this a mistake? | Isto é um erro? | **eesh**-too eh oon **eh**-roo |
| I'm rich. | Sou rico[a]. | soh **ree**-koo |
| I'm poor. | Sou pobre. | soh **paw**-breh |
| I'm broke. | Estou teso[a]. | ish-**toh** tay-zoo |
| $50 | cinquenta escudos | seeng-**kwayn**-tah ish-**koo**-doosh |
| Where is a cash machine? | Onde é que é uma caixa automática? | **ohn**-deh eh keh eh **oo**-mah **kī**-shah ow-toh-**mah**-tee-kah |

**MONEY**

## Key money words:

| bank | banco | **bang**-koo |
| money | dinheiro | deen-**yay**-roo |
| change money | troca de dinheiro | **troo**-kah deh deen-**yay**-roo |
| exchange | troca | **troo**-kah |
| buy / sell | comprar / vender | kohn-**prar** / vayn-**dar** |
| commission | comissão | koo-mee-**sow** |
| traveler's check | cheques de viagem | **sheh**-keh deh vee-**ah**-zhayn |
| credit card | cartão de crédito | kar-**tow** deh **kreh**-dee-too |
| cash advance | avanço de dinheiro | ah-**van**-soo deh deen-**yay**-roo |
| cash machine | caixa automática, Multibanco | **kī**-shah ow-toh-**mah**-tee-kah, mool-tee-**bahng**-koo |
| cashier | caixa | **kī**-shah |

| cash | **dinheiro** | deen-**yay**-roo |
| bills | **notas** | **naw**-tahsh |
| coins | **moedas** | moo-**eh**-dahsh |
| receipt | **recibo** | reh-**see**-boo |

Commissions for changing traveler's checks can be steep in Portugal. It's easier and cheaper to use your ATM or debit card to withdraw cash from a *caixa automática* or *Multibanco* (cash machine). Here are a few words you might see on a cash machine: *anular* (cancel), *corrigir* (change), and *continuar* (continue). The Portuguese currency, *escudo*, will disappear in July, 2002, when the *euro* (€ ) will rule as the sole currency of Europe's 11-country Euroland.

# Time

| What time is it? | **Que horas são?** | keh **aw**-rahsh sow |
| It's... | **São...** | sow |
| ...8:00 in the morning. | **...oito horas da manhã.** | **oy**-too aw-rahsh dah ming-**yah** |
| ...16:00. | **...dezasseis horas.** | deh-zah-**saysh** **aw**-rahsh |
| ...4:00 in the afternoon. | **...das quarto da tarde.** | dahsh kwar-too dah **tar**-deh |
| ...10:30 (in the evening). | **...dez horas e meia (da noite).** | dehsh **aw**-rahsh ee **may**-ah (dah **noy**-teh) |
| ...a quarter past nine. | **...nove e um quarto.** | **naw**-veh ee oon **kwar**-too |
| ...a quarter to eleven. | **...um quarto para as onze.** | oon **kwar**-too pah-rah ahsh **ohn**-zeh |

| ...noon. | ...melo-dia. | may-oo-dee-ah |
| ...midnight. | ...meia-noite. | may-ah-noy-teh |
| ...sunrise. | ...nascer do sol. | nahsh-sehr doo sohl |
| ...sunset. | ...por do sol. | poor doo sohl |
| ...early / late. | ...cedo / tarde. | say-doo / tar-deh |
| ...on time. | ...pontual. | pohn-too-ahl |

In Portugal, the 24-hour clock (or military time) is used mainly for train, bus, and ferry schedules. Informally, the Portuguese use the same "12-hour clock" we do.

**TIME**

## Timely words:

| minute | minuto | mee-noo-too |
| hour | hora | aw-rah |
| in the morning | da manhã | dah ming-yah |
| in the afternoon | da tarde | dah tar-deh |
| in the evening | da noite | dah noy-teh |
| night | noite | noy-teh |
| day | dia | dee-ah |
| today | hoje | oh-zheh |
| yesterday | ontem | ohn-tayn |
| tomorrow | amanhã | ah-ming-yah |
| tomorrow morning | amanhã de manhã | ah-ming-yah deh ming-yah |
| anytime | a qualquer hora | ah kwahl-kehr aw-rah |
| immediately | imediatamente | ee-meh-dee-ah-tah-mayn-teh |
| in one hour | em uma hora | ayn oo-mah aw-rah |
| every hour | todas as horas | toh-dahsh ahs aw-rahsh |
| every day | todos os dias | toh-doosh oosh dee-ahs |
| last | último | ool-tee-moo |
| this | este | aysh-teh |

| | | |
|---|---|---|
| next | **próximo** | **praw**-see-moo |
| May 15 | **quinze de Maio** | **keen**-zeh deh **mah**-yoo |
| high season | **época alta** | **eh**-poh-kah **ahl**-tah |
| low season | **época baixa** | **eh**-poh-kah bī-shah |
| in the future | **no futuro** | noo foo-**too**-roo |
| in the past | **no passado** | noo pah-**sah**-doo |
| | | |
| week | **semana** | seh-**mah**-nah |
| Monday | **segunda-feira** | seh-goon-dah-**fay**-rah |
| Tuesday | **terça-feira** | tehr-sah-**fay**-rah |
| Wednesday | **quarta-feira** | kwar-tah-**fay**-rah |
| Thursday | **quinta-feira** | keen-tah-**fay**-rah |
| Friday | **sexta-feira** | saysh-tah-**fay**-rah |
| Saturday | **sábado** | **sah**-bah-doo |
| Sunday | **domingo** | doo-**meeng**-goo |
| | | |
| month | **mês** | maysh |
| January | **Janeiro** | zhah-**nay**-roo |
| February | **Fevereiro** | feh-veh-**ray**-roo |
| March | **Março** | **mar**-soo |
| April | **Abril** | ah-**breel** |
| May | **Maio** | **mah**-yoo |
| June | **Junho** | **zhoon**-yoo |
| July | **Julho** | **zhool**-yoo |
| August | **Agosto** | ah-**gohsh**-too |
| September | **Setembro** | seh-**tayn**-broo |
| October | **Outubro** | oh-**too**-broo |
| November | **Novembro** | noo-**vayn**-broo |
| December | **Dezembro** | deh-**zayn**-broo |
| | | |
| year | **ano** | **ah**-noo |
| spring | **primavera** | pree-mah-**veh**-rah |
| summer | **verão** | veh-**row** |

| fall | **outono** | oh-**toh**-noo |
| winter | **inverno** | een-**vehr**-noo |

## Holidays and happy days:

| holiday | **feriado** | feh-ree-**ah**-doo |
| national holiday | **feriado nacional** | feh-ree-**ah**-doo nah-see-oo-**nahl** |
| religious holiday | **feriado religioso** | feh-ree-**ah**-doo ray-lee-zhee-**oh**-zoo |
| Is today / tomorrow a holiday? | **Hoje / amanhã é feriado?** | **oh**-zheh / ah-ming-**yah** eh feh-ree-**ah**-doo |
| What is the holiday? | **Qual é o feriado?** | kwahl eh oo feh-ree-**ah**-doo |
| Merry Christmas! | **Feliz Natal!** | feh-**leesh** nah-**tahl** |
| Happy New Year! | **Feliz Ano Novo!** | feh-**leesh** ah-noo **noh**-voo |
| Happy wedding anniversary! | **Feliz aniversário de casamento!** | feh-**leesh** ah-nee-vehr-**sah**-ree-oo deh kah-zah-**mayn**-too |
| Happy birthday! | **Feliz aniversário!** | feh-**leesh** ah-nee-vehr-**sah**-ree-oo |

The Portuguese sing "Happy birthday" to the same tune we do, but they sing the tune twice, using these words: *Parabéns a você, nesta data querida, muitas felicidades, muitos anos de vida. Hoje é dia de festa, cantam as nossas almas, para* (fill in name), *uma salva de palmas!* Whew!

Portugal celebrates its independence day on December 1st. Other major holidays include Liberty Day (April 25), Good Friday and Easter (unlike Holy Week in Spain), *Dia de Camões* (June 10th, in honor of the Portuguese poet Luis de Camões), *Ascenção de Maria* (August 15th), and *Dia da República* (October 5th).

TIME

# Transportation

## Trains:

| Is this the line for...? | Esta é a fila para...? | **ehsh**-tah eh ah **fee**-lah **pah**-rah |
| ...tickets | ...bilhetes | beel-**yeh**-tish |
| ...reservations | ...reservas | reh-**zehr**-vahsh |
| How much is a ticket to...? | Quanto custa o bilhete para...? | **kwahn**-too **koosh**-tah oo beel-**yeh**-teh **pah**-rah |
| A ticket to ___. | Um bilhete para ___. | oon beel-**yeh**-teh **pah**-rah |
| When is the next train? | Quando é o próximo comboio? | **kwahn**-doo eh oo **praw**-see-moo koh<u>n</u>-**boy**-oo |
| I'd like to leave... | Gostaria de ir embora... | goosh-tah-**ree**-ah deh eer ay<u>n</u>-**boh**-rah |
| I'd like to arrive... | Gostaria de chegar... | goosh-tah-**ree**-ah deh shay-**gar** |
| ...by ___. | ...por ___. | poor |
| ...in the morning. | ...de manhã. | deh ming-**yah** |
| ...in the afternoon. | ...de tarde. | deh **tar**-deh |
| ...in the evening. | ...ao anoitecer. | ow ah-noy-teh-**sehr** |
| Is there a...? | Será que á um...? | seh-**rah** keh ah oo<u>n</u> |
| ...earlier train | ...comboio mais cedo | koh<u>n</u>-**boy**-oo mïsh **say**-doo |

| | | |
|---|---|---|
| ...later train | ...comboio mais tarde | kohn-**boy**-oo mīsh **tar**-deh |
| ...overnight train | ...comboio durante a noite | kohn-**boy**-oo doo-**rayn**-teh ah **noy**-teh |
| ...supplement | ...suplemento | soo-pleh-**mayn**-too |
| Does my railpass cover the supplement? | O suplemento fica incluido no passe? | oo soo-pleh-**mayn**-too **fee**-kah een-kloo-ee-doo noo **pah**-seh |
| Is there a discount for...? | Tem desconto para...? | tayn dish-**kohn**-too **pah**-rah |
| ...youth | ...jovens | **zhaw**-vaynsh |
| ...seniors | ...pessoas de terceira idade | peh-**soh**-ahsh deh tehr-**say**-rah ee-**dah**-deh |
| Is a reservation required? | É preciso reservar? | eh preh-**see**-zoo reh-zehr-**var** |
| I'd like to reserve a... | Gostaria de reservar um... | goosh-tah-**ree**-ah deh reh-zehr-**var** oon |
| ...seat. | ...assento. | ah-**sayn**-too |
| ...berth. | ...beliche. | beh-**lee**-sheh |
| Where does (the train) leave from? | De onde é que parte? | deh **ohn**-deh eh keh **par**-teh |
| What track? | Que linha? | keh **leen**-yah |
| On time? | Pontual? | pohn-too-**ahl** |
| Late? | Atrasado? | ah-trah-**zah**-doo |
| When will it arrive? | Quando é que vai chegar? | **kwahn**-doo eh keh vī shay-**gar** |
| Is it direct? | É directo? | eh dee-**reh**-too |
| Must I transfer? | É preciso mudar? | eh preh-**see**-zoo moo-**dar** |
| When? Where? | Quando? Onde? | **kwahn**-doo / **ohn**-deh |
| Which train to...? | Que comboio para...? | keh kohn-**boy**-yoo **pah**-rah |
| Which train car for...? | Que carruagem para...? | keh kar-**wah**-zhayn **pah**-rah |

| | | |
|---|---|---|
| Where is first class? | **Onde é a primeira classe?** | ohn-deh eh ah pree-**may**-rah **klah**-seh |
| ...front / middle / back | **...frente / meio / trás** | **frayn**-teh / **may**-oh / trahsh |
| Is this (seat) free? | **Está livre?** | ish-**tah lee**-vreh |
| That's my seat. | **Este é o meu lugar.** | **aysh**-teh eh oo **meh**-oo loo-**gar** |
| Save my place? | **Guarde o meu lugar?** | **gwar**-deh oo **meh**-oo loo-**gar** |
| Where are you going? | **Onde é que vai?** | ohn-deh eh keh vī |
| I'm going to... | **Vou para...** | voh **pah**-rah |
| Tell me when to get off? | **Diga-me quando vou sair?** | **dee**-gah-meh **kwahn**-doo voh sah-**eer** |

## Ticket talk:

| | | |
|---|---|---|
| ticket window | **Bilhetes** | beel-**yay**-tish |
| reservations window | **Reservas** | reh-**zehr**-vahsh |
| national / international | **Nacional / Internacional** | nah-see-oh-**nahl** / **een**-tehr-nah-see-oh-nahl |
| ticket | **bilhete** | beel-**yeh**-teh |
| one way | **uma ida** | **oo**-mah **ee**-dah |
| roundtrip | **ida e volta** | **ee**-dah ee **vohl**-tah |
| first class | **primeira classe** | pree-**may**-rah **klah**-seh |
| second class | **segunda classe** | seh-**goon**-dah **klah**-seh |
| non-smoking | **não fumador** | now foo-mah-**dor** |
| validate | **validade** | vah-lee-**dah**-deh |
| schedule | **horário** | aw-**rah**-ree-oo |
| departure | **partida** | par-**tee**-dah |
| direct | **directo** | dee-**reh**-too |
| transfer (verb) | **mudar** | moo-**dar** |
| connection | **conexão** | koo-nehk-**sow** |
| with supplement | **com suplemento** | kohn soo-pleh-**mayn**-too |

| reservation | **reserva** | ray-**zehr**-vah |
| seat... | **assento...** | ah-**sayn**-too |
| ...by the window | **...à janela** | ah zhah-**neh**-lah |
| ...on the aisle | **...sobre corredor** | **soh**-breh koo-ray-**dor** |
| berth | **beliche** | beh-**lee**-sheh |
| refund | **reembolso** | reh-ayn-**bohl**-soo |

*TRANSPORTATION*

## *At the train station:*

| Portuguese State Railways | **Caminhos de Ferro** | kah-**meen**-yoosh deh **fehr**-roo |
| train station | **estação de comboio** | ish-tah-**sow** deh kohn-**boy**-yoo |
| train information | **informação sobre comboios** | een-for-mah-**sow soh**-breh kohn-**boy**-yoosh |
| train | **comboio** | kohn-**boy**-yoo |
| high-speed train | **alfa service** | **ahl**-fah **sehr**-vees |
| arrival | **chegada** | shay-**gah**-dah |
| departure | **partida** | par-**tee**-dah |
| delay | **atraso** | ah-**trah**-zoo |
| toilet | **casa de banho** | **kah**-zah deh **bahn**-yoo |
| waiting room | **sala de espera** | **sah**-lah deh ish-**peh**-rah |
| lockers | **depósito de bagagem automático** | deh-**paw**-zee-too deh bah-**gah**-zhayn ow-too-**mah**-tee-koo |
| baggage check room | **despacho de bagagem** | dish-**pah**-shoo deh bah-**gah**-zhayn |
| lost and found office | **perdidos e achados** | pehr-**dee**-doosh ee ah-**shah**-doosh |
| tourist information | **informação turistica** | een-for-mah-**sow** too-**reesh**-tee-kah |

| to the platforms | **acesso ao cais** | ah-**seh**-soo ow kīsh |
| platform | **cais** | kīsh |
| track | **linha** | **leen**-yah |
| train car | **carruagem** | kar-**wah**-zhay<u>n</u> |
| dining car | **carruagem** | kar-**wah**-zhay<u>n</u> |
| | **restaurante** | rish-toh-**rahn**-teh |
| sleeper car | **carruagem** | kar-**wah**-zhay<u>n</u> |
| | **cama** | **kah**-mah |
| conductor | **fiscal** | **fish**-kahl |

## *Reading Portuguese train and bus schedules:*

| | |
| --- | --- |
| **até** | until |
| **atrasado** | late |
| **chegada** | arrival |
| **de** | from |
| **destino** | destination |
| **diário** | daily |
| **dias** | days |
| **dias de semana** | weekdays |
| **domingos e feriados** | Sundays and holidays |
| **excepto** | except |
| **hora** | time |
| **linha** | track |
| **para** | to |
| **partida** | departure |
| **sabádo** | Saturday |
| **só** | only |
| **também** | also |
| **todo** | every |
| **1-5, 6, 7** | Monday-Friday, Saturday, Sunday |

## Buses and subways:

| | | |
|---|---|---|
| How do I get to..? | **Como é que vou para...?** | **koh**-moo eh keh voh **pah**-rah |
| Which bus to...? | **Que autocarro para...?** | keh ow-too-**kah**-roo **pah**-rah |
| Does it stop at...? | **Para em...?** | **pah**-rah ayn |
| Which metro stop for...? | **Qual é a paragem para...?** | kwahl eh ah pah-**rah**-zhayn **pah**-rah |
| Which direction for...? | **Para...?** | **pah**-rah |
| Must I transfer? | **É preciso mudar?** | eh preh-**see**-zoo moo-**dar** |
| How much is a ticket? | **Quanto custa um bilhete?** | **kwahn**-too **koosh**-tah oon beel-**yeh**-teh |
| Where can I buy a ticket? | **A onde posso comprar um bilhete?** | ah **ohn**-deh **paw**-soo kohn-**prar** oon beel-**yeh**-teh |
| When does the... leave? | **Quando é que... parte?** | **kwahn**-doo eh keh... **par**-teh |
| ...first | **...primeiro** | pree-**may**-roo |
| ...next | **...próximo** | **praw**-see-moo |
| ...last | **...último** | **ool**-tee-moo |
| ...bus / subway | **...autocarro / metro** | ow-too-**kah**-roo / **meh**-troo |
| What's the frequency per hour / day? | **Qual é a frequência por hora / dia?** | kwahl eh ah freh-**kayn**-see-ah poor **aw**-rah / **dee**-ah |
| I'm going to... | **Vou para...** | voh **pah**-rah |
| Tell me when to get off? | **Diga-me quando vou sair?** | **dee**-gah-meh **kwahn**-doo voh sah-**eer** |

## *Handy bus and subway words:*

| | | |
|---|---|---|
| ticket | **bilhete** | beel-**yeh**-teh |
| city bus | **autocarro** | ow-too-**kah**-roo |
| long-distance bus | **camioneta** | kahm-yoo-**neh**-tah |
| bus stop | **paragem de autocarro** | pah-**rah**-zhayn deh ow-too-**kah**-roo |
| bus station | **terminal das camionetas** | tehr-mee-**nahl** dahsh kahm-yoo-**neh**-tahsh |
| subway | **metro** | **meh**-troo |
| subway station | **estação de metro** | ish-tah-**sow** deh **meh**-troo |
| direct | **directo** | dee-**reh**-too |
| connection | **conexão** | koo-nehk-**sow** |
| pick-pocket | **carteirista** | kar-teh-**rish**-tah |

## Taxis:

| | | |
|---|---|---|
| Taxi! | **Táxi!** | **tahk**-see |
| Can you call a taxi? | **Pode chamar um táxi?** | **paw**-deh shah-**mar** oon **tahk**-see |
| Where can I get a taxi? | **Onde posso apanhar um táxi?** | **ohn**-deh **paw**-soo ah-pahn-**yar** oon **tahk**-see |
| Are you free? | **Está livre?** | ish-**tah** **lee**-vreh |
| Occupied. | **Ocupado.** | oo-koo-**pah**-doo |
| How much will it cost to go to...? | **Quanto é que custa a viagem para...?** | **kwahn**-too eh keh **koosh**-tah ah vee-ah-**zhayn** **pah**-rah |
| ...the airport | **...o aeroporto** | oo ah-roh-**por**-too |
| ...the train station | **...estação do comboio** | ish-tah-**sow** doo kohn-**boy**-oo |
| ...this address | **...este endereço** | **aysh**-teh ayn-deh-**ray**-soo |
| Too much. | **É muito caro.** | eh **mween**-too **kah**-roo |

|  |  |  |
|---|---|---|
| This is all I have. | Isto é só o que tenho. | **eesh**-too eh saw oo keh **tayn**-yoo |
| Can you take ___ people? | Pode levar ___ pessoas? | **paw**-deh leh-**var** ___ peh-**soh**-ahsh |
| Any extra fee? | A taxa extra? | ah **tah**-shah **ish**-trah |
| The meter, please. | O medidor, por favor. | oo may-dee-**dor** poor fah-**vor** |
| Where is the meter? | Onde está o medidor? | **ohn**-deh ish-**tah** oo may-dee-**dor** |
| The most direct route. | O caminho mais direto. | oo kah-**meen**-yoo mīsh dee-**reh**-too |
| I'm in a hurry. | Estou com pressa. | ish-**toh** kohn **preh**-sah |
| Slow down. | Mais devagar. | mīsh deh-vah-**gar** |
| If you don't slow down, I'll throw up. | Se não for mais devagar, vou vomitar. | seh now for mīsh day-vah-**gar** voh voo-mee-**tar** |
| Stop here. | Pare aqui. | **pah**-rah ah-**kee** |
| Can you wait? | Pode esperar? | **paw**-deh ish-peh-**rar** |
| I'll never forget this ride. | Nunca vou esquecer esta viagem. | **noon**-kah voh ish-keh-**sehr** **ehsh**-tah vee-ah-**zhayn** |
| Where did you learn to drive? | Onde é que aprendeu a conduzir? | **ohn**-deh eh keh ah-**prayn**-doo ah kohn-doo-**zeer** |
| I'll only pay what's on the meter. | Só pago o que o medidor diz. | saw **pah**-goo oo keh oo may-dee-**dor** deesh |
| My change, please. | O meu troco, por favor. | oo **meh**-oo **troh**-koo poor fah-**vor** |
| Keep the change. | Fique com o troco. | **fee**-keh kohn oo **troh**-koo |

## Rental wheels:

| | | |
|---|---|---|
| I'd like to rent... | **Gostaria de alugar...** | goosh-tah-**ree**-ah deh ah-loo-**gar** |
| ...a car. | **...um carro.** | oo<u>n</u> **kah**-roo |
| ...a station wagon. | **...uma carrinha.** | **oo**-mah kah-**reen**-yah |
| ...a van. | **...uma furgoneta.** | **oo**-mah foor-goo-**nay**-tah |
| ...a motorcycle. | **...uma mota.** | **oo**-mah **moh**-tah |
| ...a motor scooter. | **...uma motocicleta.** | **oo**-mah moh-toh-see-**kleh**-tah |
| ...a bicycle. | **...uma bicicleta.** | **oo**-mah bee-see-**kleh**-tah |
| How much...? | **Quanto custa...?** | **kwahn**-too **koosh**-tah |
| ...per hour | **...á hora** | ah **aw**-rah |
| ...per day | **...ao dia** | ow **dee**-ah |
| ...per week | **...á semana** | ah seh-**mah**-nah |
| Unlimited mileage? | **Quilómetragem ilimitada?** | kee-**loh**-meh-trah-zhay<u>n</u> ee-lee-mee-**tah**-dah |
| I brake for bakeries. | **Paro em todas as padarias.** | **pah**-roo ay<u>n</u> toh-dahsh ahsh pah-dah-**ree**-ahsh |
| Is there...? | **Há...?** | ah |
| ...a helmet | **...um capacete** | oo<u>n</u> kah-pah-**say**-teh |
| ...a discount | **...um desconto** | oo<u>n</u> dish-**kohn**-too |
| ...a deposit | **...um deposito** | oo<u>n</u> deh-**poh**-zee-too |
| ...insurance | **...seguro** | say-**goo**-roo |
| When do I bring it back? | **Quando devolvo para traz?** | **kwahn**-doo deh-**vohl**-voo **pah**-rah trahsh |

## Driving:

| | | |
|---|---|---|
| gas station | **bomba de gasolina** | **bohn**-bah deh gah-zoo-**lee**-nah |

| | | |
|---|---|---|
| The nearest gas station? | A próxima bomba de gasolina? | ah **praw**-see-mah **bohn**-bah deh gah-zoo-**lee**-nah |
| Is it self-service? | É self-service? | eh "self-service" |
| Fill the tank. | Abastecer o carro. | ah-bahsh-teh-**sehr** oo **kah**-roo |
| I need... | Preciso... | preh-**see**-zoo |
| ...gas. | ...gasolina. | gah-zoo-**lee**-nah |
| ...unleaded. | ...sem chumbo. | sayn **shoon**-boo |
| ...regular. | ...normal. | nor-**mahl** |
| ...super. | ...super. | soo-**pehr** |
| ...diesel. | ...diesel. | dee-**zehl** |
| Check... | Verificar... | veh-ree-fee-**kar** |
| ...the oil. | ...o óleo. | oo **awl**-yoo |
| ...the air in the tires. | ...o ar nos pneus. | oo ar noosh **pehn**-yoosh |
| ...the radiator. | ...o radiador. | oo rah-dee-ah-**dor** |
| ...the battery. | ...a bateria. | ah bah-teh-**ree**-ah |
| ...sparkplugs. | ...as velas. | ahsh veh-**lahsh** |
| ...headlights. | ...os faróis da frente. | oosh fah-**roysh** dah **frayn**-teh |
| ...tail lights. | ...as luzes traseiras. | ahsh **loo**-shish trah-**zay**-rahsh |
| ...directional signal. | ...a pisca-pisca. | ah **pish**-kah-**pish**-kah |
| ...the brakes. | ...os travões. | oosh trah-**vohnsh** |
| ...my pulse. | ...a minha pulsação. | ah **meen**-yah pool-sah-**sow** |

Rather than dollars and gallons, gas pumps in Portugal will read escudos and liters (basically 4 liters in a gallon). Drive carefully. Statistically, Portugal's roads are the most dangerous in Europe.

## Car trouble:

| | | |
|---|---|---|
| accident | **acidente** | ah-see-**dayn**-teh |
| breakdown | **parado** | pah-**rah**-doo |
| funny noise | **barulho estranho** | bah-**rool**-yoo ish-**trahn**-yoo |
| electrical problem | **problema elétrico** | proo-**blay**-mah eh-**leh**-tree-koo |
| flat tire | **pneu furado** | pehn-yoo foo-**rah**-doo |
| My car won't start. | **O meu carro não arranca.** | oo **meh**-oo **kah**-roo now ah-**rang**-kah |
| This doesn't work. | **Isto não trabalha.** | **eesh**-too now trah-**bahl**-yah |
| It's overheating. | **Está muito quente.** | ish-**tah** mween-too **kayn**-teh |
| It's a lemon (rattletrap). | **É um calhambeque.** | eh oon kahl-yahm-**beh**-keh |
| I need... | **Preciso...** | preh-**see**-zoo |
| ...a tow truck. | **...um reboque.** | oon reh-**baw**-keh |
| ...a mechanic. | **...um mecânico.** | oon meh-**kahn**-nee-koo |
| ...a stiff drink. | **...whiskey.** | "whiskey" |

For help with repair, look up "Repair" under Shopping.

## Parking:

| | | |
|---|---|---|
| parking garage | **garagem** | gah-**rah**-zhayn |
| Where can I park? | **Onde é que posso estacionar?** | **ohn**-deh eh keh paw-soo ish-tah-see-oo-nar |
| Is parking nearby? | **É perto do estacionamento?** | eh **pehr**-too doo ish-tah-see-oo-nah-**mayn**-too |
| Can I park here? | **Posso fazer parking aqui?** | paw-soo fah-**zehr** par-**keeng** ah-**kee** |
| How long can I park here? | **Quanto tempo posso estacionar aqui?** | **kwahn**-too **tayn**-poo paw-soo ish-tah-see-oo-**nar** ah-**kee** |

| Must I pay to park here? | É preciso pagar para estacionar aqui? | eh preh-**see**-zoo pah-**gar** **pah**-rah ish-tah-see-oo-**nar** ah-**kee** |
| Is this a safe place to park? | É seguro estacionar aqui? | eh say-**goo**-roo ish-tah-see-oo-**nar** ah-**kee** |

## Finding your way:

| I'm going to... | Vou para... | voh **pah**-rah |
| How do I get to...? | Como é que vou para...? | **koh**-moo eh keh voh **pah**-rah |
| Do you have a map? | Tem um mapa? | tay<u>n</u> oo<u>n</u> **mah**-pah |
| How many minutes / hours...? | Quantos minutos / horas...? | **kwahn**-toosh mee-**noo**-toosh / **aw**-rahsh |
| ...on foot | ...a pé | ah peh |
| ...on bicycle | ...de bicicleta | deh bee-see-**kleh**-tah |
| ...by car | ...de carro | deh **kah**-roo |
| How many kilometers to...? | Quantos kilómetros para...? | **kwahn**-toosh kee-**law**-meh-troosh **pah**-rah |
| What's the... route to Lisbon? | Qual é... estrada para Lisboa? | kwahl eh... ish-**trah**-dah **pah**-rah leezh-**boh**-ah |
| ...best | ...a melhor | ah mil-**yor** |
| ...fastest | ...a mais rápida | ah mīsh **rah**-pee-dah |
| ...most interesting | ...a mais interessante | ah mīsh een-teh-reh-**sahn**-teh |
| Point it out? | Aponte? | ah-**poh**<u>n</u>-teh |
| I'm lost. | Estou perdido[a]. | ish-**toh** pehr-**dee**-doo |
| Where am I? | Onde é que estou? | **ohn**-deh eh keh ish-**toh** |
| Who am I? | Quem é que sou? | kay<u>n</u> eh keh soh |
| Where is...? | Onde é que é...? | **ohn**-deh eh keh eh |
| The nearest...? | O próximo...? | oo **praw**-see-moo |
| Where is this address? | Onde é este endereço? | **ohn**-deh eh **aysh**-teh ay<u>n</u>-deh-**ray**-soo |

## *Key route-finding words:*

| | | |
|---|---|---|
| map | **mapa** | **mah**-pah |
| downtown | **centro** | **sayn**-troo |
| straight ahead | **em frente** | ay<u>n</u> **frayn**-teh |
| left | **esquerda** | ish-**kehr**-dah |
| right | **direita** | dee-**ray**-tah |
| first | **primeira** | pree-**may**-rah |
| next | **próximo** | **praw**-see-moo |
| intersection | **cruzamento** | kroo-zah-**mayn**-too |
| roundabout | **rotunda** | roh-**toon**-dah |
| stoplight | **sinal de luz** | see-**nahl** deh loosh |
| square | **praça** | **prah**-sah |
| street | **rua** | **roo**-ah |
| bridge | **ponte** | **pohn**-teh |
| tunnel | **túnel** | **too**-nehl |
| highway | **autoestrada** | ow-too-ish-**trah**-dah |
| north | **norte** | **nor**-teh |
| south | **sul** | sool |
| east | **este** | **ehsh**-teh |
| west | **oeste** | **wehsh**-teh |

## *Reading road signs:*

| | |
|---|---|
| **abrandar** | yield |
| **baixa** | to the center of town |
| **construção na estrada** | workers ahead |
| **cuidado** | caution |
| **desvio** | detour |
| **devagar** | slow |
| **entrada** | entrance |
| **estacionamento proibido** | no parking |
| **obras** | construction |
| **outras as direcções** | other directions (out of town) |
| **pare** | stop |

| peões | pedestrians |
| próxima saída | next exit |
| saída | exit |
| sentido único | one-way street |
| todas as direcçoes | all directions (out of town) |

*Other signs you may bump into:*

| aberto das... ás... | open from... to... |
| água não potável | undrinkable water |
| casa de banho, WC | toilet |
| cuidado | be careful |
| cuidado com o cão | mean dog |
| empurre / puxe | push / pull (but pronounced push!) |
| fechado para férias | closed for vacation |
| fechado para restauração | closed for restoration |
| homens | men |
| ocupado | occupied |
| mulheres | women |
| para alugar / venda | for rent / sale |
| perigo | danger |
| proibido | forbidden |
| proíbida a entrada | no entry |
| proibido fumar | no smoking |
| puxe / empurre | pull / push |
| saída de emergência | emergency exit |
| Turismo | tourist information office |

TRANSPORTATION

# Sleeping

## Places to stay:

| | | |
|---|---|---|
| hotel | **hotel** | oh-**tehl** |
| family-run hotel | **pensão,** **residência** | payn-**sow**, reh-zee-**dayn**-see-ah |
| fancy historic hotel | **pousada** | poh-**zah**-dah |
| room in private home | **quarto** | **kwar**-too |
| youth hostel | **pousada de** **juventude** | poh-**zah**-dah deh zhoo-vayn-**too**-deh |
| vacancy sign (literally "rooms") | **quartos** | **kwar**-toosh |

## Reserving a room:

A good time to reserve a room by phone is the morning of the day you plan to arrive. To reserve from the U.S. by fax, use the handy form in the appendix.

| | | |
|---|---|---|
| Hello. | **Olá.** | oh-**lah** |
| Do you speak English? | **Fala inglês?** | **fah**-lah een-**glaysh** |
| Do you have a room for...? | **Tem um quarto** **para...?** | tayn oon **kwar**-too **pah**-rah |
| ...one person | **...uma pessoa** | oo-mah peh-**soh**-ah |
| ...two people | **...duas pessoas** | doo-ahsh peh-**soh**-ahsh |
| ...tonight | **...esta noite** | **ehsh**-tah **noy**-teh |
| ...two nights | **...duas noites** | doo-ahsh **noy**-tehsh |
| ...Friday | **...sexta-feira** | saysh-tah-**fay**-rah |
| ...June 21 | **...21 de Junho** | **veen**-teh ee oon deh **zhoon**-yoo |
| Yes or no? | **Sim ou não?** | seeng oh now |

| I'd like... | Gostaria... | goosh-tah-**ree**-ah |
|---|---|---|
| ...a private bathroom. | ...uma casa de banho privada. | **oo**-mah **kah**-zah deh **bahn**-yoo pree-**vah**-dah |
| ...your cheapest room. | ...o quarto mais barato. | oo **kwar**-too mĩsh bah-**rah**-too |
| ...___ bed(s) for ___ people in ___ room(s). | ...___ cama(s) para ___ pessoas no ___ quarto(s). | ___ **kah**-mah(sh) **pah**-rah ___ peh-**soh**-ahsh noo ___ **kwar**-too(sh) |
| How much is it? | Quanto custa? | **kwahn**-too **koosh**-tah |
| Anything cheaper? | Nada mais barato? | **nah**-dah mĩsh bah-**rah**-too |
| I'll take it. | Eu fico. | **eh**-oo **fee**-koo |
| My name is... | Chamo-me... | **shah**-moo-meh |
| I'll stay / We'll stay... | Fico / Ficamos... | **fee**-koo / fee-**kah**-moosh |
| ...for ___ night(s). | ...por ___ noite(s). | poor ___ **noy**-teh(sh) |
| I'll come / We'll come... | Venho / Vimos... | **vehn**-yoo / **vee**-moosh |
| ...in one hour. | ...dentro de uma hora. | ...**dayn**-troo deh **oo**-mah **aw**-rah |
| ...before 4:00 in the afternoon. | ...antes das quatro da tarde. | **ahn**-tish dahsh **kwah**-troo dah **tar**-deh |
| ...Friday before 6 p.m. | ...sexta-feira antes das seis horas da tarde. | saysh-tah-**fay**-rah **ahn**-tish dahsh saysh **aw**-rahsh dah **tar**-deh |
| Thank you. | Obrigado[a]. | oh-bree-**gah**-doo |

## Getting specific:

| I'd like a room... | Gostaria um quarto... | goosh-tah-**ree**-ah oon **kwar**-too |
|---|---|---|
| ...with / without / and | ...com / sem / e | kohn / sayn / ee |
| ...toilet | ...casa de banho | **kah**-zah deh **bahn**-yoo |
| ...shower | ...chuveiro | shoo-**vay**-roo |

SLEEPING

## 154 Portuguese

| | | |
|---|---|---|
| ...shower down the hall | ...chuveiro é no fundo do corredor | shoo-**vay**-roo eh noo **foon**-doo doo koo-ray-**dor** |
| ...bathtub | ...banheira | bahn-**yay**-rah |
| ...double bed | ...cama grande | **kah**-mah **grahn**-deh |
| ...twin beds | ...camas gémeas | **kah**-mahsh **zheh**-may-ahsh |
| ...balcony | ...varanda | vah-**rahn**-dah |
| ...view | ...vista | **veesh**-tah |
| ...with only a sink | ...só com um lavatório | saw kohn oon lah-vah-**taw**-ree-oo |
| ...on the ground floor. | ...no rés-do-chão | noo **raysh**-doo-show |
| ...television | ...televisão | teh-leh-vee-**zow** |
| ...telephone | ...telefone | teh-leh-**foh**-neh |
| Is there an elevator? | Tem elevador? | tayn eh-leh-vah-**dor** |
| We arrive Monday, depart Wednesday. | Vamos chegar segunda-feira, e partir quarta-feira. | **vah**-moosh shay-**gar** seh-goon-dah-**fay**-rah, ee par-**teer** kwar-tah-**fay**-rah |
| I'll sleep anywhere. | Dormo em qualquer lugar. | **dor**-moo ayn kwahl-**kehr** loo-**gar** |
| I have a sleeping bag. | Tenho um saco de cama. | **tayn**-yoo oon **sah**-koo deh **kah**-mah |
| Will you call another hotel? | Pode contactar outro hotel? | **paw**-deh kohn-tahk-**tar** **oh**-troo oh-**tehl** |

### Confirming, changing, and canceling reservations:
You can use this template for your telephone call.

| | | |
|---|---|---|
| I have a reservation. | Tenho reserva. | **tayn**-yoo ray-**zehr**-vah |
| My name is... | Chamo-me... | **shah**-moo-meh |
| I want to... my reservation. | Quero... minha reserva. | **keh**-roo... **meen**-yah reh-**zehr**-vah |
| ...confirm | ...confirmar | kohn-feer-**mar** |

| ...cancel | ...cancelar | kahn-seh-**lar** |
| ...change | ...trocar | troh-**kar** |
| The reservation is / was for... | A reserva é / foi para... | ah reh-**zehr**-vah eh / foy **pah**-rah |
| ...one person | ...uma pessoa | oo-mah peh-**soh**-ah |
| ...two people | ...duas pessoas | **doo**-ahsh peh-**soh**-ahsh |
| ...today / tomorrow | ...hoje / amanhã | **oh**-zheh / ah-ming-**yah** |
| ...August 13 | ...13 de Agosto | **tray**-zeh deh ah-**gohsh**-too |
| ...one night / two nights | ...uma noite / duas noites | oo-mah **noy**-teh / **doo**-ahsh **noy**-tehsh |
| Did you find my reservation? | Encontrou a minha reserva? | ayn-**kohn**-troh ah **meen**-yah reh-**zehr**-vah |
| I'd like to arrive instead on... | Em vez, gostaria de chegar... | ayn vaysh goosh-tah-**ree**-ah deh shay-**gar** |
| Is everything O.K.? | Tudo bem? | **too**-doo bayn |
| Thank you. I'll see you then. | Obrigado[a], até a próxima. | oh-bree-**gah**-doo ah-**teh** ah **praw**-see-mah |
| I'm sorry I need to cancel. | Desculpe eu tenho de cancelar. | dish-**kool**-peh **eh**-oo **tayn**-yoo deh kahn-seh-**lar** |

## Nailing down the price:

| How much is...? | Quanto custa...? | **kwahn**-too **koosh**-tah |
| ...a room for ___ people | ...um quarto para ___ pessoas | oon **kwar**-too **pah**-rah ___ peh-**soh**-ahsh |
| ...your cheapest room | ...o quarto mais barato | oo **kwar**-too mīsh bah-**rah**-too |
| Breakfast included? | Pequeno almoço incluído? | peh-**kay**-noo ahl-**moh**-soo een-kloo-**ee**-doo |
| How much without breakfast? | Quanto custa sem o pequeno almoço? | **kwahn**-too **koosh**-tah sayn oo peh-**kay**-noo ahl-**moh**-soo |

| Complete price? | **Preço total?** | **pray**-soo toh-**tahl** |
| Is it cheaper if I stay ___ nights? | **É mais barato se ficar ___ noites?** | eh mīsh bah-**rah**-too seh fee-**kar** ___ **noy**-tehsh |
| I'll stay ___ nights. | **Vou ficar ___ noites.** | voh fee-**kar** ___ **noy**-tehsh |

## Choosing a room:

| Can I see the room? | **Posso ver o quarto?** | **paw**-soo vehr oo **kwar**-too |
| Show me another room? | **Mostre-me outro quarto?** | **mohsh**-treh-meh **oh**-troo **kwar**-too |
| Do you have something...? | **Tem alguma coisa...?** | tayn ahl-**goo**-mah **koy**-zah |
| ...larger / smaller | **...maior / pequeno** | mī-**yor** / peh-**kay**-noo |
| ...better / cheaper | **...melhor / barato** | mil-**yor** / bah-**rah**-too |
| ...brighter | **...claridade** | klah-ree-**dah**-deh |
| ...in the back | **...nas traseiras** | nahsh trah-**zay**-rahsh |
| ...quieter | **...calmo** | **kahl**-moo |
| I'll take it. | **Eu fico.** | **eh**-oo **fee**-koo |
| My key, please. | **A minha chave, por favor.** | ah **meen**-yah **shah**-veh poor fah-**vor** |
| Sleep well. | **Dorme bem.** | **dor**-meh bay̱n |
| Good night. | **Boa-noite.** | boh-ah-**noy**-teh |

## Hotel help:

| I'd like... | **Gostaria...** | goosh-tah-**ree**-ah |
| ...a / another | **...um / outro** | oo̱n / **oh**-troo |
| ...towel. | **...toalha.** | too-**ahl**-yah |
| ...pillow. | **...almofada.** | ahl-moh-**fah**-dah |
| ...clean sheets. | **...lençóis limpos.** | **lay̱n**-soysh **leem**-poosh |
| ...blanket. | **...cobertor.** | koo-behr-**tor** |

| ...glass. | ...copo. | **koh**-poo |
|---|---|---|
| ...sink stopper. | ...tampa para lava louça. | **tahn**-pah **pah**-rah **lah**-vah **loh**-sah |
| ...soap. | ...sabão. | sah-**bow** |
| ...toilet paper. | ...papel higiénico. | pah-**pehl** ee-zhee-**ehn**-ee-koo |
| ...crib. | ...berço. | **behr**-soo |
| ...small extra bed. | ...pequena cama extra. | peh-**kay**-nah **kah**-mah **ish**-trah |
| ...different room. | ...quarto diferente. | **kwar**-too dee-feh-**rehn**-teh |
| ...silence. | ...silêncio. | see-**layn**-see-oo |
| Where can I wash / hang my laundry? | Onde é que posso lavar / pendurar a minha roupa? | **ohn**-deh eh keh **paw**-soo lah-**var** / payn-doo-**rar** ah **meen**-yah **roh**-pah |
| I'd like to stay another night. | Gostaria de ficar outra noite. | goosh-tah-**ree**-ah deh fee-**kar** **oh**-trah **noy**-teh |
| Where can I park? | Onde é que estaciono? | **ohn**-deh eh keh ish-tah-see-**oh**-noo |
| What time do you lock up? | A que horas fecha? | ah keh **aw**-rahsh **fay**-shah |
| What time is breakfast? | A que horas é o pequeno almoço? | ah keh **aw**-rahsh eh oo peh-**kay**-noo ahl-**moh**-soo |
| Please wake me at 7:00. | Acorde-me ás sete da manhã, por favor. | ah-**kor**-deh-meh ahsh **seh**-teh dah ming-**yah** poor fah-**vor** |

## Hotel hassles:

| Come with me. | Venha comigo. | **vayn**-yah koo-**mee**-goo |
|---|---|---|
| I have a problem in my room. | Tenho um problema no meu quarto. | **tayn**-yoo oon proo-**blay**-mah noo **meh**-oo **kwar**-too |
| It smells bad. | Cheira mal. | **shay**-rah mahl |

| bugs | **Insectos** | een-**seh**-toosh |
| mice | **rato** | **rah**-too |
| prostitutes | **prostitutas** | proosh-tee-**too**-tahsh |
| The bed is too soft / hard. | **Esta cama é muito mole / dura.** | **ehsh**-tah kah-mah eh mween-too **maw**-leh / **doo**-rah |
| Lamp... | **Candeeiro...** | kahn-dee-**yay**-roo |
| Lightbulb... | **Lâmpada...** | **lahm**-pah-dah |
| Electrical outlet... | **Tomada...** | toh-**mah**-dah |
| Key... | **Chave...** | **shah**-veh |
| Lock... | **Fechadura...** | feh-shah-**doo**-rah |
| Window... | **Janela...** | zhah-**neh**-lah |
| Faucet... | **Torneira...** | tor-**nay**-rah |
| Sink... | **Lava louça...** | **lah**-vah **loh**-sah |
| Toilet... | **Lavatórios...** | lah-vah-**taw**-ree-oosh |
| Shower... | **Chuveiro...** | shoo-**vay**-roo |
| ...doesn't work. | **...não trabalha.** | now trah-**bahl**-yah |
| There is no hot water. | **Não hà água quente.** | now ah ah-gwah **kayn**-teh |
| When is the water hot? | **Quando hà água quente?** | **kwahn**-doo ah ah-gwah **kayn**-teh |

## Checking out:

| I'll leave... | **Parto...** | **par**-too |
| We'll leave... | **Partimos...** | par-**tee**-moosh |
| ...today / tomorrow. | **...hoje / amanhã.** | **oh**-zheh / ah-ming-**yah** |
| ...very early. | **...muito cedo.** | mween-too **say**-doo |
| When is check-out time? | **A que horas é preciso pagar a conta e sair?** | ah keh **aw**-rahsh eh preh-**see**-zoo pah-**gar** ah **kohn**-tah ee **sah**-eer |
| Can I pay now? | **Posso pagar agora?** | **paw**-soo pah-**gar** ah-**gor**-ah |

| The bill, please. | A conta, por favor. | ah **kohn**-tah poor fah-**vor** |
| Credit card O.K.? | Cartão de crédito O.K.? | kar-**tow** deh **kreh**-dee-too "O.K." |
| Everything was great. | Tudo foi óptimo. | **too**-doo foy **awp**-tee-moo |
| Will you call my next hotel for me? | Pode telefonar para o meu próximo hotel? | **paw**-deh teh-leh-foh-**nar** **pah**-rah oo **meh**-oo **praw**-see-moo oh-**tehl** |
| Can I...? | Posso ...? | **paw**-soo |
| Can we...? | Podemos...? | poo-**day**-moosh |
| ...leave baggage here until ___? | ...deixar a bagagem aqui até ___? | day-**shar** ah bah-**gah**-zhayn ah-**kee** ah-**teh** |

## Camping:

| tent | tenda | **tayn**-dah |
| camping | campismo | kahm-**peesh**-moo |
| The nearest campground? | O próximo parque de campismo? | oo **praw**-see-moo **par**-keh deh kahm-**peesh**-moo |
| Can I...? | Posso...? | **paw**-soo |
| Can we...? | Podemos...? | poo-**day**-moosh |
| ...camp here for one night | ...campar aqui por uma noite | kahm-**par** ah-**kee** poor **oo**-mah **noy**-teh |
| Are showers included? | Os chuveiros estam incluidos? | oosh shoo-**vay**-roosh ish-**tayn** ee-kloo-**ee**-doosh |

## Laundry:

| self-service laundry | self-service lavandaria | "self-service" lah-vahn-dah-**ree**-ah |
| wash / dry | lavar / secar | lah-**var** / say-**kar** |
| washer / dryer | máquina de lavar roupa / secador | **mah**-kee-nah deh lah-**var** **roh**-pah / **seh**-kah-dor |

| | | |
|---|---|---|
| detergent | **detergente** | deh-tehr-**zhayn**-teh |
| token | **ficha** | **fee**-shah |
| whites | **roupa branca** | **roh**-pah **brahng**-kah |
| colors | **roupa de cor** | **roh**-pah deh kor |
| delicates | **roupa delicada** | **roh**-pah deh-lee-**kah**-dah |
| handwash | **lavar à mão** | lah-**var** ah mow |
| How does this work? | **Como funciona?** | **koh**-moo foon-see-**oh**-nah |
| I need change. | **Preciso de troco.** | pray-**see**-zoo deh **troh**-koo |
| full-service laundry | **lavandaria** | lah-vahn-dah-**ree**-ah |
| Same-day service? | **No própria dia?** | noo **praw**-pree-ah **dee**-ah |
| By when do I need to drop off my clothes? | **Quando é que tenho de deixar as minhas roupas?** | **kwahn**-doo eh keh **tayn**-yoo deh day-**shar** ahsh **meen**-yahsh **roh**-pahsh |
| When will my clothes be ready? | **Quando é que as minhas roupas estão prontas?** | **kwahn**-doo eh keh ahsh **meen**-yahsh **roh**-pahsh ish-**tow** **prawn**-tahsh |
| Dried? | **Secas?** | **say**-kahsh |
| Folded? | **Dobradas?** | doo-**brah**-dahsh |

# Eating

EATING

## Finding a restaurant:

| | | |
|---|---|---|
| Where's a good... restaurant? | Onde hà um bom restaurante...? | ohn-deh ah oon bohn rish-toh-rahn-teh |
| ...cheap | ...barato | bah-rah-too |
| ...local-style | ...estilo regional | ish-tee-loo ray-zhee-oh-nahl |
| ...untouristy | ...não turístico | now too-reesh-tee-koo |
| ...Chinese | ...chinês | shee-naysh |
| ...fast food | ...comida rápida | koo-mee-dah rah-pee-dah |
| ...self-service buffet | ...de auto-serviço | deh ow-toh-sehr-vee-see-oo |
| fried chicken restaurant | churrasqueira | shoo-rahsh-kway-rah |
| beer garden | cervejaria | sehr-vay-zhah-ree-ah |
| with terrace | com esplanada | kohn ish-plah-nah-dah |
| with candles | com velas | kohn veh-lahsh |
| romantic | romântico | roh-mahn-tee-koo |
| moderate price | preço razoável | pray-soo rah-zwah-vehl |
| a splurge | extravagância | ish-trah-vah-gahn-see-ah |

## Getting a table and menu:

| | | |
|---|---|---|
| I'd like... | Gostaria... | goosh-tah-ree-ah |
| ...a table for one / two. | ...uma mesa para uma / duas. | oo-mah may-zah pah-rah oo-mah / doo-ahsh |
| ...non-smoking. | ...não fumador. | now foo-mah-dor |
| ...just a drink. | ...só uma bebida. | saw oo-mah beh-bee-dah |
| ...a snack. | ...um petisco. | oon peh-teesh-koo |
| ...just a salad. | ...só uma salada. | saw oo-mah sah-lah-dah |
| ...a half portion. | ...meia dose. | may-ah doh-zeh |
| ...a tourist menu. | ...uma ementa turística. | oo-mah eh-mayn-tah too-reesh-tee-kah |
| ...to see the menu. | ...de ver a ementa. | deh vehr ah eh-mayn-tah |
| ...to order. | ...encomendar. | ayn-koo-mayn-dar |

| ...to eat. | ...de comer. | deh koo-**mehr** |
| ...to pay. | ...de pagar. | deh pah-**gar** |
| ...to throw up. | ...de vomitar. | deh voh-mee-**tar** |
| What do you recommend? | O que é que recomenda? | oo keh eh keh ray-koo-**mayn**-dah |
| What's your favorite dish? | Qual é a seu prato preferido? | kwahl eh ah **seh**-oo **prah**-too pray-feh-**ree**-doo |
| Is it...? | Isto é...? | **eesh**-too eh |
| ...good | ...bom | boh<u>n</u> |
| ...expensive | ...caro | **kah**-roo |
| ...light | ...leve | **leh**-veh |
| ...filling | ...para encher | pah-rah ay<u>n</u>-**shehr** |
| What's local? | O que é da região? | oo keh eh dah rayzh-**yow** |
| What is...? | O que é...? | oo keh eh |
| ...that | ...aquilo | ah-**kee**-loo |
| ...fast | ...rápido | **rah**-pee-doo |
| ...cheap and filling | ...barato e enche | bah-**rah**-too ee ay<u>n</u>-sheh |
| Do you have...? | Tem...? | tay<u>n</u> |
| ...an English menu | ...uma ementa em inglês | **oo**-mah eh-**mayn**-tah ay<u>n</u> een-**glaysh** |
| ...a children's portion | ...uma refeição para criança | **oo**-mah reh-fay-**sow** pah-rah kree-**ahn**-sah |

Portuguese restaurants are not Spanish—no tapas, but cheaper prices and earlier, more "normal" hours (lunch from noon to 2 p.m., dinner from 7:30 to 10:00 p.m.). Save money by considering a *meia dose* (half portion) and *prato do dia* (menu of the day).

## The menu:

| | | |
|---|---|---|
| menu | **ementa** | eh-**mayn**-tah |
| tourist menu | **ementa turistica** | eh-**mayn**-tah too-**reesh**-tee-kah |
| special of the day | **prato do dia** | **prah**-too doo **dee**-ah |
| specialty of the house | **especialidade da casa** | ish-peh-see-ah-lee-**dah**-deh dah **kah**-zah |
| breakfast | **pequeno almoço** | peh-**kay**-noo ahl-**moh**-soo |
| lunch | **almoço** | ahl-**moh**-soo |
| dinner | **jantar** | zhahn-**tar** |
| munchies (tapas) | **petiscos** | peh-**teesh**-koosh |
| appetizers | **entradas** | ayn-**trah**-dah |
| bread | **pão** | pow |
| salad | **salada** | sah-**lah**-dah |
| soup | **sopa** | **soh**-pah |
| meat | **carne** | **kar**-neh |
| poultry | **aves** | **ah**-vish |
| fish | **peixes** | **pay**-sheesh |
| shellfish | **marisco** | mah-**reesh**-koo |
| vegetables | **legumes** | lay-**goo**-mish |
| cheese | **queijo** | **kay**-zhoo |
| dessert | **sobremesa** | soo-breh-**may**-zah |
| beverages | **bebidas** | beh-**bee**-dahsh |
| beer | **cerveja** | sehr-**vay**-zhah |
| wine | **vinho** | **veen**-yoo |
| with / and / or / without | **com / e / ou / sem** | kohn / ee / oh / sayn |

## Dietary restrictions:

| | | |
|---|---|---|
| I'm allergic to... | **Sou alérgico[a] a...** | soh ah-**lehr**-zhee-koo ah |
| I cannot eat... | **Não posso comer...** | now **paw**-soo koo-**mehr** |
| ...dairy products. | **...produtos lácteos.** | proh-**doo**-toosh **lahk**-teh-oosh |
| ...meat / pork. | **...carne / porco.** | **kar**-neh / **por**-koo |
| ...salt / sugar. | **...sal / açúcar.** | sahl / ah-**soo**-kar |
| I am diabetic. | **Sou diabético[a].** | soh dee-ah-**beh**-tee-koo |
| No fat. | **Sem gordura.** | sayn gor-**doo**-rah |
| Minimal fat. | **Pouca gordura.** | **poh**-kah gor-**doo**-rah |
| Low cholesterol. | **Colesterol baixo.** | koo-**lehsh**-teh-rohl **bī**-shoo |
| No caffeine. | **Descaféinado.** | dish-kah-feh-ee-**nah**-doo |
| No alcohol. | **Sem alcool.** | sayn **ahl**-kahl |
| I'm a... | **Sou...** | soh |
| ...vegetarian. | **...vegetariano[a].** | veh-zheh-tar-ree-**ah**-noo |
| ...strict vegetarian. | **...rigorosamente vegetariano[a].** | ree-goh-roh-zah-**mayn**-teh veh-zheh-tar-ree-**ah**-noo |
| ...carnivore. | **...carnivoro[a].** | kar-nee-**voh**-roo |

## Tableware and condiments:

| | | |
|---|---|---|
| plate | **prato** | **prah**-too |
| extra plate | **outro prato** | **oh**-troo **prah**-too |
| napkin | **guardanapo** | gwar-dah-**nah**-poo |
| silverware | **talheres** | tahl-**yehr**-ish |
| knife | **faca** | **fah**-kah |
| fork | **garfo** | **gar**-foo |
| spoon | **colher** | **kool**-yehr |
| cup | **chávena** | **shah**-veh-nah |
| glass | **copo** | **kaw**-poo |
| carafe | **jarro** | **jah**-roo |

EATING

| water | **água** | **ah**-gwah |
|---|---|---|
| bread | **pão** | pow |
| butter | **manteiga** | mahn-**tay**-gah |
| margarine | **margarina** | mar-gah-**ree**-nah |
| salt / pepper | **sal / pimenta** | sahl / pee-**mayn**-tah |
| sugar | **açúcar** | ah-**soo**-kar |
| artificial sweetener | **sacarina** | sah-kah-**ree**-nah |
| honey | **mel** | mehl |
| mustard | **mostarda** | moosh-**tar**-dah |
| ketchup | **ketchup** | "ketchup" |
| mayonnaise | **maionese** | mah-yoh-**neh**-zeh |

Sometimes the waiter will put appetizers on your table as a temptation. You can decline, ignore, or eat. You pay (usually a per-person charge) only if you consume.

## Restaurant requests and regrets:

| A little. | **Um pouco.** | oon **poh**-koo |
|---|---|---|
| More. / Another. | **Mais. / Outro.** | mīsh / **oh**-troo |
| The same. | **O mesmo.** | oo **mehsh**-moo |
| I did not order this. | **Não encomendei isto.** | now ayn-koo-mayn-**day eesh**-too |
| I've changed my mind. | **Mudei de ideia.** | **moo**-day deh ee-**day**-ah |
| Is this included with the meal? | **Isto está incluido com a refeição?** | **eesh**-too ish-**tah** een-kloo-**ee**-doo kohn ah reh-fay-**sow** |
| What time does this open / close? | **A que horas é que abre / fecha?** | ah keh **aw**-rahsh eh keh **ah**-breh / **fay**-shah |
| I'm in a hurry. | **Estou com pressa.** | ish-**toh** kohn **preh**-sah |
| I must leave at... | **Tenho que sair às...** | **tayn**-yoo keh sah-**eer** ahsh |
| When will the food be ready? | **Quando é que a comida vai estar pronta?** | **kwahn**-doo eh keh ah koo-**mee**-dah vī ish-**tar prohn**-tah |
| "To go"? (for the road) | **Para o caminho?** | **pah**-rah oo kah-**meen**-yoo |

| This is... | Isto é... | **eesh**-too eh |
| ...dirty. | ...sujo. | **soo**-zhoo |
| ...greasy. | ...gorduroso. | gor-doo-**roh**-zoo |
| ...salty. | ...salgado. | sahl-**gah**-doo |
| ...undercooked. | ...malcozinhado. | mahl-koo-zeen-**yah**-doo |
| ...overcooked. | ...queimado. | kay-**mah**-doo |
| ...inedible. | ...não comestível. | now koo-mish-**tee**-vehl |
| ...cold. | ...frio. | **free**-oo |
| Can you heat this up? | Pode aquecer a comida? | **paw**-deh ah-kay-**sehr** ah koo-**mee**-dah |
| Enjoy your meal! | Bom-apetite! | bohn-ah-peh-**tee**-teh |
| Enough. | Chega. | **shay**-gah |
| Finished? | Acabou? | ah-kah-**bow** |
| Yuck! | Porcaria! | poor-kah-**ree**-ah |
| Yummy! | Optimo! | **awp**-tee-moo |
| Delicious! | Delicioso! | deh-lee-see-**oh**-zoo |
| Very tasty! | Muito gostoso! | **mween**-too goosh-**toh**-zoo |

## Paying for your meal:

| The bill, please. | A conta, por favor. | ah **kohn**-tah poor fah-**vor** |
| Together. | Junta. | **zhoon**-tah |
| Separate. | Separada. | seh-pah-**rah**-dah |
| Credit card O.K.? | Cartão de crédito O.K.? | kar-**tow** deh **kreh**-dee-too "O.K." |
| This is not correct. | Isto não está certo. | **eesh**-too now ish-**tah** **sehr**-too |
| Can you explain this? | Pode-me explicar isto? | **paw**-deh-meh ish-plee-**kar** **eesh**-too |
| What if I wash the dishes? | E se eu lavar os pratos? | ee seh **eh**-oo lah-**var** oosh **prah**-toosh |
| tip | gorjeta | gor-**zheh**-tah |

| | | |
|---|---|---|
| Keep the change. | **Fique com o troco.** | **fee**-keh koh<u>n</u> oo **troh**-koo |
| This is for you. | **Isto é para si.** | **eesh**-too eh **pah**-rah see |

To get your waiter's attention, say, *"Por favor"* (please). For fun, ask for the bill by saying, *"A dolorosa"* (meaning roughly "OK, make me suffer"). The tip (*gorjeta*) is never included in the bill. Just leave some coins rather than bills.

## Breakfast:

| | | |
|---|---|---|
| breakfast | **pequeno almoço** | peh-**kay**-noo ahl-**moh**-soo |
| bread | **pão** | pow |
| toast | **torrada** | too-**rah**-dah |
| butter | **manteiga** | mahn-**tay**-gah |
| jelly | **geleia** | zheh-**lay**-ah |
| pastry | **pastelaria** | pahsh-teh-lah-**ree**-ah |
| omelet | **omeleta** | aw-meh-**leh**-tah |
| eggs... | **ovos...** | **aw**-voosh |
| ...fried | **...estrelados** | ish-treh-**lah**-doosh |
| ...scrambled | **...mexidos** | mish-**ee**-doosh |
| ham | **fiambre** | fee-**ahm**-breh |
| cheese | **queijo** | **kay**-zhoo |
| yogurt | **yogurte** | yoo-**goor**-teh |
| cereal | **cereal** | seh-ree-**ahl** |
| milk | **leite** | **lay**-teh |
| hot chocolate | **chocolate quente** | shoo-koo-**lah**-teh **kay<u>n</u>**-teh |
| fruit juice | **sumo de fruta** | **soo**-moo deh **froo**-tah |
| orange juice | **sumo de laranja** | **soo**-moo deh lah-**rahn**-zhah |
| coffee / tea (see Drinking) | **café / chá** | kah-**feh** / shah |
| Is breakfast included? | **O pequeno almoço está incluido?** | oo peh-**kay**-noo ahl-**moh**-soo ish-**tah** een-kloo-**ee**-doo |

## Sandwiches:

| | | |
|---|---|---|
| I'd like a sandwich. | **Gostaria uma sanduich.** | goosh-tah-**ree**-ah oo-mah sahnd-**weesh** |
| toasted ham & cheese | **tosta mista** | **tosh**-tah meesh-tah |
| cheese | **queijo** | **kay**-zhoo |
| tuna | **atum** | ah-**too<u>n</u>** |
| chicken | **frango** | **frang**-goo |
| turkey | **peru** | peh-**roo** |
| ham | **fiambre** | fee-**ahm**-breh |
| salami | **salame** | sah-**lah**-meh |
| egg salad | **salada de ovo** | sah-**lah**-dah deh **aw**-voo |
| lettuce | **alface** | ahl-**fah**-seh |
| tomatoes | **tomates** | toh-**mah**-tish |
| onions | **cebolas** | seh-**boh**-lahsh |
| mustard | **mostarda** | moosh-**tar**-dah |
| mayonnaise | **maionese** | mah-yoh-**nay**-zeh |

**EATING**

## Soups and salads:

| | | |
|---|---|---|
| soup... | **sopa...** | **soh**-pah |
| ...of the day | **...do dia** | doo **dee**-ah |
| ...fish | **...de peixe** | deh **pay**-sheh |
| ...vegetable | **...de legumes** | deh lay-**goo**-mish |
| ...with egg, bread, herbs & garlic | **...Alentejana** | ah-lay<u>n</u>-teh-**zhah**-nah |
| potato & cabbage soup | **caldo verde** | **kahl**-doo **vehr**-deh |
| salad... | **salada...** | sah-**lah**-dah |
| ...green | **...de alface** | deh ahl-**fah**-seh |
| ...mixed | **...mista** | **meesh**-tah |
| ...with octopus | **...de polvo** | deh **pohl**-voo |

| ...with green peppers and grilled sardines | ...de pimento | deh pee-**mayn**-too |
| ...tuna, potatoes, & egg | ...de atum | deh ah-**toon** |
| ...Russian (tuna with lots of mayo) | ...de russa | deh **roo**-sah |
| lettuce | alface | ahl-**fah**-seh |
| tomato | tomate | too-**mah**-teh |
| onion | cebola | sheh-**boh**-lah |
| cucumbers | pepinos | peh-**pee**-noosh |
| oil / vinegar | óleo / vinagre | awl-yoo / vee-**nah**-greh |
| What is in this salad? | O que é isto na salada? | oo keh eh **eesh**-too nah sah-**lah**-dah |

## Portuguese specialties:

| | |
|---|---|
| açorda de marisco | stew of shellfish and bread |
| arroz de polvo | stew of octopus and rice |
| arroz de tomate con filetes | fried fish with rice—standard cheap dish |
| caldo verde | potato and cabbage soup |
| caracóis | snails (summer only) |
| chouriço | smoked pork sausage |
| bacalhau | cod (prepared a thousand different ways) |
| bacalhau cozido | boiled cod with beans and carrots |
| caldeirada | bouillabaisse-type stew with mixed fish |
| coelho à caçador | rabbit with carrots and potatoes |
| costeletas de porco à alentejana | pork chops, Alentejo-style, with tomatoes and onions |
| feijoada | beans with pork and sausage |
| filetes | fried white fish |
| leitão | small roasted suckling pig |
| pastas | appetizer of bread with sardines |
| pasteis de bacalhau | codfish balls |
| perna de cabrito | roasted leg of baby goat |

## Seafood:

|  |  |  |
|---|---|---|
| seafood | **marisco** | mah-**reesh**-koo |
| assorted seafood | **diversos mariscos** | dee-**vehr**-soosh mah-**reesh**-koosh |
| fish | **peixe** | **pay**-sheh |
| fried white fish | **filetes** | feh-**leh**-tish |
| cod | **bacalhau** | bah-kahl-**yow** |
| salmon | **salmão** | sahl-**mow** |
| trout | **truta** | **troo**-tah |
| tuna | **atum** | ah-**toon** |
| sardines | **sardinhas** | sar-**deen**-yahsh |
| anchovies | **anchovas** | ahn-**shoh**-vahsh |
| bream (fish) | **pargo** | **par**-goo |
| scad (like mackerel) | **carapaus** | kah-rah-**powsh** |
| swordfish | **espadarte** | ish-pah-**dar**-teh |
| clams | **amêijoas** | ah-**may**-zhoo-ahsh |
| mussels | **mexilhões** | meh-sheel-**yohnsh** |
| oysters | **ostras** | **ohsh**-trahsh |
| shrimp | **camarão** | kah-mah-**row** |
| tiger shrimp | **tigres** | **tee**-grish |
| prawns | **gambas** | **gahm**-bahsh |
| barnacles | **percebes** | pehr-**sheh**-bish |
| crab | **caranguejo** | kah-rahn-**gay**-zhoo |
| dungeness crab | **sapateira** | sah-pah-**tay**-rah |
| lobster | **lagosta** | lah-**gohsh**-tah |
| octopus | **polvo** | **pohl**-voo |
| squid | **lulas** | **loo**-lahsh |
| How much for a portion? | **Quanto para uma dose?** | **kwahn**-too **pah**-rah **oo**-mah **doh**-seh |

EATING

In restaurants, seafood is sold by the *"KG"* (kilogram) or *"dose"* (portion). *KG* is dangerous. Ask, *"Quanto para uma dose?"* ("How much for a portion?")

*Percebes* (boiled barnacles) are sold as munchies on the street, in bars, and sometimes in restaurants. To eat a barnacle, peel off and discard the outer skin, then wash it down with beer.

## Poultry and meat:

| | | |
|---|---|---|
| poultry | **aves** | **ah**-vish |
| chicken | **frango** | **frang**-goo |
| stewing chicken | **galinha** | gah-**leen**-yah |
| turkey | **peru** | peh-**roo** |
| partridge | **perdiz** | pehr-**deesh** |
| duck | **pato** | **pah**-too |
| meat | **carne** | **kar**-neh |
| beef | **carne de vaca** | **kar**-neh deh **vah**-kah |
| roast beef | **carne assada** | **kar**-neh ah-**sah**-dah |
| beef steak | **bife** | **bee**-feh |
| ribsteak | **costelas** | kohsh-**teh**-lahsh |
| veal | **vitela** | vee-**teh**-lah |
| cutlet | **costeleta** | koosh-teh-**lay**-tah |
| pork | **porco** | **por**-koo |
| ham | **fiambre** | fee-**ahm**-breh |
| smoked ham | **presunto** | preh-**zoon**-too |
| suckling pig | **leitão** | lay-**tow** |
| sausage | **salsicha** | sahl-**see**-shah |
| lamb | **borrego** | bor-**reh**-goo |
| baby goat | **cabrito** | kah-**bree**-too |
| bunny | **coelho** | **kwayl**-yoo |
| snails | **caracóis** | kah-rah-**koysh** |
| brains | **mioleira** | mee-oh-**lay**-rah |

| tongue | lingua | leeng-gwah |
| liver | fígado | fee-gah-doo |
| tripe | tripas | tree-pahsh |
| How long has this been dead? | À quanto tempo é que isto está morto? | ah kwahn-too tayn-poo eh keh eesh-too ish-tah mor-too |

## How it's prepared:

| hot | quente | kayn-teh |
| cold | frio | free-oo |
| raw | crú | kroo |
| cooked | cozido | koo-zee-doo |
| assorted | diversos | dee-vehr-soosh |
| baked | no forno | noo for-noo |
| boiled | cozido | koo-zee-doo |
| fresh | fresco | fraysh-koo |
| fried | frito | free-too |
| grilled | grelhado | grehl-yah-doo |
| homemade | caseiro | kah-zay-roo |
| medium | meio passado | may-oo pah-sah-doo |
| microwave | micro ondas | mee-kroo ohn-dahsh |
| mild | médio | meh-dee-oo |
| mixed | mista | meesh-tah |
| poached | escalfado | ish-kahl-fah-doo |
| rare | mal passado | mahl pah-sah-doo |
| roasted | assado | ah-sah-doo |
| smoked | fumado | foo-mah-doo |
| Spanish-style (peppers & tomatoes) | Espanhola | ish-pahn-yoh-lah |
| spicy hot | picante | pee-kahn-teh |
| steamed | cozido ao vapor | koo-zee-doo ow vah-por |
| stuffed | recheio | reh-shay-oo |

| | | |
|---|---|---|
| well-done | **bem passado** | bay<u>n</u> pah-**sah**-doo |
| with rice | **arroz** | ah-**rohsh** |

## Veggies, beans, and rice:

| | | |
|---|---|---|
| vegetables | **legumes** | lay-**goo**-mish |
| asparagus | **espargos** | ish-**par**-goosh |
| beans | **feijões** | fay-**zhoh**<u>n</u>**sh** |
| beets | **beterraba** | beh-teh-**rah**-bah |
| broccoli | **brócolos** | **braw**-koo-loosh |
| cabbage | **couve** | **koh**-veh |
| carrots | **cenoura** | seh-**noh**-rah |
| cauliflower | **couve-flor** | **koh**-veh-flor |
| corn | **milho** | **meel**-yoo |
| cucumbers | **pepinos** | peh-**pee**-noosh |
| eggplant | **berinjela** | beh-reen-**zheh**-lah |
| French fries | **batatas fritas** | bah-**tah**-tahsh **free**-tahsh |
| garlic | **alho** | **ahl**-yoo |
| green beans | **feijões verdes** | fay-**zhoh**<u>n</u>**sh vehr**-dish |
| mushrooms | **cogumelos** | koo-goo-**meh**-loosh |
| olives | **azeitonas** | ah-zay-**toh**-nahsh |
| onions | **cebolas** | seh-**boh**-lahsh |
| peas | **ervilhas** | ehr-**veel**-yahsh |
| pepper... | **pimento...** | pee-**may**<u>n</u>-too |
| ...green / hot | **...verde / picante** | **vehr**-deh / pee-**kahn**-teh |
| pickle | **pepino de** | peh-**pee**-noo deh |
| | **conserva** | koh<u>n</u>-**sehr**-vah |
| potatoes | **batatas** | bah-**tah**-tahsh |
| rice | **arroz** | ah-**rohsh** |
| spaghetti | **esparguete** | ish-par-**geh**-teh |
| spinach | **espinafre** | ish-pee-**nah**-freh |
| tomatoes | **tomates** | too-**mah**-tish |

You can usually get green beans and carrots (*feijes verdes e cenoura*) instead of the standard French fries by just asking.

## Fruits and nuts:

| | | |
|---|---|---|
| almond | **amêndoa** | ah-**mayn**-doh-ah |
| apple | **maçã** | mah-**sah** |
| apricot | **damasco** | dah-**mahsh**-koo |
| banana | **banana** | bah-**nah**-nah |
| canteloupe | **meloa** | meh-**low** |
| cherry | **cereja** | seh-**ray**-zhah |
| chestnut | **castanha** | kahsh-**tahn**-yah |
| coconut | **coco** | **koh**-koo |
| date | **fruto seco** | **froo**-too **say**-koo |
| fig | **figo** | **fee**-goo |
| fruit | **fruta** | **froo**-tah |
| grapefruit | **toranja** | toh-**rahn**-zhah |
| grapes | **uvas** | **oo**-vahsh |
| hazelnut | **avelã** | ah-veh-**lah** |
| honeydew melon | **melão** | meh-**low** |
| lemon | **limão** | lee-**mow** |
| orange | **laranja** | lah-**rahn**-zhah |
| peach | **pêssego** | **pay**-seh-goo |
| peanut | **amendoim** | ah-mayn-**dweem** |
| pear | **pêra** | **pay**-rah |
| pineapple | **ananás** | ah-nah-**nahsh** |
| pistachio | **pistácio** | peesh-**tah**-see-oo |
| plum | **ameixa** | ah-**may**-shah |
| prune | **ameixa seca** | ah-**may**-shah **say**-kah |
| raspberry | **framboesa** | frahm-boo-**ay**-zah |
| strawberry | **morango** | moo-**rang**-goo |
| tangerine | **tangerina** | tahn-zheh-**ree**-nah |
| walnut | **noz** | nawsh |
| watermelon | **melancia** | meh-**lahn**-see-ah |

## Just desserts:

| | | |
|---|---|---|
| dessert | **sobremesa** | soo-breh-**may**-zah |
| caramel custard | **flan** | flahn |
| cake | **bolo** | **boh**-loo |
| cream cake | **pastel de nata** | **pahsh**-tehl deh **nah**-tah |
| cream custard | **leite creme** | **lay**-teh **kreh**-mah |
| ice cream... | **gelado...** | zheh-**lah**-doo |
| ...cone | **...cone** | **koh**-neh |
| ...cup | **...chávena** | **shah**-veh-nah |
| ...vanilla | **...baunilha** | bow-**neel**-yah |
| ...chocolate | **...chocolate** | shoo-koo-**lah**-teh |
| ...strawberry | **...morango** | moo-**rang**-goo |
| fruit cup | **salada de fruta** | sah-**lah**-dah deh **froo**-tah |
| tart | **tarte** | **tar**-teh |
| whipped cream | **chântily** | **shahn**-tee-lee |
| chocolate mousse | **mousse** | **moo**-seh |
| pudding | **pudim** | **poo**-deem |
| rice pudding | **arroz doce** | ah-**rohsh doh**-sheh |
| sweet egg pudding | **fios de ovos** | **fee**-oosh deh **aw**-voosh |
| sweet egg rolls | **trouxas de ovos** | **troo**-shahsh deh **aw**-voosh |
| pastry | **pastelaria** | pahsh-teh-lah-**ree**-ah |
| cookies | **bolos** | **boh**-loosh |
| candy | **rebuçados** | ray-boo-**sah**-doosh |
| low calorie | **poucas calorias** | **poh**-kahsh kah-loo-**ree**-ahsh |
| homemade | **caseiro** | kah-**zay**-roo |
| Exquisite! | **Requintado!** | ray-keen-**tah**-doo |
| It's heavenly! | **É divinal!** | eh dee-vee-**nahl** |

# Drinking

## Water, milk, and juice:

| | | |
|---|---|---|
| mineral water... | **água mineral...** | **ah**-gwah mee-neh-**rahl** |
| ...with / without gas | **...com / sem gás** | kohn / sayn gahsh |
| tap water | **água da torneira** | **ah**-gwah dah tor-**nay**-rah |
| whole milk | **leite gordo** | **lay**-teh **gor**-doo |
| skim milk | **leite magro** | **lay**-teh **mah**-groo |
| fresh milk | **leite fresco** | **lay**-teh **fraysh**-koo |
| hot chocolate | **chocolate quente** | shoo-koo-**lah**-teh **kayn**-teh |
| fruit juice | **sumo de fruta** | **soo**-moo deh **froo**-tah |
| orange juice (pure) | **sumo de laranja (puro)** | **soo**-moo deh lah-**rahn**-zhah (**poo**-roo) |
| apple juice | **sumo de maçã** | **soo**-moo deh mah-**sah** |
| lemonade | **limonada** | lee-moh-**nah**-dah |
| with / without... | **com / sem...** | kohn / sayn |
| ...sugar | **...açúcar** | ah-**soo**-kar |
| ...ice | **...gelo** | **zhay**-loo |
| glass / cup | **copo / chávena** | **kaw**-poo / **shah**-veh-nah |
| small / large | **pequena / grande** | peh-**kay**-nah / **grahn**-deh |
| bottle | **garrafa** | gah-**rah**-fah |
| Is this water safe to drink? | **Posso beber esta água?** | **paw**-soo beh-**behr ehsh**-tah **ah**-gwah |

Tap water is free at restaurants—ask for *água da torneira*.
If you like mineral water, your big decision is *com* or *sem
gás* (with or without carbonation). *Com gas* is a taste well
worth acquiring. The light, sturdy plastic water bottles are
great to pack along and re-use as you travel.

## Coffee and tea:

| | | |
|---|---|---|
| coffee... | café... | kah-**feh** |
| ...with milk | ...com leite | koh<u>n</u> **lay**-teh |
| ...with sugar | ...com açucar | koh<u>n</u> ah-**soo**-kar |
| ...decaffeinated | ...descaféinado | dish-kah-feh-ee-**nah**-doo |
| ...instant | ...Nescafe | **nehsh**-kah-feh |
| coffee with a little milk | meia de leite | **may**-ah deh **lay**-teh |
| coffee with lots of milk | galão | gah-**low** |
| espresso | bica | **bee**-kah |
| espresso with milk | garoto | gah-**roh**-too |
| hot water | água quente | **ah**-gwah **kay**<u>n</u>-teh |
| tea / lemon | chá / limão | shah / lee-**mow** |
| herbal tea | chá de ervas | shah deh **ehr**-vahsh |
| fruit tea | chá de frutas | shah deh **froo**-tahsh |
| iced tea | chá gelado | shah zheh-**lah**-doo |
| small / large | pequeno / grande | peh-**kay**-noo / **grahn**-deh |
| Another cup. | Outra chávena. | **oh**-trah **shah**-veh-nah |

Only tourists take milk with their coffee throughout the day. The Portuguese add milk only at breakfast.

## Wine:

| | | |
|---|---|---|
| I would like... | Gostaria... | goosh-tah-**ree**-ah |
| We would like... | Gostaríamos... | goosh-tah-**ree**-ah-moosh |
| ...a glass | ...um copo | oo<u>n</u> **kaw**-poo |
| ...a carafe | ...um jarro | oo<u>n</u> jah-roo |
| ...a bottle | ...uma garrafa | **oo**-mah gah-**rah**-fah |
| ...of red wine | ...de vinho tinto | deh **veen**-yoo **teen**-too |
| ...of white wine | ...de vinho branco | deh **veen**-yoo **brang**-koo |

| ...the wine list | ...a lista de vinhos | ah **leesh**-tah deh **veen**-yoosh |
|---|---|---|

## Wine words:

| wine | vinho | **veen**-yoo |
|---|---|---|
| select wine (good year) | vinho reserva | **veen**-yoo reh-**zehr**-vah |
| table wine | vinho de mesa | **veen**-yoo deh **may**-zah |
| cheap house wine | vinho da casa | **veen**-yoo dah **kah**-zah |
| local | local | loo-**kahl** |
| red | tinto | **teen**-too |
| white | branco | **brang**-koo |
| rose | rosado | roh-**zah**-doo |
| sparkling | espumante | ish-poo-**mahn**-teh |
| sweet | doce | **doh**-seh |
| medium | médio | **meh**-dee-oo |
| dry | seco | **say**-koo |
| very dry | muito seco | **mween**-too **say**-koo |
| cork | rolha | **rohl**-yah |

**EATING**

For good, cheap wine, try the *vinho de casa* (house wine). A Portuguese specialty is *vinho verde*. This sparkling wine, which goes well with shellfish, comes in red or white—while many argue that both are bad, the white is clearly better.

## Beer:

| beer | cerveja | sehr-**vay**-zhah |
|---|---|---|
| small glass of draft beer | imperial | ay<u>n</u>-peh-ree-**ahl** |
| glass of draft beer | fino | **fee**-noo |
| big glass of draft beer | caneca | kah-**neh**-kah |
| bottle | garrafa | gah-**rah**-fah |

| light / dark | leve / escura | leh-veh / ish-koo-rah |
| local / imported | local / importada | loo-kahl / eem-poor-tah-dah |
| small / large | pequena / grande | peh-kay-nah / grahn-deh |
| cold | fresca | frehsh-kah |
| colder | mais fresca | mīsh frehsh-kah |
| beer garden | cervejaria | sehr-vay-zhah-ree-ah |

Portuguese beer is stronger than its Spanish cousin—
*cuidado* (be careful)! For a meal with your beer, look for a
*cervejaria* (beer garden).

A popular local drink is *água ardente* (firewater), made
from grape seeds. In Lisbon, hole-in-the-wall bars sell
*ginjinha* (zheen-zheen-yah), a sweet liqueur of cherry-like
ginja berries, sugar, and schnapps.

## Bar talk:

| What would you like? | O que é que gostaria? | oo keh eh keh goosh-tah-ree-ah |
| What is the local specialty? | Qual é a especialidade local? | kwahl eh ah ish-peh-see-ah-lee-dah-deh loo-kahl |
| Straight. | Puro. | poo-roo |
| With / Without... | Com / Sem... | kohn / sayn |
| ...alcohol. | ...alcool. | ahl-kahl |
| ...ice. | ...gelo. | zhay-loo |
| One more. | Mais uma. | mīsh oo-mah |
| Cheers! | Saúde! | sah-oo-deh |
| Long live Portugal! | Vida longa Portugal! | vee-dah lohn-gah poor-too-gahl |
| I'm... | Estou... | ish-toh |
| ...tipsy. | ...tocado[a]. | toh-kah-doo |
| ...drunk. | ...bêbado[a]. | bay-bah-doo |

# Picnicking

## At the market:

| | | |
|---|---|---|
| Is it self-service? | **É self-service?** | eh "self-service" |
| Ripe for today? | **Está maduro?** | ish-**tah** mah-**doo**-roo |
| Does it need to be cooked? | **Isto precisa de ser cozinhado?** | eesh-too preh-**see**-zah deh sehr koo-zeen-**yah**-doo |
| A little taste? | **Um pouco do sabor?** | oon poh-koo deh sah-**bor** |
| Fifty grams. | **Cinquenta gramas.** | seeng-**kwayn**-tah **grah**-mahsh |
| One hundred grams. | **Cem gramas.** | sayn **grah**-mahsh |
| More. / Less. | **Mais. / Menos.** | mīsh / **may**-noosh |
| A piece. | **Um pedaço.** | oon peh-**dah**-soo |
| A slice. | **Uma fatia.** | oo-mah fah-**tee**-ah |
| Sliced. | **Ás fatias.** | ahsh fah-**tee**-ahsh |
| A small bag. | **Um saco pequeno.** | oon sah-koo peh-**kay**-noo |
| A bag, please. | **Um saco, por favor.** | oon sah-koo poor fah-**vor** |
| Will you make me a sandwich? | **Pode-me fazer uma sande?** | paw-deh-meh fah-**zehr** oo-mah **sahn**-deh |
| To take out. | **Levar para fora.** | leh-**var** pah-rah **for**-rah |
| Is there a park nearby? | **Há algum parque perto?** | ah **ahl**-goon par-keh **pehr**-too |
| Is picnicking allowed here? | **É permitido fazer piquenique aqui?** | eh pehr-mee-**tee**-doo fah-**zehr** peek-**neek** ah-**kee** |
| Enjoy your meal! | **Bom-apetite!** | bohn-ah-peh-**tee**-teh |

## Picnic prose:

| | | |
|---|---|---|
| open air market | **mercado municipal** | mehr-**kah**-doo moo-nee-see-**pahl** |
| grocery store | **mercearia** | mehr-see-ah-**ree**-ah |
| supermarket | **supermercado** | soo-pehr-mehr-**kah**-doo |
| picnic | **piquenique** | peek-**neek** |
| sandwich | **sanduích, sande** | sahnd-**weesh**, **sahn**-deh |
| bread (whole wheat) | **pão (de trigo)** | pow (deh **tree**-goo) |
| ham | **fiambre** | fee-**ahm**-breh |
| sausage | **salsicha** | sahl-**see**-shah |
| cheese | **queijo** | **kay**-zhoo |
| mustard | **mostarda** | moosh-**tar**-dah |
| mayonnaise | **maionese** | mah-yoh-**neh**-zeh |
| yogurt | **yogurte** | yoo-**goor**-teh |
| fruit | **fruta** | **froo**-tah |
| box of juice | **pacote de sumo** | pah-**koh**-teh deh **soo**-moo |
| spoon / fork... | **colher / garfo...** | **kool**-yehr / **gar**-foo |
| ...made of plastic | **...plástica** | **plahsh**-tee-koo |
| cup / plate... | **chávena / prato...** | **shah**-veh-nah / **prah**-too |
| ...made of paper | **...de papel** | deh pah-**pehl** |

You can shop at a *supermercado,* but smaller shops are more fun. Get bread for your *sanduíche* at a *padaria* and order meat and cheese by the gram at a *mercearia*. For a meal on the run on a bun, try a *prego no pão* (meat & egg roll) or a *tosta mista* (toasted cheese & ham sandwich).

# Portuguese-English Menu Decoder

This won't contain every word on your menu, but it'll help you get *mexilhões* (mussels) instead of *mioleira* (brains).

**açorda**  chowder
**açúcar**  sugar
**água**  water
**alentejana**  with tomatoes & onions
**alcool**  alcohol
**alho**  garlic
**almoço**  lunch
**amêijoas**  clams
**ameixa**  plum
**ameixa seca**  prune
**amêndoa**  almond
**amendoim**  peanut
**amoras**  berries
**ananás**  pineapple
**anchovas**  anchovies
**arenque**  herring
**arroz**  rice
**arroz doce**  rice pudding
**assado**  roasted
**atum**  tuna
**avelã**  hazelnut
**aves**  poultry
**azeitonas**  olives
**bacalhau**  cod
**batatas**  potatoes
**batatas fritas**  French fries
**baunilha**  vanilla
**bebidas**  beverages
**berinjela**  eggplant
**beterraba**  beets

**bica**  espresso
**bife**  beef steak
**bola**  scoop
**bola de Berlin**  cream cake
**bolo**  cake
**bolos**  cookies
**branco**  white
**brócolos**  broccoli
**cabrito**  baby goat
**cachorro**  hot dog
**café**  coffee
**caldeirada**  fish stew
**caldo verde**  potato & cabbage soup
**camarão**  shrimp
**caneca**  large draft beer
**caracóis**  snails
**caranguejo**  crab
**carapaus**  scad (like mackerel)
**carne**  meat
**carneiro**  lamb
**casa**  house
**caseiro**  homemade
**castanha**  chestnut
**cebolas**  onions
**cenoura**  carrots
**cereja**  cherry
**cerveja**  beer
**chá**  tea
**chântily**  whipped cream

**chávena**  cup
**chinês**  Chinese
**chocolate quente**  hot chocolate
**chouriço**  smoked pork sausage
**coco**  coconut
**coelho**  bunny
**cogumelos**  mushrooms
**com**  with
**comida**  food
**compota**  jam
**cone**  cone
**copo**  glass
**costelas**  ribsteak
**costeleta**  cutlet
**couve**  cabbage
**couve-flor**  cauliflower
**cozido**  cooked
**crú**  raw
**damasco**  apricot
**de**  of
**descaféenado**  decaffeinated
**diversos**  assorted
**doce**  sweet
**e**  and
**ementa**  menu
**entradas**  appetizers
**ervas**  herbs
**ervilhas**  peas
**escalfado**  poached
**espadarte**  swordfish
**Espanhola**  with peppers & tomatoes
**espargos**  asparagus
**esparguete**  spaghetti
**especialidade**  speciality
**espinafre**  spinach

**espumante**  sparkling
**estilo**  style
**estrelados**  fried
**fatia**  slice
**fatias**  sliced
**feijoada**  beans with pork & sausage
**feijões**  beans
**fiambre**  ham
**fígado**  liver
**figo**  fig
**filetes**  fried white fish
**fino**  draft beer
**fios de ovos**  sweet egg pudding
**flan**  caramel custard
**forno**  baked
**framboesa**  raspberry
**frango**  chicken
**fresco**  fresh
**frio**  cold
**frito**  fried
**fruta**  fruit
**fruto seco**  date
**fumado**  smoked
**galão**  coffee with lots of milk
**galinha**  stewing chicken
**gambas**  prawns
**garrafa**  bottle
**gelado**  ice cream, iced
**geleia**  jelly
**gelo**  ice
**gordura**  fat
**gostoso**  tasty
**grande**  large
**grelhado**  grilled
**imperial**  small draft beer

importada  imported
incluido  included
jantar  dinner
jarro  carafe
lagosta  lobster
laranja  orange
legumes  vegetable
leitão  small roasted pig
leite  milk
leite creme  cream custard
levar para fora  "to go"
leve  light
limão  limon
lingua  tongue
lista  list
lulas  squid
maçã  apple
maionese  mayonnaise
manteiga  butter
margarina  margarine
marisco  shellfish
massa  pasta
médio  mild
meia dose  half portion
mel  honey
melancia  watermelon
melão  honeydew melon
meloa  canteloupe
mesa  table
mexidos  scrambled
mexilhões  mussels
micro ondas  microwave
milho  corn
miolos  brains
mista  mixed
morango  strawberry

mostarda  mustard
mousse  chocolate mousse
não  not
no forno  baked
noz  walnut
óleo  oil
omeleta  omelet
ostras  oysters
ou  or
ovos  eggs
pão  bread
pão de trigo  whole wheat bread
pargo  bream (fish)
pastas  bread with sardine spread
pastel de nata  cream cake
pastelaria  pastry
pato  duck
pedaço  piece
peixe  fish
pepinos  cucumbers
pepinos de conserva  pickles
pequeno  small
pequeno almoço  breakfast
pêra  pear
percebes  barnacles
perdiz  partridge
perna de cabrito  leg of baby goat
peru  turkey
pêssego  peach
petiscos  munchies (tapas)
picante  spicy hot
pimento  bell pepper
pimento verde  green pepper
pistácio  pistachio
polvo  octopus
porco  pork

**prato** plate
**prato do dia** special of the day
**prego no pão** meat & egg roll
**presunto** smoked ham
**pudim** pudding
**puro** pure
**queijo** cheese
**quente** hot
**rebuçados** candy
**recheio** stuffed
**refeição** meal
**região** local
**regional** local
**sal** salt
**salada** salad
**salmão** salmon
**salsicha** sausage
**sande** sandwich
**sapateira** dungeness crab
**sardinhas** sardines
**seco** dry
**sem** without
**sobremesa** dessert
**sopa** soup
**sumo** juice
**tangerina** tangerine
**tarte** tart
**tigres** tiger shrimp
**tinto** red
**tomates** tomatoes
**toranja** grapefruit
**torrada** toast
**tosta mista** toasted ham & cheese
   sandwich
**toucinho** bacon
**tripas** tripe

**trouxas de ovos** sweet egg rolls
**truta** trout
**uvas** grapes
**vaca** beef
**vapor** steamed
**verde** green
**vinagre** vinegar
**vinho** wine
**vitela** veal
**yogurte** yogurt

# Sightseeing

| Where is...? | Onde é...? | **ohn**-deh eh |
| ...the best view | ...a melhor vista | ah mil-**yor veesh**-tah |
| ...the main square | ...a praça principal | ah **prah**-sah preen-see-**pahl** |
| ...the old town center | ...a parte da cidade velha | ah **par**-teh dah see-**dah**-deh **vehl**-yah |
| ...the town hall | ...a câmara da cidade | ah **kah**-mah-rah dah see-**dah**-dah |
| ...the museum | ...o museu | oo moo-**zeh**-oo |
| ...the castle | ...o castelo | oo kahsh-**teh**-loo |
| ...the ruins | ...as ruínas | ahsh roo-**ee**-nahsh |
| ...the tourist information office | ...a informação turística | ah een-for-mah-**sow** too-**reesh**-tee-kah |
| ...the toilet | ...a casa de banho | ah **kah**-zah deh **bahn**-yoo |
| ...the entrance / exit | ...a entrada / saída | ah ayn-**trah**-dah / sah-**ee**-dah |
| Is there a festival nearby? | Há um festival aqui perto? | ah oon fehsh-tee-**vahl** ah-**kee** pehr-too |
| Do you have...? | Tem...? | tayn |
| ...information | ...informações | een-for-mah-**sohwsh** |
| ...a guidebook | ...um guia | oon **gee**-ah |
| ...a guided tour | ...uma visita guiada | **oo**-mah vee-**zee**-tah gee-**ah**-dah |
| ...in English | ...em inglês | ayn een-**glaysh** |
| When is the next tour in English? | Quando é a próxima visita guiada em inglês? | **kwahn**-doo eh ah **praw**-see-mah vee-**zee**-tah gee-**ah**-dah ayn een-**glaysh** |
| Is it free? | É grátis? | eh **grah**-teesh |
| How much is it? | Quanto custa? | **kwahn**-too **koosh**-tah |

| Is the ticket good all day? | O bilhete é bom para o dia inteiro? | oo beel-**yeh**-teh eh boh<u>n</u> **pah**-rah oo **dee**-ah een-**tay**-roo |
|---|---|---|
| Can I get back in? | Posso reentrar? | **paw**-soo reh-ayn-**trar** |
| What time does this open / close? | A que horas é que abre / fecha? | ah keh **aw**-rahsh eh keh **ah**-breh / **fay**-shah |
| What time is the last entry? | A que horas é a última entrada? | ah keh **aw**-rahsh eh ah **ool**-tee-mah ayn-**trah**-dah |
| PLEASE let me in. | POR FAVOR deixe-me entrar. | poor fah-**vor** **day**-sheh-meh ayn-**trar** |
| I've traveled all the way from... | Estou a viajar de muito longe... | ish-**toh** ah vee-ah-**zhar** deh **mween**-too loh<u>n</u>-zheh |
| I must leave tomorrow. | Tenho que partir amanhã. | **tayn**-yoo keh par-**teer** ah-ming-**yah** |
| I promise I'll be fast. | Prometo que faço rápido[a]. | proo-**may**-too keh **fah**-soo **rah**-pee-doo |

To help you decipher entrance signs, *adultos* is the price an adult pays, an *obra* is an exhibit, a *visita guiada* is a guided tour, and the words *"Você está aqui"* on a map mean "You are here."

## Discounts:
You may be eligible for discounts at tourist sites, hotels, or on buses and trains—ask.

| Is there a discount for...? | Tem desconto para...? | tay<u>n</u> dish-**kohn**-too **pah**-rah |
|---|---|---|
| ...youth | ...jovens | **zhaw**-vay<u>n</u>sh |
| ...students | ...estudantes | ish-too-**dahn**-tish |
| ...families | ...famílias | fah-**meel**-yahsh |
| ...seniors | ...idosos | id-**oh**-zoosh |

| I am... | Tenho... | **tayn**-yoo |
| He / She is... | Ele / Ela tem... | **eh**-leh / **eh**-lah tay<u>n</u> |
| ... ___ years old. | ... ___ anos. | ___ ah-noosh |

## In the museum:

| Where is...? | Onde é...? | **oh<u>n</u>**-deh eh |
| I'd like to see... | Gostaria de ver... | goosh-tah-**ree**-ah deh vehr |
| Photo / Video O.K? | Foto / Vídeo O.K.? | **foh**-too / **vee**-day-oo "O.K." |
| No flash / tripod. | Não flash / tripé. | now flahsh / tree-**peh** |
| I like it. | Gosto desta. | **gawsh**-too **dehsh**-tah |
| It's so... | É tão... | eh to<u>w</u> |
| ...beautiful. | ...lindo. | **leen**-doo |
| ...ugly. | ...feio. | **fay**-oo |
| ...strange. | ...estranho. | ish-**trahn**-yoo |
| ...boring. | ...enfadonho. | ay<u>n</u>-fah-**dohn**-yoo |
| ...interesting. | ...interessante. | een-teh-reh-**sahn**-teh |
| Wow! | Fiche! | **fee**-sheh |
| My feet hurt! | Os meus pés | oosh **meh**-oosh pehsh |
| | estão cansados! | ish-**tow** kahn-**sah**-doosh |
| I'm exhausted! | Estou estoirado! | ish-**toh** ish-toy-**rah**-doo |

## Art and architecture:

| art | arte | **ar**-teh |
| artist | artista | ar-**teesh**-tah |
| painting | pintura | peeng-**too**-rah |
| self portrait | auto-retrato | ow-too-reh-**trah**-too |
| sculptor | escultor | ish-kool-**tor** |
| sculpture | escultura | ish-kool-**too**-rah |
| architect | arquiteto | ar-kee-**teh**-too |
| architecture | arquitetura | ar-kee-teh-**too**-rah |
| original | original | oo-ree-zhee-**nahl** |

SIGHTSEEING

| restored | restaurado | rish-too-**rah**-doo |
|---|---|---|
| B.C. | A.C. | ah say |
| A.D. | D.C. | day say |
| century | secúlo | seh-**koo**-loo |
| style | estilo | ish-**tee**-loo |
| Abstract | abstrato | ahbsh-**trah**-too |
| Ancient | antigo | ahn-**tee**-goo |
| Art Nouveau | arte nova | **ar**-teh **noh**-vah |
| Baroque | barroco | bah-**roh**-koo |
| Classical | clássico | **klah**-see-koo |
| Gothic | gótico | **gaw**-tee-koo |
| Impressionist | impressionista | eem-preh-see-oo-**neesh**-tah |
| Medieval | mediaval | meh-dee-ah-**vahl** |
| Moorish | mouro | **moh**-roo |
| Renaissance | renascimento | reh-nahsh-see-**mayn**-too |
| Romanesque | românico | roo-**mah**-nee-koo |
| Romantic | romântico | roo-**mahn**-tee-koo |

Portugal's golden age of trade and exploration gave birth to a lavish, flamboyant Gothic style called "Manueline," named after King Manuel of the early 16th century.

## Castles and palaces:

| castle | castelo | kahsh-**teh**-loo |
|---|---|---|
| palace | palâcio | pah-**lah**-see-oo |
| kitchen | cozinha | koh-**zeen**-yah |
| cellar | celeiro | seh-**lay**-roo |
| dungeon | masmorra | mahsh-**moh**-rah |
| moat | fosso | **foh**-soo |
| fortified walls | fortificação | for-tee-fee-kah-**sow** |
| tower | torre | **tor**-reh |
| fountain | fonte | **fohn**-teh |
| garden | jardim | zhar-**deem** |

| king | **rei** | ray |
| queen | **raínha** | rah-**een**-yah |
| knights | **cavaleiros** | kah-vah-**lay**-roosh |

## Religious words:

| cathedral | **catedral** | kah-teh-**drahl** |
| church | **igreija** | ee-**gray**-zhah |
| monastery | **monestério** | moo-nish-**teh**-ree-oo |
| mosque | **mesquita** | mehsh-**kee**-tah |
| synagogue | **sinagoga** | see-nah-**goh**-gah |
| chapel | **capela** | kah-**peh**-lah |
| altar | **altar** | ahl-**tar** |
| cross | **cruz** | kroosh |
| treasury | **tesoraria** | teh-zoh-**rah**-ree-ah |
| crypt | **caixão** | kī-**show** |
| dome | **cúpula** | **koo**-poo-lah |
| bells | **sinos** | **see**-noosh |
| organ | **orgão** | or-**gow** |
| relic | **rélica** | **reh**-lee-kah |
| saint | **santo[a]** | **sahn**-too |
| God | **Deus** | **deh**-oosh |
| Jewish | **Judeu** | **zhoo**-deh-oo |
| Muslim | **Muçulmano** | moo-sool-**mah**-noo |
| Christian | **Cristão** | kreesh-**tow** |
| Protestant | **Protestante** | proh-tish-**tayn**-teh |
| Catholic | **Católico** | kah-**taw**-lee-koo |
| agnostic | **agnóstico** | ahg-**naw**-stee-koo |
| atheist | **ateu** | ah-**teh**-oo |
| When is the mass / service? | **Quando é que é a missa / serviço?** | **kwahn**-doo eh keh eh ah **mee**-sah / sehr-**vee**-soo |
| Are there concerts in the church? | **Dão concertos na igreija?** | dow kohn-**sehr**-toosh nah ee-**gray**-zhah |

# Shopping

## Names of Portuguese shops:

| | | |
|---|---|---|
| Where is a...? | **Onde é que é um...?** | **ohn**-deh eh keh eh oo<u>n</u> |
| antique shop | **antiquário** | ahn-tee-**kwah**-ree-oo |
| art gallery | **galeria de arte** | gah-leh-**ree**-ah deh **ar**-teh |
| bakery | **padaria** | pah-dah-**ree**-ah |
| barber shop | **barbeiro** | bar-**bay**-roo |
| beauty salon | **cabelareiro** | kah-beh-lah-**ray**-roo |
| book shop | **livraria** | leev-rah-**ree**-ah |
| camera shop | **loja fotográfica** | **law**-zhah foh-toh-**grah**-fee-kah |
| coffee shop | **café** | kah-**feh** |
| department store | **grande armazen** | **grahn**-deh ar-mah-**zay<u>n</u>** |
| flea market | **feira** | **fay**-rah |
| flower market | **mercado de flores** | mehr-**kah**-doo deh **floh**-rish |
| grocery store | **mercearia** | mehr-see-ah-**ree**-ah |
| hardware store | **casa de ferragens** | **kah**-zah deh feh-rah-**zhay<u>n</u>** |
| jewelry shop | **joalheria** | zhoo-ahl-yeh-**ree**-ah |
| laundromat | **lavandaria** | lah-vahn-dah-**ree**-ah |
| newsstand | **quiosque** | kee-**awsh**-keh |
| office supplies | **papelaria** | pah-peh-lah-**ree**-ah |
| open air market | **mercado municipal** | mehr-**kah**-doo moo-nee-see-**pahl** |
| optician | **oculista** | aw-koo-**leesh**-tah |
| pastry shop | **pastelaria** | pahsh-teh-lah-**ree**-ah |
| pharmacy | **farmácia** | far-**mah**-see-ah |

| photocopy shop | casa de fotocopias | kah-zah deh foh-tee-koh-pee-ahsh |
| shopping mall | centro comercial | sayn-troo koo-mehr-see-ahl |
| souvenir shop | loja de lembranças | law-zah deh layn-brang-sahsh |
| supermarket | supermercado | soo-pehr-mehr-kah-doo |
| toy store | loja de brinquedos | law-zah deh breeng-kay-doosh |
| travel agency | agência de viagens | ah-zhayn-see-ah deh vee-ah-zhaynsh |
| used bookstore | loja de livros usados | law-zah deh leev-roosh oo-zah-doosh |
| wine shop | loja de vinhos | law-zah deh veen-yoosh |

In Portugal, most shops close for lunch from about 13:00 till 15:00, and all day on Sundays.

## Shop till you drop:

| opening hours | horário | oh-rah-ree-oo |
| sale | saldo | sahl-doo |
| How much is it? | Quanto custa? | kwahn-too koosh-tah |
| I'm / We're... | Estou / Estamos... | ish-toh / ish-tah-moosh |
| ...just browsing. | ...só a olhar. | saw ah ohl-yar |
| I'd like... | Gostaria... | goosh-tah-ree-ah |
| Do you have...? | Tem...? | tayn |
| ...something cheaper | ...alguma coisa mais barato | ahl-goo-mah koy-zah mish bah-rah-too |
| ...more | ...mais | mish |
| Better quality, please. | Melhor qualidade, por favor. | mil-yor kwah-lee-dah-deh poor fah-vor |

| Can I see...? | Posso ver...? | paw-soo vehr |
|---|---|---|
| This one. | Este aqui. | aysh-teh ah-kee |
| Can I try it on? | Posso exprimentar? | paw-soo ish-pree-mayn-tar |
| Do you have a mirror? | Tem um espelho? | tayn oon ish-payl-yoo |
| Too... | Muito... | mween-too |
| ...big. | ...grande. | grahn-deh |
| ...small. | ...pequeno. | peh-kay-noo |
| ...expensive. | ...caro. | kah-roo |
| Did you make this? | Foi você que fez isto? | foy voh-say keh fehsh eesh-too |
| What is this made of? | Isto é feito de quê? | eesh-too eh fay-too deh kay |
| Is it machine washable? | Posso lavar á máquina? | paw-soo lah-var ah mah-kee-nah |
| Will it shrink? | Vai encolher? | vĩ ayn-kohl-yehr |
| Credit card O.K.? | Cartão de crédito O.K.? | kar-tow deh kreh-dee-too "O.K." |
| Can you ship this? | Pode enviar isto? | paw-deh ayn-vee-ar eesh-too |
| Tax-free? | Livre de impostos? | lee-vreh deh eem-pohsh-toosh |
| I'll think about it. | Vou pensar. | voh payn-sar |
| What time do you close? | A que horas é que fecha? | ah keh aw-rahsh eh keh fay-shah |
| What time do you open tomorrow? | A que horas é que abre amanhã? | ah keh aw-rahsh eh keh ah-breh ah-ming-yah |
| Is that your best price? | É o seu melhor preço? | eh oo seh-oo mil-yor pray-soo |
| My last offer. | A minha última oferta. | ah meen-yah ool-tee-mah oo-fehr-tah |
| Good price. | Bom preço. | bohn pray-soo |
| I'll take it. | Eu fico. | eh-oo fee-koo |

| | | |
|---|---|---|
| I'm nearly broke. | **Estou quase sem dinheiro.** | ish-**toh** kwah-zeh say<u>n</u> deen-**yay**-roo |
| My male friend... | **O meu amigo...** | oo **meh**-oo ah-**mee**-goo |
| My female friend... | **A minha amiga...** | ah **meen**-yah ah-**mee**-gah |
| My husband... | **O meu marido...** | oo **meh**-oo mah-**ree**-doo |
| My wife... | **A minha mulher...** | ah **meen**-yah **mool**-yehr |
| ...has the money. | **...é que tem o dinheiro.** | eh keh tay<u>n</u> oo deen-**yay**-roo |

## Repair:

These handy lines can apply to any repair, whether it's a ripped rucksack, bad haircut, or crabby camera.

| | | |
|---|---|---|
| This is broken. | **Isto está avariado.** | **eesh**-too aysh-**tah** ah-vah-ree-**ah**-doo |
| Can you fix it? | **Pode reparar isto?** | **paw**-deh reh-pah-**rar eesh**-too |
| Just do the essentials. | **Faça só o que for preciso.** | **fah**-sah saw oo keh for preh-**see**-zoo |
| How much will it cost? | **Quanto vai custar?** | **kwahn**-too vĭ koosh-**tar** |
| When will it be ready? | **Quando é que vai estar pronto?** | **kwahn**-doo eh keh vĭ ish-**tar praw**<u>n</u>-too |
| I need it by ___. | **Preciso até ___.** | preh-**see**-zoo ah-**teh** |

# Entertainment

| | | |
|---|---|---|
| What's happening tonight? | O que se passa esta noite? | oo keh seh **pah**-sah **ehsh**-tah **noy**-teh |
| What do you recommend? | O que é que recomenda? | oo keh eh keh ray-koo-**mayn**-dah |
| movie... | filme... | **feel**-meh |
| ...original version | ...versão original | vehr-**sow** oo-ree-zhee-**nahl** |
| ...in English | ...em inglês | ayn een-**glaysh** |
| ...with subtitles | ...com legendas | koh<u>n</u> leh-**zhayn**-dahsh |
| ...dubbed | ...dobrado | doo-**brah**-doo |
| music... | música... | **moo**-zee-kah |
| ...live | ...ao vivo | ow **vee**-voo |
| ...classical | ...clássico | **klah**-see-koo |
| ...folk | ...folclore | fool-**klaw**-reh |
| rock / jazz / blues | rock / jazz / blues | "rock" / zhahz / bloosh |
| singer | cantor[a] | kahn-**tor** |
| concert | concerto | koh<u>n</u>-**sehr**-too |
| show | espetáculo | ish-peh-**tah**-koo-loo |
| (folk) dancing | dança (folclórica) | **dahn**-sah (fool-**klaw**-ree-kah) |
| disco | disco | **deesh**-koo |
| cover charge | entrada | ay<u>n</u>-**trah**-dah |

*Fado* is Portugal's mournful style of folk singing. An evening absorbed in these fishermen's "blues" can leave you with sorrow creases. A good show is powerful stuff. For livelier fun, try Lisbon's *Feira Popular*, a family af-*fair* with lots of food, wine, rides, and friendly chaos.

# Phoning

| The nearest phone? | **O próximo telefone?** | oo **praw**-see-moo teh-leh-**foh**-neh |
| Where is the post office? | **Onde é que são os correios?** | oh<u>n</u>-deh eh keh so<u>w</u> oosh koo-**ray**-oosh |
| I'd like to telephone... | **Gostaria de telefonar para...** | goosh-tah-**ree**-ah deh teh-leh-foh-**nar pah**-rah |
| ...the United States. | **...os Estados Unidos.** | oosh ish-**tah**-doosh oo-**nee**-doosh |
| How much per minute? | **Quanto custa por minuto?** | **kwahn**-too **koosh**-tah poor mee-**noo**-too |
| I'd like to make a... call. | **Gostaria de fazer uma chamada...** | goosh-tah-**ree**-ah deh fah-**zeer oo**-mah shah-**mah**-dah |
| ...local | **...local.** | loo-**kahl** |
| ...collect | **...à cobrança.** | ah koo-**brang**-sah |
| ...credit card | **...com o meu cartão de crédito.** | koh<u>n</u> oo **meh**-oo kar-**tow** deh **kreh**-dee-too |
| ...long distance (within Portugal) | **...para fora da cidade.** | **pah**-rah **foh**-rah dah see-**dah**-deh |
| ...international | **...internacional.** | een-tehr-nah-see-oo-**nahl** |
| It doesn't work. | **Não funciona.** | no<u>w</u> foon-see-**oh**-nah |
| May I use your phone? | **Posso utilizar o seu telefone?** | **paw**-soo oo-tee-lee-**zar** oo **seh**-oo teh-leh-**foh**-neh |
| Can you dial for me? | **Pode fazer a ligação por mim?** | **paw**-deh fah-**zehr** ah lee-gah-**sow** poor meeng |
| Can you talk for me? | **Pode falar por mim?** | **paw**-deh fah-**lar** poor meeng |
| It's busy. | **Está ocupado.** | ish-**tah** oo-koo-**pah**-doo |
| Will you try again? | **Pode tentar novamente?** | **paw**-deh tayn-**tar** noo-vah-**mayn**-teh |

| Hello. (on phone) | **Está.** | ish-**tah** |
| My name is... | **Chamo-me...** | **shah**-moo-meh |
| My number is... | **O meu número é...** | oo **meh**-oo **noo**-may-roo eh |
| Speak slowly. | **Fale devagar.** | **fah**-leh deh-vah-**gar** |
| Wait a moment. | **Um momento.** | oo<u>n</u> moo-**mayn**-too |
| Don't hang up. | **Não desligue.** | no<u>w</u> dish-**lee**-geh |

## Key telephone words:

| telephone | **telefone** | teh-leh-**foh**-neh |
| telephone card | **cartão telefónico** | kar-to<u>w</u> teh-leh-**foh**-nee-koo |
| post office | **correios** | koo-**ray**-oosh |
| operator | **telefonista** | teh-leh-foh-**neesh**-tah |
| international assis- | **assistência** | ah-seesh-**tayn**-see-ah |
| tance | **internacional** | een-tehr-nah-see-oo-**nahl** |
| country code | **código do país** | **kaw**-dee-goo doo pah-**eesh** |
| area code | **código da area** | **kaw**-dee-goo dah ah-**ray**-ah |
| telephone book | **lista telefónica** | **leesh**-tah teh-leh-**foh**-nee-kah |
| toll-free | **taxa grátis** | **tah**-shah **grah**-teesh |
| out of service | **desligado** | dish-lee-**gah**-doo |

Use a handy phone card (*cartão telefónico*) instead of coins to make your calls. See "Let's Talk Telephones" near the end of this book for more phone tips.

# E-mail

| e-mail | **e-mail** | **ee**-mayl |
| internet | **internet** | **in**-tehr-neht |
| May I check my e-mail? | **Posso verificar o meu e-mail?** | **pos**-soh veh-ree-fee-**kar** oo **meh**-oo **ee**-mayl |

| Where can I get access to the internet? | **Onde posso ter acesso à internet?** | **ohn**-deh **pos**-soh tehr ah-**seh**-soo ah **in**-tehr-neht |

## On the computer screen:

| **abrir** | open |
| **eliminar** | delete |
| **enviar** | send |
| **ficheiro** | file |
| **guardar** | save |
| **imprimir** | print |
| **mensagem** | message |

# Mailing

| Where is the post office? | **Onde é que é os correios?** | **ohn**-deh eh keh eh oosh koo-**ray**-oosh |
| Which window for...? | **Que janela para...?** | keh zhah-**neh**-lah **pah**-rah |
| Is this the line for...? | **Esta é a fila para...?** | **ehsh**-tah eh ah **fee**-lah **pah**-rah |
| ...stamps | **...selos** | **say**-loosh |
| ...packages | **...embrulhos** | ayn-**brool**-yoosh |
| To the United States... | **Para os Estados Unidos...** | **pah**-rah oosh ish-**tah**-doosh oo-**nee**-doosh |
| ...by air mail. | **...por avião.** | poor ahv-**yow** |
| ...by surface mail. | **...de barco.** | deh **bar**-koo |
| How much is it? | **Quanto custa?** | **kwahn**-too **koosh**-tah |
| How many days will it take? | **Quantos dias é que demora?** | **kwahn**-toosh **dee**-ahsh eh keh deh-**moh**-rah |

POST OFFICE

In Portugal, you can often get stamps at a *quiosque* (newsstand) or *tabacaria* (tobacco shop). As long as you know which stamps you need, this is a great convenience.

## Handy postal words:

| | | |
|---|---|---|
| post office | **correios** | koo-**ray**-oosh |
| stamp | **selo** | **say**-loo |
| post card | **cartão postal** | kar-**tow** poosh-**tahl** |
| letter | **carta** | **kar**-tah |
| aerogram | **telegrama aéreo** | teh-leh-**grah**-mah ah-**eh**-ray-oo |
| envelope | **envelope** | ayn-veh-**loh**-peh |
| package | **embrulho** | ayn-**brool**-yoo |
| box | **caixa** | kī-shah |
| string | **cordão** | kor-**dow** |
| tape | **adesivo** | ah-deh-**zee**-voo |
| mailbox | **caixa postal** | kī-shah poosh-**tahl** |
| air mail | **por avião** | poor ahv-**yow** |
| express | **expresso** | ish-**preh**-soo |
| surface mail (slow and cheap) | **de barco** | deh **bar**-koo |
| book rate | **á tabela do livro** | ah tah-**beh**-lah doo **leev**-roo |
| weight limit | **limite de peso** | lee-**mee**-teh deh **pay**-zoo |
| registered | **registrado** | ray-zheesh-**trah**-doo |
| insured | **seguro** | say-**goo**-roo |
| fragile | **frágil** | **frah**-zheel |
| contents | **conteúdo** | kohn-teh-**oo**-doo |
| customs | **alfândega** | ahl-**fahn**-deh-gah |
| to / from | **para / de** | **pah**-rah / deh |
| address | **endereço** | ayn-deh-**ray**-soo |
| zip code | **código postal** | **kaw**-dee-goo poosh-**tahl** |
| general delivery | **Posta Restante** | **pawsh**-tah rish-**tahn**-teh |

# Red Tape & Profanity

## Filling out forms:

| | |
|---|---|
| **Sr. / Sra. / Menina** | Mr. / Mrs. / Miss |
| **nome** | first name |
| **apelido** | last name |
| **endereço** | address |
| **rua** | street |
| **cidade** | city |
| **estado** | state |
| **pais** | country |
| **nacionalidade** | nationality |
| **origem / destino** | origin / destination |
| **idade** | age |
| **dia de nascimento** | date of birth |
| **lugar de nascimento** | place of birth |
| **sexo** | sex |
| **masculino** | male |
| **feminino** | female |
| **casado / casada** | married man / married woman |
| **solteiro / solteira** | single man / single woman |
| **profissão** | profession |
| **adulto** | adult |
| **criança / rapaz / rapariga** | child / boy / girl |
| **crianças** | children |
| **familia** | family |
| **assinatura** | signature |
| **data** | date |

**RED TAPE**

When filling out dates, use this order: day/month/year (Christmas is 25/12/01).

## Portuguese profanity:

In any country, red tape inspires profanity. In case you're wondering what the more colorful locals are saying...

| | | |
|---|---|---|
| Darn it! | **Caramba!** | kah-**rahm**-bah |
| Go to hell! | **Vá para o inferno!** | vah **pah**-rah oo een-**fehr**-noo |
| bastard | **bastardo** | bahsh-**tar**-doo |
| bitch | **puta** | **poo**-tah |
| breasts (colloq.) | **mamas** | **mah**-mahsh |
| penis (colloq.) | **caralho** | kah-**rahl**-yoo |
| shit | **merda** | **mehr**-dah |
| drunk | **bêbado** | **bay**-bah-doo |
| idiot | **idiota** | ee-dee-**oh**-tah |
| imbecile | **parvo** | **par**-voo |
| jerk | **palerma** | pah-**lehr**-mah |
| stupid | **estúpido[a]** | ish-**too**-pee-doo |
| cretin | **cretino** | kreh-**tee**-noo |
| Did someone fart? | **Alguem deu um peido?** | ahl-gay<u>n</u> **deh**-oo oo<u>n</u> **pay**-doo |
| I burped. | **En arrotei.** | ay<u>n</u> ah-**roh**-tay |

# Help!

| Help! | Socorro! | soo-**koh**-roo |
| Help me! | Ajude-me! | ah-**zhoo**-deh-meh |
| Call a doctor! | Chame um médico! | **shah**-meh oon **meh**-dee-koo |
| ambulance | ambulância | ay<u>n</u>-boo-**lahn**-see-ah |
| accident | acidente | ah-see-**day<u>n</u>**-teh |
| injured | ferido | feh-**ree**-doo |
| emergency | emergência | ee-mehr-**zhay<u>n</u>**-see-ah |
| fire | fogo | **foh**-goo |
| police | polícia | poo-**lee**-see-ah |
| thief | ladrão | lah-**dro<u>w</u>** |
| pick-pocket | carteirista | kar-tay-**rish**-tah |
| I've been ripped off. | Fui roubado[a]. | fwee roh-**bah**-doo |
| I've lost my... | Perdi o meu... | **pehr**-dee oo **meh**-oo |
| ...passport. | ...passaporte. | pah-sah-**por**-teh |
| ...ticket. | ...bilhete. | beel-**yeh**-teh |
| ...bag. | ...saco. | **sah**-koo |
| I've lost my... | Perdi a minha... | **pehr**-dee ah **meen**-yah |
| ...purse. | ...bolsa. | **bohl**-sah |
| ...wallet. | ...carteira. | kar-**tay**-rah |
| ...faith in humankind. | ...fé na humanidade. | feh nah oo-mah-nee-**dah**-deh |
| I'm lost. | Estou perdido[a]. | ish-**toh** pehr-**dee**-doo |

## Help for women:

| Leave me alone. | Deixe-me em paz. | **day**-sheh-meh ay<u>n</u> pahsh |
| I *vant* to be alone. | Quero estar só. | **keh**-roo ish-**tar** saw |
| I'm not interested. | Não estou interessada. | no<u>w</u> ish-**toh** een-teh-reh-**sah**-dah |
| I'm married. | Sou casada. | soh kah-**zah**-dah |
| I'm a lesbian. | Sou lésbia. | soh **lehzh**-bee-ah |
| I have a contagious disease. | Tenho uma doença contagiosa. | **tayn**-yoo **oo**-mah doo-**ayn**-sah koh<u>n</u>-tah-zhee-**oh**-zah |
| He is bothering me. | Ele está a incomodar-me. | **eh**-leh ish-**tah** ah een-koo-moo-**dar**-meh |
| Don't touch me. | Não me toque. | no<u>w</u> meh **taw**-keh |
| You're disgusting. | Tu dás-me nojo. | too **dahsh**-meh **noh**-zhoo |
| Stop following me. | Pare de me seguir. | **pah**-reh deh meh seh-**geer** |
| Enough! | Chega! | **shay**-gah |
| Go away. | Vá-se embora. | **vah**-seh ay<u>n</u>-**boh**-rah |
| Get lost! | Desapareça! | day-zah-pah-**ray**-sah |
| Drop dead! | Quero que morra! | **keh**-roo keh **moh**-rah |
| I'll call the police! | Vou chamar a polícia! | voh shah-**mar** ah poo-**lee**-see-ah |

# Health

| I am sick. | Estou doente. | ish-**toh** doo-**ayn**-teh |
| I need a doctor... | Preciso de um médico... | preh-**see**-zoo deh oo<u>n</u> meh-dee-koo |
| ...who speaks English. | ...que fale inglês. | keh **fah**-leh een-**glaysh** |
| It hurts here. | Doi aqui. | doy ah-**kee** |
| I'm allergic to... | Sou alérgico[a] a... | soh ah-**lehr**-zhee-koo ah |
| ...penicillin. | ...penecilina. | peh-neh-see-**lee**-nah |
| I am diabetic. | Sou diabético[a]. | soh dee-ah-**beh**-tee-koo |
| I've missed a period. | Tenho faltar o periodo. | **tayn**-yoo fahl-**tar** oo peh-ree-**oh**-doo |
| My friend has... | O meu amigo[a]... | oo **meh**-oo ah-**mee**-goo |
| I have... | Tenho... | **tayn**-yoo |
| ...asthma. | ...asma. | **ahzh**-mah |
| ...athlete's foot (fungus). | ...pé de atleta (fungo). | peh deh aht-**leh**-teh (**foong**-goo) |
| ...bad breath. | ...mau halito. | mow ah-**lee**-too |
| ...bug bites. | ...picadelas. | pee-kah-**deh**-lahsh |
| ...a burn. | ...uma queimadura. | **oo**-mah kay-mah-**doo**-rah |
| ...chest pains. | ...uma dor no peito. | **oo**-mah dor noo **pay**-too |
| ...a cold. | ...uma constipação. | **oo**-mah koh<u>n</u>sh-tee-pah-**sow** |
| ...constipation. | ...prisão de ventre. | pree-**zow** deh **vayn**-treh |
| ...a cough. | ...uma tosse. | **oo**-mah **taw**-seh |
| ...diarrhea. | ...diarreia. | dee-ah-**ray**-ah |
| ...dizziness. | ...tonturas. | toh<u>n</u>-**too**-rahsh |
| ...a fever. | ...febre. | **feh**-breh |
| ...the flu. | ...uma gripe. | **oo**-mah **gree**-peh |
| ...hay fever. | ...febre dos fenos. | **feh**-breh doosh **feh**-noosh |

**HEALTH**

| | | |
|---|---|---|
| ...a headache. | ...uma dor de cabeça. | oo-mah dor deh kah-**beh**-sah |
| ...hemorrhoids. | ...hemorróidas. | eh-moh-**raw**-dahsh |
| ...high blood pressure. | ...tensão alta. | tayn-**sow** ahl-tah |
| ...indigestion. | ...uma indigestão. | oo-mah een-dee-zhish-**tow** |
| ...an infection. | ...uma infecção. | oo-mah een-fehk-**sow** |
| ...a migraine. | ...uma enxaqueca. | oo-mah ayn-shah-**keh**-kah |
| ...nausea. | ...tonturas. | tohn-**too**-rahsh |
| ...a rash. | ...uma erupção. | oo-mah ee-roop-**sow** |
| ...a sore throat. | ...uma dor de garganta. | oo-mah dor deh gar-**gahn**-tah |
| ...a stomach ache. | ...uma dor de estômago. | oo-mah dor deh ish-**toh**-mah-goo |
| ...a swelling. | ...um inchado. | oon een-**shah**-doo |
| ...a toothache. | ...uma dor de dente. | oo-mah dor deh **dayn**-teh |
| ...a venereal disease. | ...uma doença venéria. | oo-mah doo-**ayn**-sah veh-**neh**-ree-ah |
| ...a urinary infection. | ...uma infecção urinario. | oo-mah een-fehk-**sow** oo-ree-**nah**-ree-oo |
| ...worms. | ...vermes. | **vehr**-mish |
| I have body odor. | Tenho cheiro corporal. | **tayn**-yoo **shay**-roo kor-poo-**rahl** |
| Is it serious? | É grave? | eh **grah**-veh |

## Handy health words:

| | | |
|---|---|---|
| pain | dor | dor |
| dentist | dentista | dayn-**teesh**-tah |
| doctor | doutor[a] | doh-**tor** |
| nurse | enfermeira | ayn-fehr-**may**-rah |
| health insurance | seguro de saúde | say-**goo**-roo deh sah-**oo**-deh |
| hospital | hospital | ohsh-pee-**tahl** |

| blood | sangue | **sang**-geh |
| bandage | penso | **payn**-soo |
| medicine | medicina | meh-dee-**zee**-nah |
| pharmacy | farmácia | far-**mah**-see-ah |
| prescription | receita | reh-**say**-tah |
| pill | comprimido | kohn-pree-**mee**-doo |
| aspirin | aspirina | ahsh-pee-**ree**-nah |
| antibiotic | antibiótico | ahn-tee-bee-**aw**-tee-koo |
| cold medicine | remedio para constipação | reh-meh-**dee**-oo pah-rah kohnsh-tee-pah-**sow** |
| cough drops | rebuçados da tosse | reh-boo-**sah**-doosh dah **taw**-seh |
| antacid | remédio para azia | reh-meh-**dee**-oo pah-rah ah-**zee**-ah |
| pain killer | comprimidos para as dores | kohn-pree-**mee**-doosh **pah**-rah ahsh **doh**-rish |
| Preparation H | Preparação H | preh-pah-rah-**sow** eh-**gah** |
| vitamins | vitaminas | vee-tah-**mee**-nahsh |

## Contacts and glasses:

| glasses | oculos | oo-**koo**-loosh |
| sunglasses | oculos de sol | oo-**koo**-loosh deh sohl |
| prescription | receita | reh-**say**-tah |
| contact lenses... | lentes de contacto... | **lehn**-tish deh kohn-**tahk**-too |
| ...soft | ...flexibeis | fleh-**shee**-baysh |
| ...hard | ...rigidas | ree-**zhee**-dahsh |
| solution... | solução... | soo-loo-**sow** |
| ...cleaning | ...de limpeza | deh leem-**pay**-zah |
| ...soaking | ...para molhar | **pah**-rah mool-**yar** |

HEALTH

## Toiletries:

| | | |
|---|---|---|
| comb | pente | **payn**-teh |
| conditioner | creme amaciador | **kreh**-meh ah-mah-see-ah-**dor** |
| condoms | preservativos | pray-zehr-vah-**tee**-voosh |
| dental floss | fio dental | **fee**-oo dayn-**tahl** |
| deodorant | desodorizante | deh-zoo-dor-ee-**zayn**-teh |
| hairbrush | escova do cabelo | ish-**koh**-vah doo kah-**beh**-loo |
| hand lotion | creme para as mãos | **kreh**-meh **pah**-rah ahsh **mowsh** |
| lip salve | batão de clerio | bah-**tow** deh see-**yay**-roo |
| nail clipper | corta unhas | **kor**-tah **oon**-yahsh |
| razor | lâmina | **lah**-mee-nah |
| sanitary napkins | pensos higiénicos | **payn**-soosh ee-zhee-**ehn**-ee-koosh |
| shampoo | shampoo | "shampoo" |
| shaving cream | creme de barbear | **kreh**-meh deh bar-**behr** |
| soap | sabão | sah-**bow** |
| sunscreen | protector solar | proo-tehk-**tor** soo-**lar** |
| tampons | tampões higiénicos | tahn-**powsh** ee-zhee-**ehn**-ee-koosh |
| tissues | lenços de papel | **layn**-soosh deh pah-**pehl** |
| toilet paper | papel higiénico | pah-**pehl** ee-zhee-**ehn**-ee-koo |
| toothbrush | escova de dentes | ish-**koh**-vah deh **dayn**-tish |
| toothpaste | pasta dos dentes | **pahsh**-tah doosh **dayn**-tish |
| tweezers | pinça | **peen**-sah |

# Chatting

| My name is... | Chamo-me... | shah-moo-meh |
| What's your name? | Como se chama? | koh-moo seh shah-mah |
| How are you? | Como está? | koh-moo ish-tah |
| Very well, thanks. | Muito bem, obrigado[a]. | mween-too bayn oh-bree-gah-doo |
| Where are you from? | De onde é que você é? | deh ohn-deh eh keh voh-say eh |
| What city? | De que cidade? | deh keh see-dah-deh |
| What country? | De que país? | deh keh pah-eesh |
| What planet? | De que planeta? | deh keh plah-nay-tah |
| I am American. | Sou Americano[a]. | soh ah-meh-ree-kah-noo |
| I am Canadian. | Sou Canadiano[a]. | soh kah-nah-dee-ah-noo |

## Nothing more than feelings...

| I am / You are... | Estou / Está... | ish-toh / ish-tah |
| ...happy. | ...feliz. | feh-leesh |
| ...sad. | ...triste. | treesh-teh |
| ...tired. | ...cansado[a]. | kahn-sah-doo |
| ...thirsty. | ...com sede. | kohn say-deh |
| ...hungry. | ...com fome. | kohn faw-meh |
| ...lucky. | ...afortunado[a]. | ah-for-too-nah-doo |
| ...homesick. | ...com saudades de casa. | kohn soh-dah-dish deh kah-zah |
| ...cold. | ...com frio. | kohn free-oh |
| ...hot. | ...com calor. | kohn kah-lor |

## Who's who:

| My... (male / female) | O meu / A minha... | oo **meh**-oo / ah **meen**-yah |
|---|---|---|
| ...friend. | ...amigo / amiga. | ah-**mee**-goo / ah-**mee**-gah |
| ...boyfriend / girlfriend. | ...namorado / namorada. | nah-moo-**rah**-doo / nah-moo-**rah**-dah |
| ...husband / wife. | ...marido / mulher. | mah-**ree**-doo / mool-**yehr** |
| ...son / daughter. | ...filho / filha. | **feel**-yoo / **feel**-yah |
| ...brother / sister. | ...irmão / irmã. | eer-**mow** / eer-**mah** |
| ...father / mother. | ...pai / mãe. | pī / mow |
| ...uncle / aunt. | ...tio / tia. | **tee**-oo / **tee**-ah |
| ...nephew / niece. | ...sobrinho / sobrinha. | soo-**breen**-yoo / soo-**breen**-yah |
| ...male / female cousin. | ...primo / prima. | **pree**-moo / **pree**-mah |
| ...grandpa / grandma. | ...avô / avó. | ah-**voh** / ah-**vaw** |
| ...grandson / granddaughter. | ...neto / neta. | **nay**-too / **nay**-tah |

## Family and work:

| Are you married? (asked of a man) | É casado? | eh kah-**zah**-doo |
|---|---|---|
| Are you married? (asked of a woman) | É casada? | eh kah-**zah**-dah |
| Do you have children? | Tem algumas crianças? | tayn ahl-**goo**-mahsh kree-**ahn**-sahsh |
| How many boys / girls? | Quantos rapazes / raparigas? | **kwahn**-toosh rah-**pah**-zish / rah-pah-**ree**-gahsh |
| Do you have photos? | Tem fotografias? | tayn foh-toh-grah-**fee**-ahsh |
| How old is your child? | Que idade tem a sua criança? | keh ee-**dah**-deh tayn ah **soo**-ah kree-**ahn**-sah |

| Beautiful child! | Linda criança! | leen-dah kree-ahn-sah |
| Beautiful children! | Lindas crianças! | leen-dahsh kree-ahn-sahsh |
| What is your occupation? | Qual é a sua profissão? | kwahl eh ah soo-ah proo-fee-sow |
| Do you like your work? | Gosta do seu trabalho? | gawsh-tah doo seh-oo trah-bahl-yoo |
| I'm a... | Sou... | soh |
| ...student. | ...estudante. | ish-too-dahn-teh |
| ...teacher. | ...professor[a]. | proo-feh-sor |
| ...worker. | ...trabalhador[a]. | trah-bahl-yah-dor |
| ...professional traveler. | ...viajante profissional. | vee-ah-zhahn-teh proo-feh-see-oo-nahl |
| Can I take a photo of you? | Posso tirar-lhe uma foto? | pos-soh tee-rar-leh oo-mah foh-too |

## Chatting with children:

| What's your name? | Como te chama? | koh-moo teh shah-mah |
| My name is... | Chamo-me... | shah-moo-meh |
| How old are you? | Que idade tens? | keh ee-dah-deh taynsh |
| Do you have brothers and sisters? | Tens irmãos e irmãs? | taynsh eer-mowsh ee eer-mahsh |
| Do you like school? | Gostas da escola? | goosh-tahsh dah ish-koh-lah |
| What are you studying? | O que é que estás a estudar? | oo keh eh keh ish-tahsh ah ish-too-dar |
| I'm studying... | Estou a estudar... | ish-toh ah ish-too-dar |
| What's your favorite subject? | Qual é o tua disciplina preferida? | kwahl eh oo too-ah dee-shee-plee-nah pray-feh-ree-dah |
| Do you have pets? | Tens animais de estimação? | taynsh ah-nee-mīsh deh ish-tee-mah-sow |

| | | |
|---|---|---|
| ...cat / dog / fish | ...gato / cão / peixe | **gah**-too / **kow** / **pay**-sheh |
| Will you teach me some Portuguese words? | Podes-me ensinar algumas palavras portuguêsas? | paw-dish-meh ayn-see-**nar** ahl-**goo**-mahsh pah-**lahv**-rahsh por-too-**gay**-shahsh |
| What is that? | O que é isso? | oo keh eh **ee**-soo |
| Will you teach me a simple Portuguese song? | Podes-me ensinar uma canção fácil em português? | paw-dish-meh ayn-see-**nar** oo-mah kahn-**sow** fah-seel ayn poor-too-**gaysh** |
| Guess which country I live in. | Adivinha onde eu vivo. | ah-dee-**veen**-yah **ohn**-deh eh-oo vee-voo |
| How old am I? | Quantos anos tenho? | **kwahn**-toosh ah-noosh **tayn**-yoo |
| I'm... years old. | Tenho... anos. | **tayn**-yoo... ah-noosh |
| Want to hear me burp? | Queres ouvir-me a arrotar? | **kehr**-ish oh-**veer**-meh ah ah-roo-**tar** |
| Teach me a fun game. | Ensina-me um jogo engraçado. | ayn-**see**-nah-meh oon **zhoh**-goo ayn-grah-**sah**-doo |
| Got any candy? | Tens um rebuçado? | **tayn**sh oon reh-boo-**sah**-doo |

## Travel talk:

| | | |
|---|---|---|
| I am / Are you...? | Estou / Está...? | ish-**toh** / ish-**tah** |
| ...on vacation | ...de férias | deh **feh**-ree-ahsh |
| ...on business | ...em negócios | ayn neh-**gaw**-see-oosh |
| How long have you been traveling? | Á quanto tempo é que tem estado a viajar? | ah **kwahn**-too **tayn**-poo eh keh **tayn** ish-**tah**-doo ah vee-ah-**zhar** |
| day / week | dia / semana | **dee**-ah / seh-**mah**-nah |
| month / year | mês / ano | maysh / **ah**-noo |
| When are you going home? | Quando é que vai voltar para casa? | **kwahn**-doo eh keh vī vohl-**tar** pah-rah **kah**-zah |

| | | |
|---|---|---|
| This is my first time in... | **Esta é a minha primeira vez em...** | ehsh-tah eh ah **meen**-yah pree-**may**-rah vaysh ay<u>n</u> |
| Today / Tomorrow I'm going to... | **Hoje / Amanhã vou para...** | **oh**-zheh / ah-ming-**yah** voh **pah**-rah |
| I'm happy here. | **Estou contente aqui.** | ish-**toh** koh<u>n</u>-**tay<u>n</u>**-teh ah-**kee** |
| This is paradise. | **Isto é um paraíso.** | **ish**-toh eh oo<u>n</u> pah-rah-**ee**-zoo |
| The Portuguese are friendly. | **Os Portugueses são simpáticos.** | oosh poor-too-**gay**-zish so<u>w</u> seeng-**pah**-tee-koosh |
| Portugal is wonderful. | **Portugal é maravilhoso.** | poor-too-**gahl** eh mah-rah-veel-**yoh**-zoo |
| To travel is to live. | **A maneira de viver é viajar.** | ah mah-**nay**-rah deh vee-**vehr** eh vee-ah-**zhar** |
| Have a good trip! | **Boa-viagem!** | boh-ah-vee-**ah**-zhay<u>n</u> |

## Map talk:

Use these phrases, along with the maps of Iberia, Europe, and the U.S.A. near the end of this book, to delve into family history and explore travel dreams.

| | | |
|---|---|---|
| I live here. | **Eu vivo aqui.** | **eh**-oo **vee**-voo ah-**kee** |
| I was born here. | **Eu nasci aqui.** | **eh**-oo **nahsh**-see ah-**kee** |
| My ancestors came from... | **Os meus antepassados vieram de...** | oosh **meh**-oosh ahn-teh-pah-**sah**-doosh vee-**eh**-rahm deh |
| I've traveled to... | **Ja viajei a...** | zhah vee-**ah**-zhay ah |
| Next I'll go to... | **Em seguida irei...** | ay<u>n</u> sehg-**ee**-dah ee-**ray** |
| Where do you live? | **A onde vive?** | ah **ohn**-deh **vee**-veh |
| Where were you born? | **A onde nasceu?** | ah **ohn**-deh nahsh-**seh**-oo |
| Where did your ancestors come from? | **De onde vieram os vossos antepassados?** | deh **ohn**-deh vee-**eh**-rahm oosh **vaw**-soosh ahn-teh-pah-**sah**-doosh |

**CHATTING**

| Where have you traveled? | **A onde tem viajado?** | ah **ohn**-deh tayn vee-ah-**zhah**-doo |
| Where are you going? | **A onde vai?** | ah **ohn**-deh vī |
| Where would you like to go? | **O onde gostaria de ir?** | oo **ohn**-deh goosh-tah-**ree**-ah deh eer |

## Favorite things:

| What's your favorite...? | **Qual é o seu... favorito?** | kwahl eh oo **seh**-oo... fah-voo-**ree**-too |
| ...hobby | **...passatempo** | pah-sah-**tayn**-poo |
| ...ice cream | **...gelado** | zheh-**lah**-doo |
| ...male singer | **...cantor** | kahn-**tor** |
| ...male movie star | **...actor** | ah-**tor** |
| ...movie | **...filme** | **feel**-meh |
| ...sport | **...desporto** | dish-**por**-too |
| ...vice | **...vício** | **vee**-see-oo |
| What's your favorite...? | **Qual é a sua... favorita?** | kwahl eh ah **soo**-ah... fah-voo-**ree**-tah |
| ...food | **...comida** | koo-**mee**-dah |
| ...art | **...arte** | **ar**-teh |
| ...music | **...música** | **moo**-zee-kah |
| ...female singer | **...cantora** | kahn-**toh**-rah |
| ...female movie star | **...actriz** | ah-**treesh** |

## Weather:

| What will the weather be like tomorrow? | **Qual é o tempo para amanhã?** | kwahl eh oo **tayn**-poo **pah**-rah ah-ming-**yah** |
| sunny / cloudy | **sol / nublado** | sohl / noo-**blah**-doo |
| hot / cold | **quente / frio** | **kayn**-teh / **free**-oo |

| muggy / windy | úmido / ventoso | oo-mee-doo / vayn-toh-zoo |
| rain / snow | chuva / neve | shoo-vah / neh-veh |

## Thanks a million:

| Thank you very much. | Muito obrigado[a]. | mween-too oh-bree-gah-doo |
| Thank you. (friendly, informal) | Obrigadinho[a]. | oh-bree-gah-deen-yoo |
| You are... | Você é... | voh-say eh |
| ...wonderful. | ...maravilhoso[a]. | mah-rah-veel-yoh-zoo |
| ...generous. | ...generouso[a]. | zheh-neh-roh-zoo |
| You spoil me / us. | Mimou me / nos. | mee-moh meh / nohsh |
| You've been a great help. | Você foi uma grande ajuda. | voh-say foy oo-mah grahn-deh ah-zhoo-dah |

## Responses for all occasions:

| I like that. | Gosto disto. | gawsh-too deesh-too |
| I like you. | Gosto de si. | gawsh-too deh see |
| Fantastic! | Fantástico! | fahn-tahsh-tee-koo |
| What a nice place. | Que sítio bonito. | keh see-tee-oo boh-nee-too |
| Perfect. | Perfeito. | pehr-fay-too |
| Funny. | Cómico. | kaw-mee-koo |
| Interesting. | Interessante. | een-teh-reh-sahn-teh |
| I don't smoke. | Não fumo. | now foo-moo |
| I haven't any. | Não tenho nenhuma. | now tayn-yoo nayn-oo-mah |
| Really? | A sério? | ah seh-ree-oo |
| Wow! | Fiche! | fee-sheh |
| Congratulations! | Parabéns! | pah-rah-baynsh |
| Well done! | Bem feito! | bayn fay-too |
| You're welcome. | Não tem de quê. | now tayn deh kay |

| | | |
|---|---|---|
| Bless you! (after sneeze) | **Santinho!** | sahn-**teen**-yoo |
| What a pity. | **É uma pena.** | eh **oo**-mah **pay**-nah |
| That's life. | **É a vida.** | eh ah **vee**-dah |
| No problem. | **Não tem problema.** | n<u>ow</u> tay<u>n</u> proo-**blay**-mah |
| O.K. | **Está bem.** | ish-**tah** bay<u>n</u> |
| This is the good life! | **Esta é a boa vida!** | **ehsh**-tah eh ah **boh**-ah **vee**-dah |
| Good luck! | **Boa-sorte!** | boh-ah-**sor**-teh |
| Let's go! | **Vamos!** | **vah**-moosh |

# Create Your Own Conversation

Using these lists, you can have deep (or ridiculous) conversations with the locals.

### Who:

| | | |
|---|---|---|
| I / you | **eu / você** | eh-oo / voh-**say** |
| he / she | **ele / ela** | **eh**-leh / **eh**-lah |
| we / they | **nós / eles** | nawsh / **eh**-lish |
| my / your... | **meus / seus...** | **meh**-oosh / **seh**-oosh |
| ...parents / children | **...pais / crianças** | pīsh / kree-**ahn**-sahsh |
| men / women | **homens / mulheres** | aw-may<u>n</u>sh / mool-**yeh**-rish |
| rich / poor | **rico / pobre** | **ree**-koo / **paw**-breh |
| politicians | **políticos** | poo-**lee**-tee-koosh |
| big business | **negócio grande** | neh-**gaw**-see-oo **grahn**-deh |
| mafia | **máfia** | **mah**-fee-ah |
| military | **militares** | mee-lee-**tah**-rish |
| Portuguese | **Portugueses** | poor-too-**gay**-zish |
| Spanish | **Espanhóis** | ish-pahn-**yoysh** |
| French | **Franceses** | frahn-**say**-zish |
| Germans | **Alemães** | ah-leh-**may<u>n</u>sh** |
| Americans | **Americanos** | ah-meh-ree-**kah**-noosh |

| liberals | **liberais** | lee-**beh**-raysh |
| conservatives | **conservadores** | koh<u>n</u>-sehr-vah-**doh**-rish |
| radicals | **radicais** | rah-**dee**-kaysh |
| travelers | **vijantes** | vee-**zhan**-tish |
| everyone | **todas as pessoas** | **toh**-dahsh ahsh peh-**soh**-ahsh |
| God | **Deus** | **deh**-oosh |

## *What:*

| want / need | **querer / precisar** | keh-**rehr** / preh-see-**zar** |
| take / give | **tirar / dar** | tee-**rar** / dar |
| love / hate | **amar / odiar** | ah-**mar** / oo-dee-**ar** |
| work / play | **trabalhar / jogar** | trah-bahl-**yar** / zhoo-**gar** |
| have / lack | **ter / faltar** | tehr / fahl-**tar** |
| learn / fear | **aprender / temer** | ah-pray<u>n</u>-**dar** / teh-**mehr** |
| help / abuse | **ajudar / abusar** | ah-zhoo-**dar** / ah-boo-**zar** |
| prosper / suffer | **prósperar / sofrer** | prawsh-peh-**rar** / soof-**rehr** |
| buy / sell | **comprar / vender** | koh<u>n</u>-**prar** / vay<u>n</u>-**dar** |

## *Why:*

| love / sex | **amor / sexo** | ah-**mor** / **sehk**-soo |
| money / power | **dinheiro / poder** | deen-**yay**-roo / poo-**dehr** |
| work | **trabalho** | trah-**bahl**-yoo |
| food | **comida** | koo-**mee**-dah |
| family | **familia** | fah-**meel**-yah |
| health | **saúde** | sah-**oo**-deh |
| hope | **esperança** | ish-peh-**rahn**-sah |
| education | **instrução** | eensh-troo-**sow** |
| guns | **pistolas** | peesh-**toh**-lahsh |
| religion | **religião** | ray-lee-**zhow** |
| happiness | **felicidade** | feh-lee-see-**dah**-deh |
| marijuana | **marijuana** | mah-ree-**wah**-nah |

## 218 Portuguese

| | | |
|---|---|---|
| democracy | **democracia** | deh-moo-krah-**see**-ah |
| taxes | **taxas** | **tahsh**-ahsh |
| lies | **mentiras** | may<u>n</u>-**tee**-rahsh |
| corruption | **corrupção** | koo-roop-**sow** |
| pollution | **polulção** | pool-wee-**sow** |
| television | **televisão** | teh-leh-vee-**zow** |
| relaxation | **descanso** | dish-**kahn**-soo |
| violence | **violência** | vee-oo-**lay<u>n</u>**-see-ah |
| racism | **racismo** | rah-**seesh**-moo |
| respect | **respeito** | rish-**pay**-too |
| war / peace | **guerra / paz** | **geh**-rah / pahsh |
| global perspective | **perspectiva mundial** | persh-pehk-**tee**-vah moo<u>n</u>-dee-**ahl** |

## *You be the judge:*

| | | |
|---|---|---|
| (no) problem | **(não) á problema** | (no<u>w</u>) ah proo-**blay**-mah |
| (not) good | **(não) bom** | (no<u>w</u>) boh<u>n</u> |
| (not) dangerous | **(não) perigoso** | (no<u>w</u>) peh-ree-**goh**-zoo |
| (not) fair | **(não) justo** | (no<u>w</u>) **zhoosh**-too |
| (not) guilty | **(não) culpado** | (no<u>w</u>) kool-**pah**-doo |
| (not) powerful | **(não) poderoso** | (no<u>w</u>) poo-deh-**roh**-zoo |
| (not) stupid | **(não) estúpido** | (no<u>w</u>) ish-**too**-pee-doo |
| (not) happy | **(não) feliz** | (no<u>w</u>) feh-**leesh** |
| because / for | **porque / para** | **poor**-keh / **pah**-rah |
| and / or / from | **e / ou / de** | ee / oh / deh |
| too much | **demasiado** | deh-mah-zee-**ah**-doo |
| (never) enough | **(nunca é) suficiente** | (**noon**-kah eh) soo-fee-see-**ay<u>n</u>**-teh |
| same | **mesmo** | **mehsh**-moo |
| better / worse | **melhor / pior** | mil-**yor** / pee-**or** |
| here / everywhere | **aqui / em toda parte** | ah-**kee** / ay<u>n</u> **toh**-dah **par**-teh |

## *Assorted beginnings and endings:*

| | | |
|---|---|---|
| I like... | Gosto... | **gawsh**-too |
| I don't like... | Não gosto... | no<u>w</u> **gawsh**-too |
| Do you like...? | Gosta...? | **gawsh**-tah |
| I am / Are you...? | Sou / É...? | soh / eh |
| ...an optimist / pessimist | ...um optimista / pessimista | oo<u>n</u> awp-tee-**meesh**-tah / peh-see-**meesh**-tah |
| I believe... | Acredito... | ah-kreh-**dee**-too |
| I don't believe... | Não acredito... | no<u>w</u> ah-kreh-**dee**-too |
| Do you believe...? | Acredita...? | ah-kreh-**dee**-tah |
| ...in God | ...em Deus | ay<u>n</u> **deh**-oosh |
| ...in life after death | ...vida para além da morte | **vee**-dah **pah**-rah ah-**lehm** dah **mor**-teh |
| ...in extra-terrestrial life | ...que existe vida em outros planetas | keh ee-**zeesh**-teh **vee**-dah ay<u>n</u> **oh**-troosh plah-**nay**-tahsh |
| ...in Santa Claus | ...no Pai-Natal | noo pī-nah-**tahl** |
| Yes. / No. | Sim. / Não. | seeng / no<u>w</u> |
| Maybe. / I don't know. | Talvez. / Não sei. | **tahl**-vaysh / no<u>w</u> say |
| What's most important in life? | O que é a coisa mais importante na vida? | oo keh eh ah **koy**-zah mīsh eem-poor-**tahn**-teh nah **vee**-dah |
| The problem is... | O problema é... | oo proo-**blay**-mah eh |
| The answer is... | A resposta é... | ah rish-**pohsh**-tah eh |
| We have solved the world's problems. | Nós resolvemos os problemas do mundo. | nawsh reh-zool-**vay**-moosh oosh proo-**blay**-mahsh doo **moon**-doo |

# A Portuguese Romance

## *Words of love:*

| | | |
|---|---|---|
| I / me / you | **eu / mim / tu** | **eh**-oo / meeng / too |
| flirt | **namorar** | nah-moo-**rar** |
| kiss | **beijo** | **bay**-zhoo |
| hug | **abraço** | ah-**brah**-soo |
| love | **amor** | ah-**mor** |
| make love | **fazer amor** | fah-**zehr** ah-**mor** |
| condom | **preservativo** | preh-zehr-vah-**tee**-voo |
| contraceptive | **contraceptivo** | koh<u>n</u>-trah-sehp-**tee**-voo |
| safe sex | **sexo seguro** | **sehk**-soo say-**goo**-roo |
| sexy | **sexy** | "sexy" |
| romantic | **romântico** | roh-**mahn**-tee-koo |
| my tender love | **minha ternura** | **meen**-yah tehr-**noo**-rah |
| my darling (male, female) | **meu querido / minha querida** | **meh**-oo keh-**ree**-doo / **meen**-yah keh-**ree**-dah |
| my angel | **meu anjo** | **meh**-oo **ahn**-zhoo |
| baby | **bébe** | **beh**-beh |
| my soft thing (male, female) | **meu fofinho / minha fofinha** | **meh**-oo foh-**feen**-yoo / **meen**-yah foh-**feen**-yah |

## *Ah, amor:*

| | | |
|---|---|---|
| What's the matter? | **O que é que se passa?** | oo keh eh keh seh **pah**-sah |
| Nothing. | **Nada.** | **nah**-dah |
| I am / Are you...? | **Sou / És...?** | soh / ehsh |
| ...straight | **...normal** | nor-**mahl** |
| ...gay | **...maricas** | mah-**ree**-kahsh |

| | | |
|---|---|---|
| ...undecided | ...indeciso[a] | een-day-**see**-zoo |
| ...prudish | ...puritano[a] | poo-ree-**tah**-noo |
| ...horny | ...excitado[a] | ish-see-**tah**-doo |
| We are on our honeymoon. | Nós estamos em lua de mel. | nawsh ish-**tah**-moosh ayn **loo**-ah deh mehl |
| I have a... | Tenho... | **tayn**-yoo |
| ...a boyfriend. | ...um namorado. | oon nah-moo-**rah**-doo |
| ...a girlfriend. | ...uma namorada. | **oo**-mah nah-moo-**rah**-dah |
| I'm married. | Sou casado[a]. | soh kah-**zah**-doo |
| I'm not married. | Não sou casado[a]. | now soh kah-**zah**-doo |
| I'm rich and single. | Sou rico[a] e solteiro[a]. | soh **ree**-koo ee sool-**tay**-roo |
| I'm lonely. | Sinto-me só. | **seeng**-too-meh saw |
| I have no diseases. | Não tenho nenhuma doença. | now **tayn**-yoo neen-**yoo**-mah doo-**ayn**-sah |
| I have many diseases. | Tenho muitas doenças. | **tayn**-yoo mween-tahsh doo-**ayn**-sahsh |
| Can I see you again? | Quando é que o posso voltar a ver? | **kwahn**-doo eh keh oo **paw**-soo vool-**tar** ah vehr |
| Is this an aphrodisiac? | É isto um afrodisíaco? | eh **eesh**-too oon ah-froo-dee-**zee**-ah-koo |
| This is (not) my first time. | (Não) é a minha primeira vez. | (now) eh ah **meen**-yah pree-**may**-rah vaysh |
| Do you do this often? | Faz isto regularmente? | fahsh **eesh**-too reh-goo-lar-**mayn**-teh |
| How's my breath? | Como é que cheiro da boca? | **koh**-moo eh keh **shay**-roo dah **boh**-kah |
| Let's just be friends. | Vamos ser só amigos. | **vah**-moosh sehr saw ah-**mee**-goosh |
| I'll pay for my share. | Pagarei somente a minha parte. | pah-gah-**ray** soo-**mayn**-teh ah **meen**-yah **par**-teh |

| Would you like a massage for...? | Gostaria de uma massagem para...? | goosh-tah-**ree**-ah deh **oo**-mah mah-**sah**-zhay<u>n</u> **pah**-rah |
| ...your back | ...as tuas costas | ahsh **too**-ahsh **kawsh**-tahsh |
| ...your feet | ...os seus pés | oosh **seh**-oosh pehsh |
| Why not? | Porquê não? | poor-**kay** no<u>w</u> |
| Try it. | Exprimente. | ish-pree-**mayn**-teh |
| It tickles. | Isso faz cócegas. | **ee**-soo fahsh **kaw**-see-gahsh |
| Oh my God! | Ó meu Deus! | aw **meh**-oo **deh**-oosh |
| I love you. | Eu amo-te. | **eh**-oo **ah**-moo-teh |
| Darling, will you marry me? | Querida, queres casar comigo? | keh-**ree**-dah **keh**-rish kah-**zar** koo-**mee**-goo |

## Conversing with Portuguese animals:

| rooster / cock-a-doodle-doo | galo / co-coro-cocó | **gah**-loo / koo-koo-roo-koo-**kaw** |
| bird / tweet tweet | pássaro / piu piu | **pah**-sah-roo / pee-**oo** pee-**oo** |
| cat / meow | gato / miau | **gah**-too / **mee**-ow |
| dog / woof woof | cão / ão ão | ko<u>w</u> / o<u>w</u> o<u>w</u> |
| duck / quack quack | pato / quac quac | **pah**-too / kwahk kwahk |
| cow / moo | vaca / moo | **vah**-kah / moo |
| pig / oink oink | porco / orn orn (or just snort) | **por**-koo / orn orn (or just snort) |

# English-Spanish-Portuguese Dictionary

| English | Spanish | Portuguese |
|---------|---------|------------|

## A

| English | Spanish | Portuguese |
|---------|---------|------------|
| above | encima | acima |
| accident | accidente | acidente |
| accountant | contador | contador |
| adaptor | adaptador | adaptador |
| address | dirección | endereço |
| adult | adulto | adulto |
| afraid | miedoso | medo |
| after | después | depois |
| afternoon | tarde | tarde |
| afterwards | después | depois |
| again | otra vez | outra vez |
| age | edad | idade |
| aggressive | agresivo | agressivo |
| agree | de acuerdo | de acordo |
| AIDS | SIDA | SIDA |
| air | aire | ar |
| air-conditioned | aire acondicionado | ar condicionado |
| airline | línea aérea | linha aérea |
| air mail | correo aéreo | correio aéreo |
| airport | aeropuerto | aeroporto |
| alarm clock | despertador | despertador |
| alcohol | alcohol | alcool |
| allergic | alérgico | alérgico |
| allergies | alergias | alergias |
| alone | solo | sozinho |
| already | ya | já |
| always | siempre | sempre |
| ancestors | antepasados | antepassados |
| ancient | antiguo | antigo |
| and | y | e |
| angry | enfadado | chateado |
| ankle | tobillo | tornozelo |

| English | Spanish | Portuguese |
| --- | --- | --- |
| animal | animal | animal |
| another | otro | outro |
| answer | respuesta | resposta |
| antibiotic | antibiótico | antibiótico |
| antiques | antigüedades | antiguidades |
| apartment | apartamento | apartamento |
| apology | disculpa | desculpa |
| appetizers | aperitivos | aperitivos |
| appointment | cita | apontamento |
| approximately | aproximadamente | aproximadamente |
| arrivals | llegadas | chegadas |
| arrive | llegar | chegar |
| arm | brazo | braço |
| art | arte | arte |
| artificial | artificial | artificial |
| artist | artista | artista |
| ashtray | cenicero | cinzeiro |
| ask | preguntar | perguntar |
| aspirin | aspirina | aspirina |
| at | a | á |
| attractive | atractivo | atraente |
| aunt | tía | tia |
| autumn | otoño | outono |

## B

| baby | niño, niña | bébé |
| --- | --- | --- |
| babysitter | niñera | babysitter |
| backpack | mochila | mochila |
| bad | malo | mau |
| bag | bolsa | saco |
| baggage | equipaje | bagagem |
| bakery | panadería | padaria |
| balcony | balcón | varanda |

| English | Spanish | Portuguese |
|---|---|---|
| ball | pelota | bola |
| band-aid | tirita | adesivo |
| bank | banco | banco |
| barber | barbero | barbeiro |
| basement | sótano | porão |
| basket | canasta | cesto |
| bath | baño | banho |
| bathroom | baño | casa de banho |
| bathtub | bañera | banheira |
| battery | batería | bateria |
| beach | playa | praia |
| beard | barba | barba |
| beautiful | bonito[a] | lindo[a] |
| because | porque | porquê |
| bed | cama | cama |
| bedroom | habitación | quarto |
| bedsheet | sábana | lençol de cama |
| beef | carne de vaca | bife |
| beer | cerveza | cerveja |
| before | antes | antes |
| begin | comenzar | começar |
| behind | detrás | detrás |
| below | abajo | abaixo |
| belt | cinturón | cinto |
| best | mejor | melhor |
| bib | babero | babeiro |
| bicycle | bicicleta | bicicleta |
| big | grande | grande |
| bill (payment) | cuenta | conta |
| bird | pájaro | pássaro |
| birthday | cumpleaños | aniversário |
| black | negro | preto |
| blanket | manta | corbetor |
| blond | rubio | louro |

| English | Spanish | Portuguese |
|---|---|---|
| blood | sangre | sangre |
| blouse | camisa | blusa |
| blue | azul | azul |
| boat | barco | barco |
| body | cuerpo | corpo |
| boiled | cocido | fervido |
| bomb | bomba | bomba |
| book | libro | livro |
| book shop | librería | livraria |
| boots | botas | botas |
| border | orilla | fronteira |
| borrow | pedir prestado | emprestar |
| boss | jefe | patrão |
| bottle | botella | garrafa |
| bottom | fondo | fundo |
| bowl | plato hondo | tijela |
| box | caja | caixa |
| boy | chico | rapaz |
| bra | sujetador | soutien |
| bracelet | brazalete | pulseira |
| bread | pan | pão |
| breakfast | desayuno | pequeno almoço |
| bridge | puente | ponte |
| Britain | Gran Bretaña | Grã-Bretanha |
| broken | roto | partido |
| brother | hermano | irmão |
| brown | marrón | castanho |
| bucket | cubo | balde |
| building | edificio | prédio |
| bulb | bombilla | lâmpada |
| burn (n) | quemadura | queimadura |
| bus | autobús | autocarro |
| business | negocio | negócio |
| business card | tarjeta de visita | cartão |

| English | Spanish | Portuguese |
|---|---|---|
| but | pero | mas |
| button | botón | botão |
| by (via) | en | via |

## C

| | | |
|---|---|---|
| calendar | calendario | calendário |
| calorie | caloría | caloria |
| camera | cámara | camara |
| camping | camping | campismo |
| can (n) | bote | lata |
| can (v) | poder | poder |
| Canada | Canadá | Canadá |
| can opener | abridor de latas | abertor de latas |
| canal | canal | canal |
| candle | candela | vela |
| candy | caramelo | doce |
| canoe | canoa | canoa |
| cap | gorro | boné |
| captain | capitán | capitão |
| car | coche | carro |
| carafe | garrafa | jarro |
| card | tarjeta | cartão |
| cards (deck) | naipe | cartas |
| careful | cuidadoso | cuidadoso |
| carpet | alfombra | carpete |
| carry | llevar | carregar |
| cashier | cajera | caixa |
| cassette | cinta | cassete |
| castle | castillo | castelo |
| cat | gato | gato |
| catch (v) | coger | apanhar |
| cathedral | catedral | catedral |
| cave | cueva | cave |

| English | Spanish | Portuguese |
| --- | --- | --- |
| cellar | bodega | adega |
| center | centro | centro |
| century | siglo | século |
| chair | silla | cadeira |
| change (n) | cambio | troca |
| change (v) | cambiar | mudar |
| charming | lujoso | encantador |
| cheap | barato | barato |
| check | cheque | cheque |
| Cheers! | ¡Salud! | Saúde! |
| cheese | queso | queijo |
| chicken | pollo | galinha |
| children | niños | crianças |
| Chinese (adj) | chino | chinês |
| chocolate | chocolate | chocolate |
| Christmas | Navidad | Natal |
| church | iglesia | igreija |
| cigarette | cigarrillo | cigarro |
| cinema | cine | cinema |
| city | ciudad | cidade |
| class | clase | classe |
| clean (adj) | limpio | limpo |
| clear | claro | claro |
| cliff | acantilado | falésia |
| closed | cerrado | fechado |
| cloth | tejido | tecido |
| clothes | ropa | roupa |
| clothesline | cordón para ropa | linha de roupas |
| clothes pins | pinzas | broches |
| cloudy | nuboso | nebuloso |
| coast | costa | costa |
| coat hanger | percha | cruzeta |
| coffee | café | café |
| coins | monedas | moedas |

| English | Spanish | Portuguese |
|---|---|---|
| cold (adj) | frío | frio |
| colors | colores | cores |
| comb (n) | peine | pente |
| come | venir | vir |
| comfortable | cómodo | confortável |
| compact disc | compact disc | compact disco |
| complain | quejarse | queixar |
| complicated | complicado | complicado |
| computer | computadora | computador |
| concert | concierto | concerto |
| condom | preservativo | perservativo |
| conductor | conductor | condutor |
| confirm | confirmar | confirmar |
| congratulations | felicidades | parabéns |
| connection (train) | enlace | conexão |
| constipation | estreñimiento | prisão de ventre |
| cook (v) | cocinar | cozinhar |
| cool | fresco | fresco |
| cork | corcho | rolha |
| corkscrew | sacacorchos | sacarolhas |
| corner | esquina | esquina |
| corridor | pasillo | corredor |
| cost | precio | preço |
| cot | catre | rede |
| cotton | algodón | algodão |
| cough (v) | toser | tosser |
| cough drops | gotas para la tos | rabuçados da tosse |
| country | país | país |
| countryside | campo | campo |
| cousin | primo, prima | primo, prima |
| cow | vaca | vaca |
| cozy | cómodo | confortável |
| crafts | artesanía | artesanato |
| credit card | tarjeta de crédito | cartão de crédito |

| English | Spanish | Portuguese |
|---------|---------|------------|
| crowd (n) | multitud | multidão |
| cry (v) | llorar | chorar |
| cup | taza | chávena |

## D

| | | |
|---------|---------|------------|
| dad | papá | pai |
| dance (v) | bailar | dançar |
| danger | peligro | perigo |
| dangerous | peligroso | perigoso |
| dark | oscuro | escuro |
| daughter | hija | filha |
| day | día | dia |
| dead | muerto | morto |
| delay | retraso | atraso |
| delicious | delicioso | delicioso |
| dental floss | seda dental | fio dental |
| dentist | dentista | dentista |
| deodorant | desodarante | desodorizante |
| depart | salir | partir |
| departures | salidas | partidas |
| deposit | depósito | depósito |
| dessert | postre | sobremesa |
| detour | desvío | desvio |
| diabetic | diabético | diabético |
| diamond | diamante | diamante |
| diaper | pañal | fraldas |
| diarrhea | diarrea | diarreia |
| dictionary | diccionario | dicionário |
| die | morir | morrer |
| difficult | difícil | difícil |
| dinner | cena | jantar |
| direct | directo | directo |
| direction | dirección | direção |

| English | Spanish | Portuguese |
|---|---|---|
| dirty | sucio | sujo |
| discount | descuento | desconto |
| disease | enfermedad | doença |
| disturb | molestar | incomudar |
| divorced | divorciado[a] | divorciado[a] |
| doctor | doctor | doutor |
| dog | perro | cão |
| doll | muñeca | boneca |
| donkey | burro | burro |
| door | puerta | porta |
| dormitory | dormitorio | dormitorio |
| double | doble | dobrar |
| down | abajo | abaixo |
| dream (n) | sueño | sonho |
| dream (v) | soñar | sonhar |
| dress (n) | vestido | vestido |
| drink (n) | bebida | bebida |
| drive (v) | conducir | conduzir |
| driver | conductor | condutor |
| drunk | borracho | bêbado |
| dry | seco | seco |

## E

| English | Spanish | Portuguese |
|---|---|---|
| each | cada | cada |
| ear | oreja | orelha |
| early | temprano | cedo |
| earplugs | tapón de oidos | tampões de ouvido |
| earrings | pendientes | brincos |
| earth | tierra | terra |
| east | este | este |
| Easter | Pascua | Pascoa |
| easy | fácil | fácil |
| eat | comer | comer |

DICTIONARY

| English | Spanish | Portuguese |
|---------|---------|------------|
| elbow | codo | cotovelo |
| elevator | ascensor | elevador |
| embarrassing | embarazoso | humilhante |
| embassy | embajada | embaixada |
| empty | vacío | vazio |
| engineer | ingeniero | engenheiro |
| English | inglés | inglês |
| enjoy | disfrutar | gostar |
| enough | suficiente | suficiente |
| entrance | entrada | entrada |
| envelope | sobre | envelope |
| eraser | borrador | borracha |
| Europe | Europa | Europa |
| evening | la tarde | noitecer |
| every | todo | todo |
| everything | todo | tudo |
| exactly | exactamente | exactamente |
| example | ejemplo | exemplo |
| excellent | excelente | excelente |
| except | excepto | excepto |
| exchange (n) | cambio | câmbio |
| excuse me | lo siento | desculpe |
| exhausted | agotado | esgotado |
| exit | salida | saída |
| expensive | caro | caro |
| explain | explicar | explicar |
| eye | ojo | olho |

## F

| | | |
|---------|---------|------------|
| face | cara | cara |
| factory | fábrica | fábrica |
| fall (v) | caer | cair |
| false | falso | falso |

| English | Spanish | Portuguese |
|---|---|---|
| family | familia | familia |
| famous | famoso | famoso |
| fantastic | fantástico | fantástico |
| far | lejos | longe |
| farm | granja | quinta |
| farmer | granjero | granjeiro |
| fashion | moda | moda |
| fat (adj) | gordo | gordo |
| father | padre | pai |
| faucet | grifo | torneira |
| fax | fax | fax |
| female | femenino | feminino |
| ferry | transbordador | barco |
| festival | festival | festival |
| fever | fiebre | fevre |
| few | poco | pouco |
| field | campo | campo |
| fight (n) | pelea | luta |
| fight (v) | discutir | lutar |
| fine (good) | bueno | bom |
| finger | dedo | dedo |
| finish (v) | terminar | terminar |
| fireworks | fuegos artificiales | fogo de artificio |
| first | primero | primeiro |
| first aid | primeros auxilios | pronto socorro |
| first class | primera clase | primeira classe |
| fish | pescado | peixe |
| fish (v) | pescar | pescar |
| fix (v) | arreglar | arranjar |
| fizzy | gaseoso | com gás |
| flag | bandera | bandeira |
| flashlight | linterna | lanterna a pilhas |
| flavor (n) | sabor | sabor |
| flea | pulga | pulga |

DICTIONARY

| English | Spanish | Portuguese |
|---|---|---|
| flight | vuelo | voo |
| flower | flor | flor |
| flu | gripe | gripe |
| fly | volar | voar |
| fog | nieble | nevoeiro |
| food | comida | comida |
| foot | pie | pé |
| football | fútbol | futebol |
| for | para | para |
| forbidden | prohibido | proibido |
| foreign | extranjero | estranjeiro |
| forget | olvidar | esquecer |
| fork | tenedor | garfo |
| fountain | fuente | fonte |
| France | Francia | França |
| free (no cost) | gratis | grátis |
| fresh | fresco | fresco |
| Friday | viernes | sexta-feira |
| friend | amigo, amiga | amigo, amiga |
| friendship | amistad | amizade |
| frisbee | frisbee | disco voador |
| from | de | de |
| fruit | fruta | fruta |
| fun | diversión | divertido |
| funeral | funeral | funeral |
| funny | divertido | divertido |
| furniture | muebles | mobilias |
| future | futuro | futuro |

## G

| | | |
|---|---|---|
| gallery | galería | galeria |
| game | juego | jogo |
| garage | garaje | garagem |

| English | Spanish | Portuguese |
| --- | --- | --- |
| garden | jardín | jardim |
| gardening | jardineria | jardinagem |
| gas | gas | gás |
| gas station | gasolinera | bomba de gasolina |
| gay | homosexual | homosexual |
| gentleman | caballeros | cavalheiro |
| genuine | auténtico | genuíno |
| Germany | Alemania | Alemanha |
| gift | regalo | prenda |
| girl | chica | rapariga |
| give | dar | dar |
| glass | vaso | copo |
| glasses (eye) | gafas | ocúlos |
| gloves | guantes | luvas |
| go | ir | ir |
| God | Dios | deus |
| gold | oro | ouro |
| golf | golf | golfe |
| good | bueno | bom |
| goodbye | adiós | adeus |
| good day | buenos días | bom-dia |
| go through | atravesar | atravessar |
| grammar | gramática | gramática |
| grandchild | nieto, nieta | neto, neta |
| grandfather | abuelo | avô |
| grandmother | abuela | avó |
| gray | gris | cinzento |
| greasy | grasiento | gorduroso |
| great | magnífico | magnifico |
| Greece | Grecia | Grécia |
| green | verde | verde |
| grocery store | supermercado | mercearia |
| guarantee | garantía | garantia |
| guest | invitados | convidados |

DICTIONARY

| English | Spanish | Portuguese |
|---|---|---|
| **guide** | guía | uma guia |
| **guidebook** | guía | um guia |
| **guitar** | guitarra | guitarra |
| **gum** | chicle | pastilha elástica |
| **gun** | pistola | pistola |

## H

| English | Spanish | Portuguese |
|---|---|---|
| **hair** | pelo | cabelo |
| **hairbrush** | cepillo del pelo | escova de cabelo |
| **haircut** | corte de pelo | corte de cabelo |
| **hand** | mano | mão |
| **handicapped** | minusvalidos | aleijados |
| **handicrafts** | artesanía | artesanato |
| **handle (n)** | tirador | puxador |
| **handsome** | guapo | bonito |
| **happy** | feliz | feliz |
| **harbor** | puerto | porto |
| **hard** | difícil | difícil |
| **hat** | sombrero | chapéu |
| **hate** | odiar | odiar |
| **have** | tener | ter |
| **he** | él | ele |
| **head** | cabeza | cabeça |
| **headache** | dolor de cabeza | dor de cabeça |
| **healthy** | sano | saudavel |
| **hear** | oír | ouvir |
| **heart** | corazón | coração |
| **heat (n)** | calor | calor |
| **heaven** | cielo | céu |
| **heavy** | pesado | pesado |
| **hello** | hola | olá |
| **help (n)** | ayuda | ajuda |

| English | Spanish | Portuguese |
|---|---|---|
| help (v) | ayudar | ajudar |
| hemorrhoids | hemorroides | hemorróidas |
| here | aquí | aqui |
| hi | hola | olá |
| high | alto | alto |
| highchair | silla para niños | cadeirinha alta |
| highway | autopista | autoestrada |
| hill | colina | subida |
| history | historia | história |
| hitchhike | hacer auto-stop | pedir boleia |
| hobby | pasatiempo | passatempo |
| hole | agujero | buraco |
| holiday | festivo | feriado |
| homemade | hecho en casa | á moda de casa |
| homesick | morriña | saudade |
| honest | honesto | honesto |
| honeymoon | luna de miel | lua de mel |
| horrible | horrible | horrível |
| horse | caballo | cavalo |
| horse riding | montar a caballo | montar a cavalo |
| hospital | hospital | hospital |
| hot | calor | calor |
| hotel | hotel | hotel |
| hour | hora | hora |
| house | casa | casa |
| how many | cuánto | quanto |
| how much ($) | cuánto cuesta | quanto custa |
| how | cómo | como |
| hungry | hambriento | esfomeado |
| hurry (v) | apresurarse | apressar |
| husband | marido | marido |
| hydrofoil | hidroplano | hidroplano |

| English | Spanish | Portuguese |
|---------|---------|------------|

## I

| English | Spanish | Portuguese |
|---------|---------|------------|
| I | yo | eu |
| ice | hielo | gelo |
| ice cream | helado | gelado |
| if | si | se |
| ill | enfermo | doente |
| immediately | inmediatamente | imediatamente |
| important | importante | importante |
| imported | importado | importado |
| impossible | imposible | impossível |
| in | en | em |
| included | incluido | incluido |
| incredible | increíble | inacreditável |
| independent | independiente | independente |
| indigestion | indigestión | indigestão |
| industry | industria | industria |
| information | información | informação |
| injured | herido | ferido |
| innocent | inocente | inocente |
| insect | insecto | insecto |
| insect repellant | liquido de insectos | repelente de insectos |
| inside | interior | interior |
| instant | instante | instante |
| instead | en vez de | em vez de |
| insurance | seguro | seguro |
| intelligent | inteligente | inteligente |
| interesting | interesante | interresante |
| invitation | invitación | convite |
| iodine | yodo | iodo |
| is | es | ser |
| island | isla | ilha |
| Italy | Italia | Itália |
| itch (n) | comezón | comichão |

| English | Spanish | Portuguese |
|---------|---------|------------|

### J

| English | Spanish | Portuguese |
|---------|---------|------------|
| jacket | chaqueta | casaco |
| jaw | mandíbula | maxila |
| jeans | vaqueros | jeans |
| jewelry | joyas | joalheria |
| job | trabajo | trabalho |
| jogging | footing | jogging |
| joke (n) | chiste | piada |
| journey | viaje | viagem |
| juice | zumo | sumo |
| jump | saltar | saltar |

### K

| keep | guardar | guardar |
| kettle | olla | chaleira |
| key | llave | chave |
| kill | matar | matar |
| kind | amable | simpático |
| king | rey | rei |
| kiss (n) | beso | beijo |
| kitchen | cocina | cozinha |
| knee | rodilla | joelho |
| knife | cuchillo | faca |
| know | saber | saber |

### L

| ladder | escalera de mano | escada |
| ladies | señoras | senhoras |
| lake | lago | lago |
| lamb | cordero | cordeiro |

DICTIONARY

| English | Spanish | Portuguese |
|---|---|---|
| language | lenguaje | língua |
| large | grande | grande |
| last | último | último |
| late | tarde | tarde |
| later | más tarde | mais tarde |
| laugh (v) | reír | rir |
| laundromat | lavandería | lavandaria |
| lawyer | abogado | advogado |
| lazy | perezoso | preguiçoso |
| leather | cuero | cabedal |
| leave | salir | sair |
| left | izquierda | esquerda |
| leg | pierna | perna |
| lend | prestar | emprestar |
| letter | carta | carta |
| library | biblioteca | biblioteca |
| life | vida | vida |
| light (n) | luz | luz |
| light bulb | bombilla | lâmpada |
| lighter (n) | encendedor | isqueiro |
| like (v) | gustar | gostar |
| lip | labio | lábio |
| list | lista | lista |
| listen | escuchar | escutar |
| liter | litro | litro |
| little | pequeño | pequeno |
| live (v) | vivir | viver |
| local | local | local |
| lock (v) | cerrar | fechar |
| lock (n) | cerradura | fechadura |
| lockers | casilleros | armários |
| look | mirar | olhar |
| lost | perdido | perdido |

| English | Spanish | Portuguese |
|---------|---------|------------|
| **loud** | ruidoso | ruidoso |
| **love (v)** | amar | amar |
| **lover** | amante | amante |
| **low** | bajo | baixo |
| **luck** | suerte | sorte |
| **luggage** | equipaje | bagagem |
| **lukewarm** | templado | tépido |
| **lungs** | pulmones | pulmões |

## M

| English | Spanish | Portuguese |
|---------|---------|------------|
| **macho** | macho | macho |
| **mad** | enfadado | chateado |
| **magazine** | revista | revista |
| **mail (n)** | correo | correio |
| **main** | principal | principal |
| **make (v)** | hacer | fazer |
| **male** | masculino | masculino |
| **man** | hombre | homen |
| **manager** | director | gerente |
| **many** | mucho | muito |
| **map** | mapa | mapa |
| **market** | mercado | mercado |
| **married** | casado[a] | casado[a] |
| **matches** | cerillas | fosforos |
| **maximum** | máximo | máximo |
| **maybe** | tal vez | talvez |
| **meat** | carne | carne |
| **medicine** | medicina | medicina |
| **medium** | mediano | médio |
| **men** | hombres | homens |
| **menu** | menú | ementa |
| **message** | recado | recado |

DICTIONARY

| English | Spanish | Portuguese |
|---|---|---|
| metal | metal | metal |
| midnight | medianoche | meia-noite |
| mineral water | agua mineral | água mineral |
| minimum | mínimo | mínimo |
| minutes | minutos | minutos |
| mirror | espejo | espelho |
| Miss | Señorita | Menina |
| mistake | error | erro |
| misunderstanding | malentendido | malentendido |
| mix (n) | mixto | mista |
| modern | moderno | moderno |
| mom | mamá | mãe |
| moment | momento | momento |
| Monday | lunes | segunda-feira |
| money | dinero | dinheiro |
| month | mes | mês |
| monument | monumento | monumento |
| moon | luna | lua |
| more | más | mais |
| morning | mañana | manhã |
| mosquito | mosquito | mosquito |
| mother | madre | mãe |
| mountain | montaña | montanha |
| moustache | bigote | bigode |
| mouth | boca | boca |
| movie | película | filme |
| Mr. | Señor | Senhor |
| Mrs. | Señora | Senhora |
| much | mucho | muito |
| muscle | músculo | músculo |
| museum | museo | museu |
| music | música | música |
| my | mi | meu |

| English | Spanish | Portuguese |
|---------|---------|------------|

## N

| English | Spanish | Portuguese |
|---------|---------|------------|
| nail clipper | corta uñas | corta unhas |
| naked | desnudo | nuo |
| name | nombre | nome |
| napkin | servilleta | guardanapo |
| narrow | estrecho | estreito |
| nationality | nacionalidad | nacionalidade |
| natural | natural | natural |
| nature | naturaleza | natureza |
| nausea | náusea | náusea |
| near | cerca | perto |
| necessary | necesario | necessário |
| necklace | collar | fio |
| need | necesitar | necessitar |
| needle | aguja | agulha |
| nephew | sobrino | sobrinho |
| nervous | nervioso | nervoso |
| never | nunca | nunca |
| new | nuevo | novo |
| newspaper | periódico | jornal |
| next | siguiente | próximo |
| nice | amable | simpático |
| niece | sobrina | sobrinha |
| nickname | apodo | alcunha |
| night | noche | noite |
| no | no | não |
| noisy | ruidoso | barulho |
| non-smoking | no fumadores | não fumador |
| noon | mediodía | meio-dia |
| normal | normal | normal |
| north | norte | norte |
| nose | nariz | nariz |
| not | no | não |

| English | Spanish | Portuguese |
|---|---|---|
| notebook | cuaderno | caderno |
| nothing | nada | nada |
| no vacancy | completo | cheio |
| now | ahora | agora |

## O

| English | Spanish | Portuguese |
|---|---|---|
| occupation | oficio | profissão |
| occupied | ocupado | ocupado |
| ocean | océano | oceano |
| of | de | de |
| office | oficina | escritório |
| O.K. | O.K. | O.K. |
| old | viejo | velho |
| on | sobre | sobre |
| once | una vez | uma vez |
| one way (street) | dirección única | sentido único |
| one way (ticket) | de ida | uma ida |
| only | sólo | só |
| open (adj) | abierto | aberto |
| open (v) | abrir | abrir |
| opera | ópera | ópera |
| operator | telefonista | operador |
| optician | óptico | oculista |
| or | o | ou |
| orange (color) | naranja | cor de laranja |
| orange (fruit) | naranja | laranja |
| original | original | original |
| other | otro | outro |
| oven | horno | forno |
| over (finished) | terminado | acabado |
| own (v) | poseer | possuir |
| owner | dueño | dono |

| English | Spanish | Portuguese |
|---------|---------|------------|
| | **P** | |
| pacifier | chupete | chupeta |
| package | paquete | embalagem |
| | | |
| page | página | página |
| pail | cubo | balde |
| pain | dolor | dor |
| painting | pintura | pintura |
| palace | palacio | palácio |
| panties | bragas | cuecas |
| pants | pantalones | calças |
| paper | papel | papel |
| paper clip | clip | clip |
| parents | padres | pais |
| park (v) | aparcar | estacionar |
| park (garden) | parque | parque |
| party | fiesta | festa |
| passenger | pasajero | passageiro |
| passport | pasaporte | passaporte |
| pay | pagar | pagar |
| peace | paz | paz |
| pedestrian | peatón | peão |
| pen | bolígrafo | caneta |
| pencil | lápiz | lápis |
| people | gente | pessoas |
| percent | porciento | percento |
| perfect | perfecto | perfeito |
| perfume | perfume | perfume |
| period (of time) | período | período |
| period (woman's) | regla | menstruação |
| person | persona | pessoa |
| pet (n) | animal de casa | animal de estimação |
| pharmacy | farmacia | farmácia |

| English | Spanish | Portuguese |
|---|---|---|
| photo | foto | fotografia |
| pick-pocket | carterista | carteirista |
| picnic | picnic | piquenique |
| piece | pedazo | pedaço |
| pig | cerdo | porco |
| pill | píldora | comprimido |
| pillow | almohada | almofada |
| pin | alfiler | alfinete |
| pink | rosa | cor de rosa |
| pity, it's a | que lástima | que pena |
| pizza | pizza | pizza |
| plane | avión | avião |
| plain | al natural | simples |
| plant | planta | planta |
| plastic | plástico | plástico |
| plastic bag | bolsa de plástica | saco plástico |
| plate | plato | prato |
| platform (train) | andén | cais |
| play (v) | jugar | jogar |
| please | por favor | por favor |
| pliers | alicates | alicate |
| pocket | bolsillo | bolso |
| point (v) | apuntar | apontar |
| police | policía | polícia |
| poor | pobre | pobre |
| pork | cerdo | porco |
| Portugal | Portugal | Portugal |
| possible | posible | possível |
| postcard | carta postal | cartão postal |
| poster | cartel | poster |
| practical | práctico | prático |
| pregnant | embarazada | grávida |
| prescription | prescripción | receita médica |
| present (gift) | regalo | presente |

| English | Spanish | Portuguese |
|---------|---------|------------|
| pretty | bonita | bonita |
| price | precio | preço |
| priest | sacerdote | padre |
| private | privado | privado |
| problem | problema | problema |
| profession | profesión | profissão |
| prohibited | prohibido | proibido |
| pronunciation | pronunciacion | pronúncia |
| public | público | público |
| pull | tirar | tirar |
| purple | morado | roxo |
| purse | bolsa | bolsa |
| push | empujar | empurrar |

## Q

| English | Spanish | Portuguese |
|---------|---------|------------|
| quality | calidad | qualidade |
| quarter (¼) | cuarta parte | quarto |
| queen | reina | rainha |
| question (n) | pregunta | pergunta |
| quiet | tranquilo | calado |

## R

| English | Spanish | Portuguese |
|---------|---------|------------|
| R.V. | caravana | roulote |
| rabbit | conejo | coelho |
| radio | radio | rádio |
| raft | balsa | balsa |
| railway | ferrocarril | caminho de ferro |
| rain (n) | lluvia | chuva |
| rainbow | arco iris | arco íris |
| raincoat | impermeable | casaco impermeável |

| English | Spanish | Portuguese |
|---|---|---|
| rape (n) | violación | violação |
| raw | crudo | cru |
| razor | Gilete | Gilete |
| ready | listo | pronto |
| receipt | recibo | recibo |
| receive | recibir | receber |
| receptionist | recepcionista | recepcionista |
| recipe | receta | receita |
| recommend | recomendar | recomendar |
| red | rojo | vermelho |
| refund (n) | reembolso | reembolso |
| relax | relajar | relaxar |
| religion | religión | religião |
| remember | recordar | recordar |
| rent (v) | alquilar | renda |
| repair | arreglar | reparar |
| reserve | reservar | reservar |
| reservation | reserva | reserva |
| rich | rico | rico |
| right (direction) | derecha | direita |
| right (correct) | correcto | certo |
| ring (n) | sortija | campaínha |
| ripe | maduro | maduro |
| river | río | rio |
| rock (n) | roca | rock |
| roller skates | patines | patins |
| romantic | romántico | romântico |
| roof | techo | telhado |
| room | habitación | quarto |
| rope | cuerda | corda |
| rotten | podrido | podre |
| roundtrip | ida y vuelta | ida e volta |
| rowboat | bote | barco de passeio |
| rucksack | mochila | mochila |

| English | Spanish | Portuguese |
|---|---|---|
| **rug** | alfombra | carpete |
| **ruins** | ruinas | ruínas |
| **run (v)** | correr | correr |

## S

| English | Spanish | Portuguese |
|---|---|---|
| **sad** | triste | triste |
| **safe** | seguro | seguro |
| **safety pin** | imperdible | alfinete de segurança |
| **sailing** | barco de vela | barco de vela |
| **sale** | rebajas | saldos |
| **same** | mismo | mesmo |
| **sandals** | sandalias | sandálias |
| **sandwich** | bocadillo | sande |
| **sanitary napkins** | compresas | pensos higiénicos |
| **Saturday** | sábado | sábado |
| **scandalous** | escandaloso | escandulo |
| **scarf** | bufanda | lenço |
| **school** | colegio | escola |
| **science** | ciencia | ciência |
| **scientist** | científico | cientista |
| **scissors** | tijeras | tesouras |
| **scotch tape** | cinta adhesiva | fita cola |
| **screwdriver** | destornillador | chave de parafusos |
| **sculptor** | escultor | escultor |
| **sculpture** | escultura | escultura |
| **sea** | mar | mar |
| **seafood** | marisco | marisco |
| **seat** | asiento | lugar, assento |
| **second** | segunda | segunda |
| **second class** | segunda clase | segunda classe |
| **secret** | secreto | segredo |
| **see** | ver | ver |
| **self-service** | auto-servicio | auto serviço |

DICTIONARY

| English | Spanish | Portuguese |
|---|---|---|
| sell | vender | vender |
| send | enviar | enviar |
| separate | separado | separado |
| serious | serio | sério |
| service | servicio | serviço |
| sex | sexo | sexo |
| sexy | sexy | sexy |
| shampoo | champú | xampú |
| shaving cream | espuma de afeitar | creme de barbear |
| she | ella | ela |
| sheet | sábana | lençol |
| shell | concha | concha |
| ship (n) | barco | barco |
| ship (v) | enviar | enviar |
| shirt | camisa | camisa |
| shoes | zapatos | sapatos |
| shopping | compras | compras |
| short | corto | curto |
| shorts | pantalones cortos | calções |
| shoulder | hombros | ombros |
| show (v) | enseñar | mostrar |
| show (n) | espectáculo | espectáculo |
| shower | ducha | chuveiro |
| shy | tímido | tímido |
| sick | enfermo | doente |
| sign | señal | sinal |
| signature | firma | assinatura |
| silence | silencio | silêncio |
| silk | seda | seda |
| silver | plata | prata |
| similar | similar | similar |
| simple | sencillo | simples |
| sing | cantar | cantar |
| singer | cantante | cantor |

| English | Spanish | Portuguese |
|---|---|---|
| single | soltero[a] | solteiro[a] |
| sink | lavabo | lavatório |
| sir | señor | senhor |
| sister | hermana | irmã |
| size | talla | tamanho |
| skating | patinaje | patinagem |
| ski (v) | esquiar | esquiar |
| skin | piel | pele |
| skinny | delgado | magro |
| skirt | falda | saia |
| sky | cielo | céu |
| sleep (v) | dormir | dormir |
| sleepy | soñoliento | sonolento |
| slice | rodaja | fatia |
| slide (photo) | diapositiva | slide |
| slippery | resbaladizo | escorregadio |
| slow | despacio | devagar |
| small | pequeño | pequeno |
| smell (n) | olor | cheiro |
| smile (n) | sonrisa | sorriso |
| smoking | fumadores | fumador |
| snack | pincho | petisco |
| sneeze (n) | estornudo | espirro |
| snore | roncar | ressonar |
| soap | jabón | sabão |
| soccer | futball | futebol |
| socks | calcetines | meias |
| something | alguna cosa | alguma coisa |
| son | hijo | filho |
| song | canción | canção |
| soon | pronto | cedo |
| sorry | lo siento | desculpe |
| sour | agrio | azedo |
| south | sur | sul |

DICTIONARY

| English | Spanish | Portuguese |
|---|---|---|
| Spain | España | Espanha |
| speak | hablar | falar |
| speciality | especialidad | especialidade |
| speed | velocidad | velocidade |
| spend | gastar | gastar |
| spider | araña | arranha |
| spoon | cuchara | colher |
| sport | deporte | desporto |
| spring (n) | primavera | primavera |
| square (town) | plaza | praça |
| stapler | grapadora | agrafador |
| stairs | escaleras | escadas |
| stamp | sello | selo |
| star (in sky) | estrella | estrela |
| state | estado | estado |
| station | estación | estação |
| stomach | estomago | estômago |
| stop (n) | parada | parar |
| stop (v) | parar | parar |
| storm | tormenta | tempestada |
| story (floor) | planta | andar |
| straight | derecho | em frente |
| strange | extraño | estranho |
| stream (n) | arroyo | corrente |
| street | calle | rua |
| string | cordón | fio |
| strong | fuerte | forte |
| stuck | atascado | imobilizado |
| student | estudiante | estudante |
| stupid | estúpido | estúpido |
| sturdy | robusto | sólido |
| style | estilo | estilo |
| subway | metro | metro |
| suddenly | de repente | de repente |

| English | Spanish | Portuguese |
|---------|---------|------------|
| **suitcase** | maleta | mala |
| **summer** | verano | verão |
| **sun** | sol | sol |
| **sunbathe** | tomar el sol | bronzear |
| **sunburn** | quemadura | queimadura solar |
| **Sunday** | domingo | domingo |
| **sunglasses** | gafas de sol | óculos de sol |
| **sunny** | soleado | sol |
| **sunset** | puesta de sol | pôr do sol |
| **sunscreen** | protección de sol | protector solar |
| **sunshine** | luz del sol | brilho de sol |
| **sunstroke** | insolación | insolação |
| **suntan (n)** | bronceado | bronzeado |
| **suntan lotion** | bronceador | creme de bronzear |
| **supermarket** | supermercado | supermercado |
| **supplement** | suplemento | suplemento |
| **surprise (n)** | sorpresa | surpresa |
| **swallow (v)** | tragar | engolir |
| **sweat (v)** | sudar | suar |
| **sweater** | suéter | pullover |
| **sweet** | dulce | doce |
| **swim** | nadar | nadar |
| **swimming pool** | piscina | piscina |
| **swim suit** | traje de baño | fato de banho |
| **swim trunks** | bañador | calção de banho |
| **Switzerland** | Suiza | Suiça |
| **synthetic** | sintético | sintético |

## T

| English | Spanish | Portuguese |
|---------|---------|------------|
| **table** | mesa | mesa |
| **tail** | rabo | rabo |
| **take** | tomar | tomar |
| **take out (food)** | para llevar | para levar |

DICTIONARY

| English | Spanish | Portuguese |
|---|---|---|
| talcum powder | polvos de talco | pó de talco |
| talk | hablar | falar |
| tall | alto | alto |
| tampons | tampones | tampões |
| tape (cassette) | casete | cassete |
| taste (n) | sabor | sabor |
| taste (try) | probar | provar |
| tax | impuesto | taxa |
| teacher | profesor | professor |
| team | equipo | equipa |
| teenager | joven | jovem |
| telephone | teléfono | telefone |
| television | telivisión | televisão |
| temperature | temperatura | temperatura |
| tender | tierno | tenro |
| tennis | tenis | ténis |
| tennis shoes | tenis | sapatos de ténis |
| tent | tienda de campaña | tenda |
| tent pegs | estacas de tienda | estacas de tenda |
| terrible | terrible | terrível |
| thanks | gracias | obrigado |
| theater | teatro | teatro |
| thermometer | termómetro | termómetro |
| they | ellos | eles |
| thick | grueso | grosso |
| thief | ladrón | ladrão |
| thigh | muslo | coxa |
| thin | delgado | magro |
| thing | cosa | coisa |
| think | pensar | pensar |
| thirsty | sediento | sede |
| thread | hilo | linha |
| throat | garganta | garganta |
| through | a través | através |

| English | Spanish | Portuguese |
|---|---|---|
| throw | tirar | atirar |
| Thursday | jueves | quinta-feira |
| ticket | billete | bilhete |
| tight | apretado | apretado |
| timetable | horario | horário |
| tired | cansado | cansado |
| tissues | pañuelos de papel | lenços de papel |
| to | a | para |
| today | hoy | hoje |
| toe | dedo del pie | dedo do pé |
| together | juntos | juntos |
| toilet | servicios | casa de banho |
| toilet paper | papel higiénico | papel higiénico |
| tomorrow | mañana | amanhã |
| tonight | esta noche | esta noite |
| too (much) | demasiado | demasiado |
| tooth | dientes | dentes |
| toothbrush | cepillo de dientes | escova de dentes |
| toothpaste | pasta de dientes | pasta de dentes |
| toothpick | palillo | palito |
| total | total | total |
| tour | viaje | excursão |
| tourist | turista | turista |
| towel | toalla | toalha |
| tower | torre | torre |
| town | pueblo | cidade |
| toy | juguete | brinquedo |
| track (train) | vía | linha |
| traditional | tradicional | tradicional |
| traffic | tráfico | tráfico |
| train | tren | comboio |
| translate | traducir | traduzir |
| travel (v) | viajar | viajar |
| travel agency | agencia de viajes | agência de viagens |

DICTIONARY

| English | Spanish | Portuguese |
|---------|---------|------------|
| traveler's check | cheque de viajero | cheque de viagem |
| tree | árbol | árvore |
| trip | viaje | viagem |
| trouble | dificultad | problema |
| T-shirt | camiseta | T-shirt |
| Tuesday | martes | terça-feira |
| tunnel | túnel | túnel |
| tweezers | pinzas | pinsa |
| twins | gemelos | gêmeos |

## U

| English | Spanish | Portuguese |
|---------|---------|------------|
| ugly | feo | feio |
| umbrella | paraguas | guarda-chuva |
| uncle | tío | tio |
| under | debajo | debaixo |
| underpants | calzoncillos | cuecas |
| understand | entender | entender |
| unemployed | sin empleo | desempregado |
| unfortunate | desafortunado | desventurado |
| United States | Estados Unidos | Estados Unidos |
| university | universidad | universidade |
| up | arriba | subida |
| upstairs | escaleras | escadas |
| urgent | urgente | urgente |
| us | nosotros | nós |
| use (v) | usar | usar |

## V

| English | Spanish | Portuguese |
|---------|---------|------------|
| vacancy sign | habitaciónes | quartos |
| vacant | libre | livre |

| English | Spanish | Portuguese |
|---|---|---|
| valley | valle | vale |
| vegetarian | vegetariano[a] | vegetariano[a] |
| very | muy | muito |
| vest | chaleco | colete |
| video | vídeo | vídeo |
| video camera | cámara de vídeo | video camera |
| view | vista | vista |
| village | aldea | aldeia |
| vineyard | viñedo | vinhedo |
| virus | virus | vírus |
| visit (n) | visita | visita |
| visit (v) | visitar | visitar |
| vitamins | vitaminas | vitaminas |
| voice | voz | voz |
| vomit | vomitar | vomitar |

## W

| English | Spanish | Portuguese |
|---|---|---|
| waist | cintura | cintura |
| wait (v) | esperar | esperar |
| waiter | camarero | criado |
| waitress | camarera | senhora, menina |
| wake up | despertarse | acordar |
| walk (v) | andar | andar |
| wallet | cartera | carteira |
| want | querer | querer |
| warm (adj) | caliente | quente |
| wash | lavar | lavar |
| watch (n) | reloj | relógio |
| watch (v) | vigilar | olhar |
| water | agua | água |
| water, tap | agua del grifo | água da torneira |
| waterfall | cascada | queda de água |
| we | nosotros | nós |

| English | Spanish | Portuguese |
| --- | --- | --- |
| weather | tiempo | tempo |
| wedding | boda | casamento |
| Wednesday | miércoles | quarta-feira |
| week | semana | semana |
| weight | peso | peso |
| welcome | bienvenido | bem-vindo |
| west | oeste | oeste |
| wet | mojado | molhado |
| what | qué | o quê |
| wheel | rueda | roda |
| when | cuándo | quando |
| where | dónde | donde |
| white | blanco | branco |
| who | quién | quem |
| why | por qué | porquê |
| widow | viuda | viúva |
| widower | viudo | viúvo |
| wife | esposa | esposa |
| wild | salvaje | salvagem |
| wind | viento | vento |
| window | ventana | janela |
| wine | vino | vinho |
| wing | ala | asa |
| winter | invierno | inverno |
| wish (v) | desear | desejo |
| with | con | com |
| without | sin | sem |
| woman | mujer | mulher |
| women | mujeres | mulheres |
| wood | madera | madeira |
| wool | lana | lã |
| word | palabra | palavra |
| work (n) | trabajo | trabalho |
| work (v) | trabajar | trabalhar |

| English | Spanish | Portuguese |
|---|---|---|
| **world** | mundo | mundo |
| **worst** | peor | pior |
| **wrap (v)** | envolver | embrulhar |
| **wrist** | muñeca | pulso |
| **write** | escribir | escrever |

## Y / Z

| English | Spanish | Portuguese |
|---|---|---|
| **year** | año | ano |
| **yellow** | amarillo | amarelo |
| **yes** | si | sim |
| **yesterday** | ayer | ontem |
| **you (formal)** | usted | voçê |
| **you (informal)** | tú | tu |
| **young** | joven | novo |
| **youth hostel** | albergue de juventud | albergue de juventude |
| **zero** | cero | zero |
| **zip-lock bag** | bolsa de cremallera | saco plastico com fecho |
| **zipper** | cremallera | fecho |
| **zoo** | zoo | zoo |

# Spanish-English Dictionary

## A

**a**  at
**a**  to
**a través**  through
**abajo**  below
**abajo**  down
**abierto**  open (adj)
**abogado**  lawyer
**abridor de latas**  can opener
**abrir**  open (v)
**abuela**  grandmother
**abuelo**  grandfather
**acantilado**  cliff
**accidente**  accident
**adaptador**  adaptor
**adiós**  goodbye
**adulto**  adult
**aeropuerto**  airport
**agencia de viajes**  travel agency
**agotado**  exhausted
**agresivo**  aggressive
**agrio**  sour
**agua**  water
**agua del grifo**  water, tap
**agua mineral**  mineral water
**aguja**  needle
**agujero**  hole
**ahora**  now
**aire**  air
**aire acondicionado**  air-conditioned
**al natural**  plain
**ala**  wing

**albergue de juventud**  youth hostel
**alcohol**  alcohol
**aldea**  village
**Alemania**  Germany
**alergias**  allergies
**alérgico**  allergic
**alfiler**  pin
**alfombra**  carpet
**alfombra**  rug
**algodón**  cotton
**alguna cosa**  something
**alicates**  pliers
**almohada**  pillow
**alquilar**  rent (v)
**alto**  high
**alto**  tall
**amable**  kind
**amable**  nice
**amante**  lover
**amar**  love (v)
**amarillo**  yellow
**amigo, amiga**  friend
**amistad**  friendship
**andar**  walk (v)
**andén**  platform (train)
**animal**  animal
**animal de casa**  pet (n)
**año**  year
**antepasados**  ancestors
**antes**  before
**antibiótico**  antibiotic
**antigüedades**  antiques
**antiguo**  ancient

aparcar park (v)
apartamento apartment
aperitivos appetizers
apodo nickname
apresurarse hurry (v)
apretado tight
aproximadamente approximately
apuntar point (v)
aquí here
araña spider
árbol tree
arco iris rainbow
arreglar fix (v)
arreglar repair
arriba up
arroyo stream (n)
arte art
artesanía crafts
artesanía handicrafts
artificial artificial
artista artist
ascensor elevator
asiento seat
aspirina aspirin
atascado stuck
atractivo attractive
atravesar go through
auténtico genuine
auto-servicio self-service
autobús bus
autopista highway
avión plane
ayer yesterday
ayuda help (n)
ayudar help (v)
azul blue

## B

babero bib
bailar dance (v)
bajo low
balcón balcony
balsa raft
banco bank
bañador swim trunks
bandera flag
bañera bathtub
baño bath
baño bathroom
barato cheap
barba beard
barbero barber
barco boat
barco ship (n)
barco de vela sailing
batería battery
bebida drink (n)
beso kiss (n)
biblioteca library
bicicleta bicycle
bienvenido welcome
bigote moustache
billete ticket
blanco white
boca mouth
bocadillo sandwich
boda wedding
bodega cellar
bolígrafo pen
bolsa bag
bolsa purse
bolsa de cremallera zip-lock bag

**bolsa de plástica**  plastic bag
**bolsillo**  pocket
**bomba**  bomb
**bombilla**  bulb
**bombilla**  light bulb
**bonita**  pretty
**bonito[a]**  beautiful
**borracho**  drunk
**borrador**  eraser
**botas**  boots
**bote**  can (n)
**bote**  rowboat
**botella**  bottle
**botón**  button
**bragas**  panties
**brazalete**  bracelet
**brazo**  arm
**bronceado**  suntan (n)
**bronceador**  suntan lotion
**bueno**  fine (good)
**bueno**  good
**buenos días**  good day
**bufanda**  scarf
**burro**  donkey

# C

**caballeros**  gentleman
**caballo**  horse
**cabeza**  head
**cada**  each
**caer**  fall (v)
**café**  coffee
**caja**  box
**cajera**  cashier
**calcetines**  socks
**calendario**  calendar

**calidad**  quality
**caliente**  warm (adj)
**calle**  street
**calor**  heat (n)
**calor**  hot
**caloría**  calorie
**calzoncillos**  underpants
**cama**  bed
**cámara**  camera
**cámara de vídeo**  video camera
**camarera**  waitress
**camarero**  waiter
**cambiar**  change (v)
**cambio**  change (n)
**cambio**  exchange (n)
**camisa**  blouse
**camisa**  shirt
**camiseta**  T-shirt
**camping**  camping
**campo**  countryside
**campo**  field
**Canadá**  Canada
**canal**  canal
**canasta**  basket
**canción**  song
**candela**  candle
**canoa**  canoe
**cansado**  tired
**cantante**  singer
**cantar**  sing
**capitán**  captain
**cara**  face
**caramelo**  candy
**caravana**  R.V.
**carne**  meat
**carne de vaca**  beef
**caro**  expensive

carta letter
carta postal postcard
cartel poster
cartera wallet
carterista pick-pocket
casa house
casado[a] married
cascada waterfall
casete tape (cassette)
casilleros lockers
castillo castle
catedral cathedral
catre cot
cena dinner
cenicero ashtray
centro center
cepillo de dientes toothbrush
cepillo del pelo hairbrush
cerca near
cerdo pig
cerdo pork
cerillas matches
cero zero
cerrado closed
cerradura lock (n)
cerrar lock (v)
cerveza beer
chaleco vest
champú shampoo
chaqueta jacket
cheque check
cheque de viajero traveler's
  check
chica girl
chicle gum
chico boy
chino Chinese (adj)

chiste joke (n)
chocolate chocolate
chupete pacifier
cielo heaven
cielo sky
ciencia science
científico scientist
cigarrillo cigarette
cine cinema
cinta cassette
cinta adhesiva scotch tape
cintura waist
cinturón belt
cita appointment
ciudad city
claro clear
clase class
clip paper clip
coche car
cocido boiled
cocina kitchen
cocinar cook (v)
codo elbow
coger catch (v)
colegio school
colina hill
collar necklace
colores colors
comenzar begin
comer eat
comezón itch (n)
comida food
cómo how
cómodo comfortable
cómodo cozy
compact disc compact disc
completo no vacancy

**complicado** complicated
**compras** shopping
**compresas** sanitary napkins
**computadora** computer
**con** with
**concha** shell
**concierto** concert
**conducir** drive (v)
**conductor** conductor
**conductor** driver
**conejo** rabbit
**confirmar** confirm
**contador** accountant
**corazón** heart
**corcho** cork
**cordero** lamb
**cordón** string
**cordón para ropa** clothesline
**correcto** right (correct)
**correo** mail (n)
**correo aéreo** air mail
**correr** run (v)
**corta uñas** nail clipper
**corte de pelo** haircut
**corto** short
**cosa** thing
**costa** coast
**cremallera** zipper
**crudo** raw
**cuaderno** notebook
**cuándo** when
**cuánto** how many
**cuánto cuesta** how much ($)
**cuarta parte** quarter (¼)
**cubo** bucket
**cubo** pail
**cuchara** spoon

**cuchillo** knife
**cuenta** bill (payment)
**cuerda** rope
**cuero** leather
**cuerpo** body
**cueva** cave
**cuidadoso** careful
**cumpleaños** birthday

# D

**dar** give
**de** from
**de** of
**de acuerdo** agree
**de ida** one way (ticket)
**de repente** suddenly
**debajo** under
**dedo** finger
**dedo del pie** toe
**delgado** skinny
**delgado** thin
**delicioso** delicious
**demasiado** too (much)
**dentista** dentist
**deporte** sport
**depósito** deposit
**derecha** right (direction)
**derecho** straight
**desafortunado** unfortunate
**desayuno** breakfast
**descuento** discount
**desear** wish (v)
**desnudo** naked
**desodarante** deodorant
**despacio** slow
**despertador** alarm clock

**despertarse** wake up
**después** after
**después** afterwards
**destornillador** screwdriver
**desvío** detour
**detrás** behind
**día** day
**diabético** diabetic
**diamante** diamond
**diapositiva** slide (photo)
**diarrea** diarrhea
**diccionario** dictionary
**dientes** tooth
**difícil** difficult
**difícil** hard
**dificultad** trouble
**dinero** money
**Dios** God
**dirección** address
**dirección** direction
**dirección única** one way (street)
**directo** direct
**director** manager
**disculpa** apology
**discutir** fight (v)
**disfrutar** enjoy
**diversión** fun
**divertido** funny
**divorciado[a]** divorced
**doble** double
**doctor** doctor
**dolor** pain
**dolor de cabeza** headache
**domingo** Sunday
**dónde** where
**dormir** sleep (v)
**dormitorio** dormitory

**ducha** shower
**dueño** owner
**dulce** sweet

# E

**edad** age
**edificio** building
**ejemplo** example
**él** he
**ella** she
**ellos** they
**embajada** embassy
**embarazada** pregnant
**embarazoso** embarrassing
**empujar** push
**en** by (via)
**en** in
**en vez de** instead
**encendedor** lighter (n)
**encima** above
**enfadado** angry
**enfadado** mad
**enfermedad** disease
**enfermo** ill
**enfermo** sick
**enlace** connection (train)
**enseñar** show (v)
**entender** understand
**entrada** entrance
**enviar** send
**enviar** ship (v)
**envolver** wrap (v)
**equipaje** baggage
**equipaje** luggage
**equipo** team
**error** mistake

SPANISH

**es** is
**escalera de mano** ladder
**escaleras** stairs
**escaleras** upstairs
**escandaloso** scandalous
**escribir** write
**escuchar** listen
**escultor** sculptor
**escultura** sculpture
**España** Spain
**especialidad** speciality
**espectáculo** show (n)
**espejo** mirror
**esperar** wait (v)
**esposa** wife
**espuma de afeitar** shaving
  cream
**esquiar** ski (v)
**esquina** corner
**esta noche** tonight
**estacas de tienda** tent pegs
**estación** station
**estado** state
**Estados Unidos** United States
**este** east
**estilo** style
**estomago** stomach
**estornudo** sneeze (n)
**estrecho** narrow
**estrella** star (in sky)
**estreñimiento** constipation
**estudiante** student
**estúpido** stupid
**Europa** Europe
**exactamente** exactly
**excelente** excellent
**excepto** except

**explicar** explain
**extranjero** foreign
**extraño** strange

# F

**fábrica** factory
**fácil** easy
**falda** skirt
**falso** false
**familia** family
**famoso** famous
**fantástico** fantastic
**farmacia** pharmacy
**fax** fax
**felicidades** congratulations
**feliz** happy
**femenino** female
**feo** ugly
**ferrocarril** railway
**festival** festival
**festivo** holiday
**fiebre** fever
**fiesta** party
**firma** signature
**flor** flower
**fondo** bottom
**footing** jogging
**foto** photo
**Francia** France
**fresco** cool
**fresco** fresh
**frío** cold (adj)
**frisbee** frisbee
**fruta** fruit
**fuegos artificiales** fireworks
**fuente** fountain

**fuerte** strong
**fumadores** smoking
**funeral** funeral
**futball** soccer
**fútbol** football
**futuro** future

# G

**gafas** glasses (eye)
**gafas de sol** sunglasses
**galería** gallery
**garaje** garage
**garantía** guarantee
**garganta** throat
**garrafa** carafe
**gas** gas
**gaseoso** fizzy
**gasolinera** gas station
**gastar** spend
**gato** cat
**gemelos** twins
**gente** people
**Gilete** razor
**golf** golf
**gordo** fat (adj)
**gorro** cap
**gotas para la tos** cough drops
**gracias** thanks
**gramática** grammar
**Gran Bretaña** Britain
**grande** big
**grande** large
**granja** farm
**granjero** farmer
**grapadora** stapler
**grasiento** greasy

**gratis** free (no cost)
**Grecia** Greece
**grifo** faucet
**gripe** flu
**gris** gray
**grueso** thick
**guantes** gloves
**guapo** handsome
**guardar** keep
**guía** guide
**guía** guidebook
**guitarra** guitar
**gustar** like (v)

# H

**habitación** bedroom
**habitación** room
**habitaciónes** vacancy sign
**hablar** speak
**hablar** talk
**hacer** make (v)
**hacer auto-stop** hitchhike
**hambriento** hungry
**hecho en casa** homemade
**helado** ice cream
**hemorroides** hemorrhoids
**herido** injured
**hermana** sister
**hermano** brother
**hidroplano** hydrofoil
**hielo** ice
**hija** daughter
**hijo** son
**hilo** thread
**historia** history
**hola** hello

**SPANISH**

**hola** hi
**hombre** man
**hombres** men
**hombros** shoulder
**homosexual** gay
**honesto** honest
**hora** hour
**horario** timetable
**horno** oven
**horrible** horrible
**hospital** hospital
**hotel** hotel
**hoy** today

# I

**ida y vuelta** roundtrip
**iglesia** church
**imperdible** safety pin
**impermeable** raincoat
**importado** imported
**importante** important
**imposible** impossible
**impuesto** tax
**incluido** included
**increíble** incredible
**independiente** independent
**indigestión** indigestion
**industria** industry
**información** information
**ingeniero** engineer
**inglés** English
**inmediatamente** immediately
**inocente** innocent
**insecto** insect
**insolación** sunstroke
**instante** instant

**inteligente** intelligent
**interesante** interesting
**interior** inside
**invierno** winter
**invitación** invitation
**invitados** guest
**ir** go
**isla** island
**Italia** Italy
**izquierda** left

# J

**jabón** soap
**jardín** garden
**jardineria** gardening
**jefe** boss
**joven** teenager
**joven** young
**joyas** jewelry
**juego** game
**jueves** Thursday
**jugar** play (v)
**juguete** toy
**juntos** together
**juventude** youth

# L

**la tarde** evening
**labio** lip
**ladrón** thief
**lago** lake
**lana** wool
**lápiz** pencil
**lavabo** sink
**lavandería** laundromat

**lavar** wash
**lejos** far
**lenguaje** language
**libre** vacant
**librería** book shop
**libro** book
**limpio** clean (adj)
**línea aérea** airline
**linterna** flashlight
**liquido de insectos** insect repellant
**lista** list
**listo** ready
**litro** liter
**llave** key
**llegadas** arrivals
**llegar** arrive
**llevar** carry
**llorar** cry (v)
**lluvia** rain (n)
**lo siento** excuse me
**lo siento** sorry
**local** local
**lujoso** charming
**luna** moon
**luna de miel** honeymoon
**lunes** Monday
**luz** light (n)
**luz del sol** sunshine

# M

**macho** macho
**madera** wood
**madre** mother
**maduro** ripe
**magnífico** great

**malentendido** misunderstanding
**maleta** suitcase
**malo** bad
**mamá** mom
**mañana** morning
**mañana** tomorrow
**mandíbula** jaw
**mano** hand
**manta** blanket
**mapa** map
**mar** sea
**marido** husband
**marisco** seafood
**marrón** brown
**martes** Tuesday
**más** more
**más tarde** later
**masculino** male
**matar** kill
**máximo** maximum
**mediano** medium
**medianoche** midnight
**medicina** medicine
**mediodía** noon
**mejor** best
**menú** menu
**mercado** market
**mes** month
**mesa** table
**metal** metal
**metro** subway
**mi** my
**miedoso** afraid
**miércoles** Wednesday
**mínimo** minimum
**minusvalidos** handicapped
**minutos** minutes

SPANISH

**mirar** look
**mismo** same
**mixto** mix (n)
**mochila** backpack
**mochila** rucksack
**moda** fashion
**moderno** modern
**mojado** wet
**molestar** disturb
**momento** moment
**monedas** coins
**montaña** mountain
**montar a caballo** horse riding
**monumento** monument
**morado** purple
**morir** die
**morriña** homesick
**mosquito** mosquito
**mucho** many
**mucho** much
**muebles** furniture
**muerto** dead
**mujer** woman
**mujeres** women
**multitud** crowd (n)
**mundo** world
**muñeca** doll
**muñeca** wrist
**músculo** muscle
**museo** museum
**música** music
**muslo** thigh
**muy** very

# N

**nacionalidad** nationality
**nada** nothing
**nadar** swim
**naipe** cards (deck)
**naranja** orange (color)
**naranja** orange (fruit)
**nariz** nose
**natural** natural
**naturaleza** nature
**náusea** nausea
**Navidad** Christmas
**necesario** necessary
**necesitar** need
**negocio** business
**negro** black
**nervioso** nervous
**nieble** fog
**nieto, nieta** grandchild
**niñera** babysitter
**niño, niña** baby
**niños** children
**no** no
**no** not
**no fumadores** non-smoking
**noche** night
**nombre** name
**normal** normal
**norte** north
**nosotros** us
**nosotros** we
**nuboso** cloudy
**nuevo** new
**nunca** never

# O

o  or
O.K.  O.K.
océano  ocean
ocupado  occupied
odiar  hate
oeste  west
oficina  office
oficio  occupation
oír  hear
ojo  eye
olla  kettle
olor  smell (n)
olvidar  forget
ópera  opera
óptico  optician
oreja  ear
original  original
orilla  border
oro  gold
oscuro  dark
otoño  autumn
otra vez  again
otro  another
otro  other

# P

padre  father
padres  parents
pagar  pay
página  page
país  country
pájaro  bird
palabra  word
palacio  palace
palillo  toothpick
pan  bread
panadería  bakery
pañal  diaper
pantalones  pants
pantalones cortos  shorts
pañuelos de papel  tissues
papá  dad
papel  paper
papel higiénico  toilet paper
paquete  package
para  for
para llevar  take out (food)
parada  stop (n)
paraguas  umbrella
parar  stop (v)
parque  park (garden)
pasajero  passenger
pasaporte  passport
pasatiempo  hobby
Pascua  Easter
pasillo  corridor
pasta de dientes  toothpaste
patinaje  skating
patines  roller skates
paz  peace
peatón  pedestrian
pedazo  piece
pedir prestado  borrow
peine  comb (n)
pelea  fight (n)
película  movie
peligro  danger
peligroso  dangerous
pelo  hair
pelota  ball
pendientes  earrings

SPANISH

**pensar**  think
**peor**  worst
**pequeño**  little
**pequeño**  small
**percha**  coat hanger
**perdido**  lost
**perezoso**  lazy
**perfecto**  perfect
**perfume**  perfume
**periódico**  newspaper
**período**  period (of time)
**pero**  but
**perro**  dog
**persona**  person
**pesado**  heavy
**pescado**  fish
**pescar**  fish (v)
**peso**  weight
**picnic**  picnic
**pie**  foot
**piel**  skin
**pierna**  leg
**píldora**  pill
**pincho**  snack
**pintura**  painting
**pinzas**  clothes pins
**pinzas**  tweezers
**piscina**  swimming pool
**pistola**  gun
**pizza**  pizza
**planta**  plant
**planta**  story (floor)
**plástico**  plastic
**plata**  silver
**plato**  plate
**plato hondo**  bowl
**playa**  beach

**plaza**  square (town)
**pobre**  poor
**poco**  few
**poder**  can (v)
**podrido**  rotten
**policía**  police
**pollo**  chicken
**polvos de talco**  talcum powder
**por favor**  please
**por qué**  why
**porciento**  percent
**porque**  because
**Portugal**  Portugal
**poseer**  own (v)
**posible**  possible
**postre**  dessert
**práctico**  practical
**precio**  cost
**precio**  price
**pregunta**  question (n)
**preguntar**  ask
**prescripción**  prescription
**preservativo**  condom
**prestar**  lend
**primavera**  spring (n)
**primera clase**  first class
**primero**  first
**primeros auxilios**  first aid
**primo, prima**  cousin
**principal**  main
**privado**  private
**probar**  taste (try)
**problema**  problem
**profesión**  profession
**profesor**  teacher
**prohibido**  forbidden
**prohibido**  prohibited

**pronto**  soon
**pronunciacion**  pronunciation
**protección de sol**  sunscreen
**público**  public
**pueblo**  town
**puente**  bridge
**puerta**  door
**puerto**  harbor
**puesta de sol**  sunset
**pulga**  flea
**pulmones**  lungs

## Q

**qué**  what
**que lástima**  pity, it's a
**quejarse**  complain
**quemadura**  burn (n)
**quemadura**  sunburn
**querer**  want
**queso**  cheese
**quién**  who

## R

**rabo**  tail
**radio**  radio
**rebajas**  sale
**recado**  message
**recepcionista**  receptionist
**receta**  recipe
**recibir**  receive
**recibo**  receipt
**recomendar**  recommend
**recordar**  remember
**reembolso**  refund (n)
**regalo**  gift

**regalo**  present (gift)
**regla**  period (woman's)
**reina**  queen
**reír**  laugh (v)
**relajar**  relax
**religión**  religion
**reloj**  watch (n)
**resbaladizo**  slippery
**reserva**  reservation
**reservar**  reserve
**respuesta**  answer
**retraso**  delay
**revista**  magazine
**rey**  king
**rico**  rich
**río**  river
**robusto**  sturdy
**roca**  rock (n)
**rodaja**  slice
**rodilla**  knee
**rojo**  red
**romántico**  romantic
**roncar**  snore
**ropa**  clothes
**rosa**  pink
**roto**  broken
**rubio**  blond
**rueda**  wheel
**ruidoso**  loud
**ruidoso**  noisy
**ruinas**  ruins

## S

**sábado**  Saturday
**sábana**  bedsheet
**sábana**  sheet

**saber** know
**sabor** flavor (n)
**sabor** taste (n)
**sacacorchos** corkscrew
**sacerdote** priest
**salida** exit
**salidas** departures
**salir** depart
**salir** leave
**saltar** jump
**¡Salud!** Cheers!
**salvaje** wild
**sandalias** sandals
**sangre** blood
**sano** healthy
**seco** dry
**secreto** secret
**seda** silk
**seda dental** dental floss
**sediento** thirsty
**segunda** second
**segunda clase** second class
**seguro** insurance
**seguro** safe
**sello** stamp
**semana** week
**señal** sign
**sencillo** simple
**Señor** Mr.
**señor** sir
**Señora** Mrs.
**señoras** ladies
**Señorita** Miss
**separado** separate
**serio** serious
**servicio** service
**servicios** toilet

**servilleta** napkin
**sexo** sex
**sexy** sexy
**si** yes (also if)
**SIDA** AIDS
**siempre** always
**siglo** century
**siguiente** next
**silencio** silence
**silla** chair
**silla para niños** highchair
**similar** similar
**sin** without
**sin empleo** unemployed
**sintético** synthetic
**sobre** envelope
**sobre** on
**sobrina** niece
**sobrino** nephew
**sol** sun
**soleado** sunny
**solo** alone
**sólo** only
**soltero[a]** single
**sombrero** hat
**sonrisa** smile (n)
**soñar** dream (v)
**soñoliento** sleepy
**sorpresa** surprise (n)
**sortija** ring (n)
**sótano** basement
**sucio** dirty
**sudar** sweat (v)
**sueño** dream (n)
**suerte** luck
**suéter** sweater
**suficiente** enough

**Suiza** Switzerland
**sujetador** bra
**supermercado** grocery store
**suplemento** supplement
**sur** south

# T

**tal vez** maybe
**talla** size
**tampones** tampons
**tapón de oidos** earplugs
**tarde** afternoon
**tarde** late
**tarjeta** card
**tarjeta de crédito** credit card
**tarjeta de visita** business card
**taza** cup
**teatro** theater
**techo** roof
**tejido** cloth
**telefonista** operator
**teléfono** telephone
**telivisión** television
**temperatura** temperature
**templado** lukewarm
**temprano** early
**tenedor** fork
**tener** have
**tenis** tennis
**tenis** tennis shoes
**terminado** over (finished)
**terminar** finish (v)
**termómetro** thermometer
**terrible** terrible
**tía** aunt
**tiempo** weather

**tienda de campaña** tent
**tierno** tender
**tierra** earth
**tijeras** scissors
**tímido** shy
**tío** uncle
**tirador** handle (n)
**tirar** pull
**tirar** throw
**tirita** band-aid
**toalla** towel
**tobillo** ankle
**todo** every
**todo** everything
**tomar** take
**tomar el sol** sunbathe
**tormenta** storm
**torre** tower
**toser** cough (v)
**total** total
**trabajar** work (v)
**trabajo** job
**trabajo** work (n)
**tradicional** traditional
**traducir** translate
**tráfico** traffic
**tragar** swallow (v)
**traje de baño** swim suit
**tranquilo** quiet
**transbordador** ferry
**tren** train
**triste** sad
**tú** you (informal)
**túnel** tunnel
**turista** tourist

## U

**último** last
**una vez** once
**universidad** university
**urgente** urgent
**usar** use (v)
**usted** you (formal)

## V

**vaca** cow
**vacío** empty
**valle** valley
**vaqueros** jeans
**vaso** glass
**vegetariano[a]** vegetarian
**velocidad** speed
**vender** sell
**venir** come
**ventana** window
**ver** see
**verano** summer
**verde** green
**vestido** dress (n)
**vía** track (train)
**viajar** travel (v)
**viaje** journey
**viaje** tour
**viaje** trip
**vida** life
**vídeo** video
**viejo** old
**viento** wind
**viernes** Friday
**vigilar** watch (v)
**vino** wine

**viñedo** vineyard
**violación** rape (n)
**virus** virus
**visita** visit (n)
**visitar** visit (v)
**vista** view
**vitaminas** vitamins
**viuda** widow
**viudo** widower
**vivir** live (v)
**volar** fly
**vomitar** vomit
**voz** voice
**vuelo** flight

## Y

**y** and
**ya** already
**yo** I
**yodo** iodine

## Z

**zapatos** shoes
**zoo** zoo
**zumo** juice

# Portuguese-English Dictionary

## A

**á**  at
**á moda de casa**  homemade
**abaixo**  below
**abaixo**  down
**aberto**  open (adj)
**abertor de latas**  can opener
**abrir**  open (v)
**acabado**  over (finished)
**acidente**  accident
**acima**  above
**acordar**  wake up
**adaptador**  adaptor
**adega**  cellar
**adesivo**  band-aid
**adeus**  goodbye
**adulto**  adult
**advogado**  lawyer
**aeroporto**  airport
**agência de viagens**  travel
  agency
**agora**  now
**agrafador**  stapler
**agressivo**  aggressive
**água**  water
**água da torneira**  water, tap
**água mineral**  mineral water
**agulha**  needle
**ajuda**  help (n)
**ajudar**  help (v)
**albergue de juventude**  youth
  hostel
**alcool**  alcohol
**alcunha**  nickname

**aldeia**  village
**aleijados**  handicapped
**Alemanha**  Germany
**alergias**  allergies
**alérgico**  allergic
**alfinete**  pin
**alfinete de segurança**  safety
  pin
**algodão**  cotton
**alguma coisa**  something
**alicate**  pliers
**almofada**  pillow
**alto**  high
**alto**  tall
**amanhã**  tomorrow
**amante**  lover
**amar**  love (v)
**amarelo**  yellow
**amigo, amiga**  friend
**amizade**  friendship
**andar**  story (floor)
**andar**  walk (v)
**animal**  animal
**animal de estimação**  pet (n)
**aniversário**  birthday
**ano**  year
**antepassados**  ancestors
**antes**  before
**antibiótico**  antibiotic
**antigo**  ancient
**antiguidades**  antiques
**apanhar**  catch (v)
**apartamento**  apartment
**aperitivos**  appetizers
**apontamento**  appointment

PORTUGUESE

**apontar** point (v)
**apressar** hurry (v)
**apretado** tight
**aproximadamente** approximately
**aqui** here
**ar** air
**ar condicionado** air-conditioned
**arco íris** rainbow
**armários** lockers
**arranha** spider
**arranjar** fix (v)
**arte** art
**artesanato** crafts
**artesanato** handicrafts
**artificial** artificial
**artista** artist
**árvore** tree
**asa** wing
**aspirina** aspirin
**assinatura** signature
**atirar** throw
**atraente** attractive
**atraso** delay
**através** through
**atravessar** go through
**auto serviço** self-service
**autocarro** bus
**autoestrada** highway
**avião** plane
**avô** grandfather
**avó** grandmother
**azedo** sour
**azul** blue

# B

**babeiro** bib
**babysitter** babysitter
**bagagem** baggage
**bagagem** luggage
**baixo** low
**balde** bucket
**balde** pail
**balsa** raft
**banco** bank
**bandeira** flag
**banheira** bathtub
**banho** bath
**barato** cheap
**barba** beard
**barbeiro** barber
**barco** boat
**barco** ferry
**barco** ship (n)
**barco de passeio** rowboat
**barco de vela** sailing
**barulho** noisy
**bateria** battery
**bêbado** drunk
**bébé** baby
**bebida** drink (n)
**beijo** kiss (n)
**bem-vindo** welcome
**biblioteca** library
**bicicleta** bicycle
**bife** beef
**bigode** moustache
**bilhete** ticket
**blusa** blouse
**boca** mouth
**bola** ball

bolsa   purse
bolso   pocket
bom   fine (good)
bom   good
bom-dia   good day
bomba   bomb
bomba de gasolina   gas station
boné   cap
boneca   doll
bonita   pretty
bonito   handsome
borracha   eraser
botão   button
botas   boots
braço   arm
branco   white
brilho de sol   sunshine
brincos   earrings
brinquedo   toy
broches   clothes pins
bronzeado   suntan (n)
bronzear   sunbathe
buraco   hole
burro   donkey

## C

cabeça   head
cabedal   leather
cabelo   hair
cada   each
cadeira   chair
cadeirinha alta   highchair
caderno   notebook
café   coffee
cair   fall (v)
cais   platform (train)

caixa   box
caixa   cashier
calado   quiet
calção de banho   swim trunks
calças   pants
calções   shorts
calendário   calendar
calor   heat (n)
calor   hot
caloria   calorie
cama   bed
camara   camera
câmbio   exchange (n)
caminho de ferro   railway
camisa   shirt
campaínha   ring (n)
campismo   camping
campo   countryside
campo   field
Canadá   Canada
canal   canal
canção   song
caneta   pen
canoa   canoe
cansado   tired
cantar   sing
cantor   singer
cão   dog
capitão   captain
cara   face
carne   meat
caro   expensive
carpete   carpet
carpete   rug
carregar   carry
carro   car
carta   letter

PORTUGUESE

**cartão**  card (also businiss card)
**cartão de crédito**  credit card
**cartão postal**  postcard
**cartas**  cards (deck)
**carteira**  wallet
**carteirista**  pick-pocket
**casa**  house
**casa de banho**  bathroom
**casa de banho**  toilet
**casaco**  jacket
**casaco impermeável**  raincoat
**casado[a]**  married
**casamento**  wedding
**cassete**  cassette
**cassete**  tape (cassette)
**castanho**  brown
**castelo**  castle
**catedral**  cathedral
**cavalheiro**  gentleman
**cavalo**  horse
**cave**  cave
**cedo**  early
**cedo**  soon
**centro**  center
**certo**  right (correct)
**cerveja**  beer
**cesto**  basket
**céu**  heaven
**céu**  sky
**chaleira**  kettle
**chapéu**  hat
**chateado**  angry
**chateado**  mad
**chave**  key
**chave de parafusos**  screwdriver
**chávena**  cup
**chegadas**  arrivals

**chegar**  arrive
**cheio**  no vacancy
**cheiro**  smell (n)
**cheque**  check
**cheque de viagem**  traveler's check
**chinês**  Chinese (adj)
**chocolate**  chocolate
**chorar**  cry (v)
**chupeta**  pacifier
**chuva**  rain (n)
**chuveiro**  shower
**cidade**  city
**cidade**  town
**ciência**  science
**cientista**  scientist
**cigarro**  cigarette
**cinema**  cinema
**cinto**  belt
**cintura**  waist
**cinzeiro**  ashtray
**cinzento**  gray
**claro**  clear
**classe**  class
**clip**  paper clip
**coelho**  rabbit
**coisa**  thing
**colete**  vest
**colher**  spoon
**com**  with
**com gás**  fizzy
**comboio**  train
**começar**  begin
**comer**  eat
**comichão**  itch (n)
**comida**  food
**como**  how

**compact disco**  compact disc
**complicado**  complicated
**compras**  shopping
**comprimido**  pill
**computador**  computer
**concerto**  concert
**concha**  shell
**condutor**  conductor
**condutor**  driver
**conduzir**  drive (v)
**conexão**  connection (train)
**confirmar**  confirm
**confortável**  comfortable
**confortável**  cozy
**conta**  bill (payment)
**contador**  accountant
**convidados**  guest
**convite**  invitation
**copo**  glass
**cor de laranja**  orange (color)
**cor de rosa**  pink
**coração**  heart
**corbetor**  blanket
**corda**  rope
**cordeiro**  lamb
**cores**  colors
**corpo**  body
**corredor**  corridor
**correio**  mail (n)
**correio aéreo**  air mail
**corrente**  stream (n)
**correr**  run (v)
**corta unhas**  nail clipper
**corte de cabelo**  haircut
**costa**  coast
**cotovelo**  elbow
**coxa**  thigh

**cozinha**  kitchen
**cozinhar**  cook (v)
**creme de barbear**  shaving cream
**creme de bronzear**  suntan lotion
**criado**  waiter
**crianças**  children
**cru**  raw
**cruzeta**  coat hanger
**cuecas**  panties
**cuecas**  underpants
**cuidadoso**  careful
**curto**  short

# D

**dançar**  dance (v)
**dar**  give
**de**  from
**de**  of
**de acordo**  agree
**de repente**  suddenly
**debaixo**  under
**dedo**  finger
**dedo do pé**  toe
**delicioso**  delicious
**demasiado**  too (much)
**dentes**  tooth
**dentista**  dentist
**depois**  after
**depois**  afterwards
**depósito**  deposit
**desconto**  discount
**desculpa**  apology
**desculpe**  excuse me
**desculpe**  sorry

PORTUGUESE

**desejo** wish (v)
**desempregado** unemployed
**desodorizante** deodorant
**despertador** alarm clock
**desporto** sport
**desventurado** unfortunate
**desvio** detour
**detrás** behind
**deus** God
**devagar** slow
**dia** day
**diabético** diabetic
**diamante** diamond
**diarreia** diarrhea
**dicionário** dictionary
**difícil** difficult
**difícil** hard
**dinheiro** money
**direção** direction
**directo** direct
**direita** right (direction)
**disco voador** frisbee
**divertido** fun
**divertido** funny
**divorciado[a]** divorced
**dobrar** double
**doce** candy
**doce** sweet
**doença** disease
**doente** ill
**doente** sick
**domingo** Sunday
**donde** where
**dono** owner
**dor** pain
**dor de cabeça** headache
**dormir** sleep (v)

**dormitorio** dormitory
**doutor** doctor

# E

**e** and
**ela** she
**ele** he
**eles** they
**elevador** elevator
**em** in
**em frente** straight
**em vez de** instead
**embaixada** embassy
**embalagem** package
**embrulhar** wrap (v)
**ementa** menu
**emprestar** borrow
**emprestar** lend
**empurrar** push
**encantador** charming
**endereço** address
**engenheiro** engineer
**engolir** swallow (v)
**entender** understand
**entrada** entrance
**envelope** envelope
**enviar** send
**enviar** ship (v)
**equipa** team
**erro** mistake
**escada** ladder
**escadas** stairs
**escadas** upstairs
**escandulo** scandalous
**escola** school
**escorregadio** slippery

**escova de cabelo** hairbrush
**escova de dentes** toothbrush
**escrever** write
**escritório** office
**escultor** sculptor
**escultura** sculpture
**escuro** dark
**escutar** listen
**esfomeado** hungry
**esgotado** exhausted
**Espanha** Spain
**especialidade** speciality
**espectáculo** show (n)
**espelho** mirror
**esperar** wait (v)
**espirro** sneeze (n)
**esposa** wife
**esquecer** forget
**esquerda** left
**esquiar** ski (v)
**esquina** corner
**esta noite** tonight
**estação** station
**estacas de tenda** tent pegs
**estacionar** park (v)
**estado** state
**Estados Unidos** United States
**este** east
**estilo** style
**estômago** stomach
**estranho** strange
**estranjeiro** foreign
**estreito** narrow
**estrela** star (in sky)
**estudante** student
**estúpido** stupid
**eu** I

**Europa** Europe
**exactamente** exactly
**excelente** excellent
**excepto** except
**excursão** tour
**exemplo** example
**explicar** explain

# F

**fábrica** factory
**faca** knife
**fácil** easy
**falar** speak
**falar** talk
**falésia** cliff
**falso** false
**família** family
**famoso** famous
**fantástico** fantastic
**farmácia** pharmacy
**fatia** slice
**fato de banho** swim suit
**fax** fax
**fazer** make (v)
**fechado** closed
**fechadura** lock (n)
**fechar** lock (v)
**fecho** zipper
**feio** ugly
**feliz** happy
**feminino** female
**feriado** holiday
**ferido** injured
**fervido** boiled
**festa** party
**festival** festival

PORTUGUESE

**fevre** fever
**filha** daughter
**filho** son
**filme** movie
**fio** necklace
**fio** string
**fio dental** dental floss
**fita cola** scotch tape
**flor** flower
**fogo de artificio** fireworks
**fonte** fountain
**forno** oven
**forte** strong
**fosforos** matches
**fotografia** photo
**fraldas** diaper
**França** France
**fresco** cool
**fresco** fresh
**frio** cold (adj)
**fronteira** border
**fruta** fruit
**fumador** smoking
**fundo** bottom
**funeral** funeral
**futebol** football
**futebol** soccer
**futuro** future

# G

**galeria** gallery
**galinha** chicken
**garagem** garage
**garantia** guarantee
**garfo** fork
**garganta** throat

**garrafa** bottle
**gás** gas
**gastar** spend
**gato** cat
**gelado** ice cream
**gelo** ice
**gêmeos** twins
**genuíno** genuine
**gerente** manager
**Gilete** razor
**golfe** golf
**gordo** fat (adj)
**gorduroso** greasy
**gostar** enjoy
**gostar** like (v)
**Grã-Bretanha** Britain
**gramática** grammar
**grande** big
**grande** large
**granjeiro** farmer
**grátis** free (no cost)
**grávida** pregnant
**Grécia** Greece
**gripe** flu
**grosso** thick
**guarda-chuva** umbrella
**guardanapo** napkin
**guardar** keep
**guitarra** guitar

# H

**hemorróidas** hemorrhoids
**hidroplano** hydrofoil
**história** history
**hoje** today
**homen** man

**homens** men
**homosexual** gay
**honesto** honest
**hora** hour
**horário** timetable
**horrível** horrible
**hospital** hospital
**hotel** hotel
**humilhante** embarrassing

## I

**ida e volta** roundtrip
**idade** age
**igreija** church
**ilha** island
**imediatamente** immediately
**imobilizado** stuck
**importado** imported
**importante** important
**impossível** impossible
**inacreditável** incredible
**incluido** included
**incomudar** disturb
**independente** independent
**indigestão** indigestion
**industria** industry
**informação** information
**inglês** English
**inocente** innocent
**insecto** insect
**insolação** sunstroke
**instante** instant
**inteligente** intelligent
**interior** inside
**interresante** interesting
**inverno** winter

**iodo** iodine
**ir** go
**irmã** sister
**irmão** brother
**isqueiro** lighter (n)
**Itália** Italy

## J

**já** already
**janela** window
**jantar** dinner
**jardim** garden
**jardinagem** gardening
**jarro** carafe
**jeans** jeans
**joalheria** jewelry
**joelho** knee
**jogar** play (v)
**jogging** jogging
**jogo** game
**jornal** newspaper
**jovem** teenager
**juntos** together
**juventude** youth

## L

**lã** wool
**lábio** lip
**ladrão** thief
**lago** lake
**lâmpada** bulb
**lâmpada** light bulb
**lanterna a pilhas** flashlight
**lápis** pencil
**laranja** orange (fruit)

lata   can (n)
lavandaria   laundromat
lavar   wash
lavatório   sink
lenço   scarf
lençol   sheet
lençol de cama   bedsheet
lenços de papel   tissues
limpo   clean (adj)
lindo[a]   beautiful
língua   language
linha   thread
linha   track (train)
linha aérea   airline
linha de roupas   clothesline
lista   list
litro   liter
livraria   book shop
livre   vacant
livro   book
local   local
longe   far
louro   blond
lua   moon
lua de mel   honeymoon
lugar, assento   seat
luta   fight (n)
lutar   fight (v)
luvas   gloves
luz   light (n)

# M

macho   macho
madeira   wood
maduro   ripe
mãe   mom

mãe   mother
magnífico   great
magro   skinny
magro   thin
mais   more
mais tarde   later
mala   suitcase
malentendido   misunderstanding
manhã   morning
mão   hand
mapa   map
mar   sea
marido   husband
marisco   seafood
mas   but
masculino   male
matar   kill
mau   bad
maxila   jaw
máximo   maximum
medicina   medicine
médio   medium
medo   afraid
meia-noite   midnight
meias   socks
meio-dia   noon
melhor   best
Menina   Miss
menstruação   period (woman's)
mercado   market
mercearia   grocery store
mês   month
mesa   table
mesmo   same
metal   metal
metro   subway
meu   my

**minimo** minimum
**minutos** minutes
**mista** mix (n)
**mobilias** furniture
**mochila** backpack
**mochila** rucksack
**moda** fashion
**moderno** modern
**moedas** coins
**molhado** wet
**momento** moment
**montanha** mountain
**montar a cavalo** horse riding
**monumento** monument
**morrer** die
**morto** dead
**mosquito** mosquito
**mostrar** show (v)
**mudar** change (v)
**muito** many
**muito** much
**muito** very
**mulher** woman
**mulheres** women
**multidão** crowd (n)
**mundo** world
**músculo** muscle
**museu** museum
**música** music

# N

**nacionalidade** nationality
**nada** nothing
**nadar** swim
**não** no
**não** not

**não fumador** non-smoking
**nariz** nose
**Natal** Christmas
**natural** natural
**natureza** nature
**náusea** nausea
**nebuloso** cloudy
**necessário** necessary
**necessitar** need
**negócio** business
**nervoso** nervous
**neto, neta** grandchild
**nevoeiro** fog
**noite** night
**noitecer** evening
**nome** name
**normal** normal
**norte** north
**nós** us
**nós** we
**novo** new
**novo** young
**nunca** never
**nuo** naked

# O

**o quê** what
**O.K.** O.K.
**obrigado** thanks
**oceano** ocean
**oculista** optician
**óculos** glasses (eye)
**óculos de sol** sunglasses
**ocupado** occupied
**odiar** hate
**oeste** west

olá   hello
olá   hi
olhar   look
olhar   watch (v)
olho   eye
ombros   shoulder
ontem   yesterday
ópera   opera
operador   operator
orelha   ear
original   original
ou   or
ouro   gold
outono   autumn
outra vez   again
outro   another
outro   other
ouvir   hear

# P

padaria   bakery
padre   priest
pagar   pay
página   page
pai   dad
pai   father
país   country
pais   parents
palácio   palace
palavra   word
palito   toothpick
pão   bread
papel   paper
papel higiénico   toilet paper
para   for
para   to

para levar   take out (food)
parabéns   congratulations
parar   stop (n)
parar   stop (v)
parque   park (garden)
partidas   departures
partido   broken
partir   depart
Pascoa   Easter
passageiro   passenger
passaporte   passport
pássaro   bird
passatempo   hobby
pasta de dentes   toothpaste
pastilha elástica   gum
patinagem   skating
patins   roller skates
patrão   boss
paz   peace
pé   foot
peão   pedestrian
pedaço   piece
pedir boleia   hitchhike
peixe   fish
pele   skin
pensar   think
pensos higiénicos   sanitary
  napkins
pente   comb (n)
pequeno   little
pequeno   small
pequeno almoço   breakfast
percento   percent
perdido   lost
perfeito   perfect
perfume   perfume
pergunta   question (n)

**perguntar**  ask
**perigo**  danger
**perigoso**  dangerous
**período**  period (of time)
**perna**  leg
**perservativo**  condom
**perto**  near
**pesado**  heavy
**pescar**  fish (v)
**peso**  weight
**pessoa**  person
**pessoas**  people
**petisco**  snack
**piada**  joke (n)
**pinsa**  tweezers
**pintura**  painting
**pior**  worst
**piquenique**  picnic
**piscina**  swimming pool
**pistola**  gun
**pizza**  pizza
**planta**  plant
**plástico**  plastic
**pó de talco**  talcum powder
**pobre**  poor
**poder**  can (v)
**podre**  rotten
**polícia**  police
**ponte**  bridge
**por favor**  please
**pôr do sol**  sunset
**porão**  basement
**porco**  pig
**porco**  pork
**porquê**  because
**porquê**  why
**porta**  door

**porto**  harbor
**Portugal**  Portugal
**possível**  possible
**possuir**  own (v)
**poster**  poster
**pouco**  few
**praça**  square (town)
**praia**  beach
**prata**  silver
**prático**  practical
**prato**  plate
**preço**  cost
**preço**  price
**prédio**  building
**preguiçoso**  lazy
**prenda**  gift
**presente**  present (gift)
**preto**  black
**primavera**  spring (n)
**primeira classe**  first class
**primeiro**  first
**primo, prima**  cousin
**principal**  main
**prisão de ventre**  constipation
**privado**  private
**problema**  problem
**problema**  trouble
**professor**  teacher
**profissão**  occupation
**profissão**  profession
**proibido**  forbidden
**proibido**  prohibited
**pronto**  ready
**pronto socorro**  first aid
**pronúncia**  pronunciation
**protector solar**  sunscreen
**provar**  taste (try)

**próximo** next
**público** public
**pulga** flea
**pullover** sweater
**pulmões** lungs
**pulseira** bracelet
**pulso** wrist
**puxador** handle (n)

## Q

**qualidade** quality
**quando** when
**quanto** how many
**quanto custa** how much ($)
**quarta-feira** Wednesday
**quarto** bedroom
**quarto** quarter (¼)
**quarto** room
**quartos** vacancy sign
**que pena** pity, it's a
**queda de água** waterfall
**queijo** cheese
**queimadura** burn (n)
**queimadura solar** sunburn
**queixar** complain
**quem** who
**quente** warm (adj)
**querer** want
**quinta** farm
**quinta-feira** Thursday

## R

**rabo** tail
**rabuçados da tosse** cough
  drops

**rádio** radio
**rainha** queen
**rapariga** girl
**rapaz** boy
**recado** message
**receber** receive
**receita** recipe
**receita médica** prescription
**recepcionista** receptionist
**recibo** receipt
**recomendar** recommend
**recordar** remember
**rede** cot
**reembolso** refund (n)
**rei** king
**relaxar** relax
**religião** religion
**relógio** watch (n)
**renda** rent (v)
**reparar** repair
**repelente de insectos** insect
  repellant
**reserva** reservation
**reservar** reserve
**resposta** answer
**ressonar** snore
**revista** magazine
**rico** rich
**rio** river
**rir** laugh (v)
**rock** rock (n)
**roda** wheel
**rolha** cork
**romântico** romantic
**roulote** R.V.
**roupa** clothes
**roxo** purple

**rua** street
**ruidoso** loud
**ruínas** ruins

## S

**sábado** Saturday
**sabão** soap
**saber** know
**sabor** flavor (n)
**sabor** taste (n)
**sacarolhas** corkscrew
**saco** bag
**saco plástico** plastic bag
**saco plastico com fecho** zip-
 lock bag
**saia** skirt
**saída** exit
**sair** leave
**saldos** sale
**saltar** jump
**salvagem** wild
**sandálias** sandals
**sande** sandwich
**sangre** blood
**sapatos** shoes
**sapatos de ténis** tennis shoes
**saudade** homesick
**saudavel** healthy
**Saúde!** Cheers!
**se** if
**seco** dry
**século** century
**seda** silk
**sede** thirsty
**segredo** secret
**segunda** second

**segunda classe** second class
**segunda-feira** Monday
**seguro** insurance
**seguro** safe
**selo** stamp
**sem** without
**semana** week
**sempre** always
**Senhor** Mr.
**senhor** sir
**Senhora** Mrs.
**senhora, menina** waitress
**senhoras** ladies
**sentido único** one way (street)
**separado** separate
**ser** is
**sério** serious
**serviço** service
**sexo** sex
**sexta-feira** Friday
**sexy** sexy
**SIDA** AIDS
**silêncio** silence
**sim** yes
**similar** similar
**simpático** kind
**simpático** nice
**simples** plain
**simples** simple
**sinal** sign
**sintético** synthetic
**slide** slide (photo)
**só** only
**sobre** on
**sobremesa** dessert
**sobrinha** niece
**sobrinho** nephew

**sol** sun
**sol** sunny
**sólido** sturdy
**solteiro[a]** single
**sonhar** dream (v)
**sonho** dream (n)
**sonolento** sleepy
**sorriso** smile (n)
**sorte** luck
**soutien** bra
**sozinho** alone
**suar** sweat (v)
**subida** hill
**subida** up
**suficiente** enough
**Suiça** Switzerland
**sujo** dirty
**sul** south
**sumo** juice
**supermercado** supermarket
**suplemento** supplement
**surpresa** surprise (n)

# T

**T-shirt** T-shirt
**talvez** maybe
**tamanho** size
**tampões** tampons
**tampões de ouvido** earplugs
**tarde** afternoon
**tarde** late
**taxa** tax
**teatro** theater
**tecido** cloth
**telefone** telephone
**televisão** television

**telhado** roof
**temperatura** temperature
**tempestada** storm
**tempo** weather
**tenda** tent
**ténis** tennis
**tenro** tender
**tépido** lukewarm
**ter** have
**terça-feira** Tuesday
**terminar** finish (v)
**termómetro** thermometer
**terra** earth
**terrível** terrible
**tesouras** scissors
**tia** aunt
**tijela** bowl
**tímido** shy
**tio** uncle
**tirar** pull
**toalha** towel
**todo** every
**tomar** take
**torneira** faucet
**tornozelo** ankle
**torre** tower
**tosser** cough (v)
**total** total
**trabalhar** work (v)
**trabalho** job
**trabalho** work (n)
**tradicional** traditional
**traduzir** translate
**tráfico** traffic
**triste** sad
**troca** change (n)
**tu** you (informal)

**tudo** everything
**túnel** tunnel
**turista** tourist

# U

**último** last
**um guia** guidebook
**uma guia** guide
**uma ida** one way (ticket)
**uma vez** once
**universidade** university
**urgente** urgent
**usar** use (v)

# V

**vaca** cow
**vale** valley
**varanda** balcony
**vazio** empty
**vegetariano[a]** vegetarian
**vela** candle
**velho** old
**velocidade** speed
**vender** sell
**vento** wind
**ver** see
**verão** summer
**verde** green
**vermelho** red
**vestido** dress (n)
**via** by (via)
**viagem** journey
**viagem** trip
**viajar** travel (v)
**vida** life

**video camera** video camera
**vídeo** video
**vinhedo** vineyard
**vinho** wine
**violação** rape (n)
**vir** come
**vírus** virus
**visita** visit (n)
**visitar** visit (v)
**vista** view
**vitaminas** vitamins
**viúva** widow
**viúvo** widower
**viver** live (v)
**voar** fly
**você** you (formal)
**vomitar** vomit
**voo** flight
**voz** voice

# X

**xampú** shampoo

# Z

**zero** zero
**zoo** zoo

PORTUGUESE

# Hurdling the Language Barrier

## Don't be afraid to communicate

Even the best phrase book won't satisfy your needs in every situation. To really hurdle the language barrier, you need to leap beyond the printed page, and dive into contact with the locals. Never allow your lack of foreign language skills to isolate you from the people and cultures you traveled halfway around the world to experience. Remember that in every country you visit, you're surrounded by expert, native-speaking tutors. Spend bus and train rides letting them teach you.

Start conversations by asking politely in the local language, "Do you speak English?" When you speak English with someone from another country, talk slowly, clearly, and with carefully chosen words. Use what the Voice of America calls "simple English." You're talking to people who are wishing it was written down, hoping to see each letter as it tumbles out of your mouth. Pronounce each letter, avoiding all contractions and slang. For bad examples, listen to other tourists.

Keep things caveman-simple. Make single nouns work as entire sentences ("Photo?"). Use internationally-understood words ("self-service" works in Madrid). Butcher the language if you must. The important thing is to make the effort. To get air mail stamps, you can flap your wings and say "tweet, tweet." If you want milk, moo and pull two imaginary udders. Risk looking like a fool.

If you're short on words, make your picnic a potluck. Pull out a map and point out your journey. Draw what you mean. Bring photos from home and introduce your family. Play cards or toss a Frisbee. Fold an origami bird for kids or dazzle 'em with sleight-of-hand magic.

Go ahead and make educated guesses. Many situations are easy-to-fake multiple choice questions. Practice. Read timetables, concert posters and newspaper headlines. Listen to each language on a multilingual tour. Be melodramatic. Exaggerate the local accent. Self-consciousness is the deadliest communication-killer.

Choose multilingual people to communicate with, like students, business people, urbanites, young well-dressed people, or anyone in the tourist trade. Use a small note pad to keep track of handy phrases you pick up—and to help you communicate more clearly with the locals by scribbling down numbers, maps, and so on. Some travelers carry important messages written on a small card: vegetarian, boiled water, your finest ice cream.

## Numbers and Stumblers:

■ Europeans write a few numbers differently than we do. The one has an upswing ( 1 ), the four looks like a lightning bolt ( 4 ), and the seven has a cross ( 7 ).

■ Europeans write the date in this order: day/month/year. Christmas is 25-12-01, not 12-25-01.

■ Commas are decimal points and decimals are commas. A dollar and a half is 1,50 and 5.280 feet are in a mile.

■ The European "first floor" isn't the ground floor, but the first floor up.

■ When counting with your fingers, start with your thumb. If you hold up only your first finger, you'll probably get two of something.

## International words

As our world shrinks, more and more words hop across their linguistic boundaries and become international. Savvy travelers develop a knack for choosing words most likely to be universally understood ("auto" instead of "car," "kaput" rather than "broken," "photo," not "picture"). Internationalize your pronunciation. "University," if you play around with its sound (oo-nee-vehr-see-tay), will be understood anywhere. Practice speaking English with a heavy Iberian accent. Wave your arms a lot. Be creative.

Here are a few internationally understood words. Remember, cut out the Yankee accent and give each word a pan-European sound.

| | | | |
|---|---|---|---|
| Stop | Kaput | Vino | Restaurant |
| Ciao | Bank | Hotel | Bye-bye |
| Rock 'n' roll | Post | Camping | OK |
| Auto | Picnic | Amigo | Autobus (boos) |
| Nuclear | Macho | Tourist | English |
| Yankee | Americano | Mama mia | Michelangelo |
| Beer | Oo la la | Coffee | Casanova (romantic) |
| Chocolate | Moment | Sexy | Disneyland |
| Tea | Coca-Cola | No problem | Passport |
| Telephone | Photo | Photocopy | Police |
| Europa | Self-service | Toilet | Information |
| Super | Taxi | Central | Rambo |
| Pardon | University | Fascist | U.S. profanity |

## Common Iberian gestures

**The Eyelid Pull:** Place your extended forefinger below the center of your eye, and pull the skin downward. In Spain this is a friendly warning, meaning: "Be alert, that guy is clever."

**The Fingertip Kiss:** Bring the thumb and fingers of your right hand together at your lips, kiss gently, and toss them up and away. This usually means praise in Spain, and is used as a form of salutation in Portugal.

**The Hand Purse:** Straighten the fingers and thumb of one hand, bringing them all together to make an upward point. Your hands can be held still or moved a little up and down at the wrist. In Iberia, this means "lots."

**The Cheek Screw:** Make a fist, stick out your forefinger and screw it into your cheek. This is used in southern Spain to call someone "effeminate."

**The Nose Flick:** Thumbing your nose is used as a form of mockery in Spain and Portugal.

**Hook 'em Horns:** Stick out your index finger and pinky, and hold your two middle fingers down with your thumb. Either you're a Texas Longhorns fan or you're accusing someone of impotence.

**The Forearm Jerk:** Clench your right fist, and jerk your forearm up as you slap your bicep with your left palm. This is a rude phallic gesture that Iberians use the way

Americans give someone "the finger." This extra-large version says, "I'm superior."

**Counting on fingers:** Counting begins with the thumb, so if you hold up two fingers, someone will sell you three of something.

**To beckon someone:** In Iberia, wave your hand palm downward.

## Tongue twisters
Here are a few *trabalenguas* that are sure to challenge you and amuse your Iberian hosts.

### Spanish tongue twisters:

| | |
|---|---|
| **Pablito clavó un clavito. ¿Qué clavito clavó Pablito?** | Paul stuck in a stick. What stick did Paul stick in? |
| **Un tigre, dos tigres, tres tigres comían trigo en un trigal. Un tigre, dos tigres, tres tigres.** | One tiger, two tigers, three tigers ate wheat in a wheatfield. One tiger, two tigers, three tigers. |
| **El cielo está enladrillado. ¿Quién lo desenladrillará? El desenladrillador que lo desenladrille un buen desenladrillador será.** | The sky is bricked up. Who will unbrick it? He who unbricks it, what a fine unbricker he will be. |

## *Portuguese tongue twisters:*

| | |
|---|---|
| **O rato roeu a roupa do rei de Roma.** | The mouse nibbled the clothes of the king of Rome. |
| **Um tigre, dois tigres, três tigres.** | One tiger, two tigers, three tigers. |
| **Se cá nevasse fazia-se cá ski, mas como cá não neva não se faz cá ski.** | If the snow would fall, we'd ski, but since it doesn't, we don't. |

## *English tongue twisters:*

After your Iberian friends have laughed at you, let them try these tongue twisters in English:

If neither he sells seashells, nor she sells seashells, who shall sell seashells? Shall seashells be sold?

Peter Piper picked a peck of pickled peppers.

Rugged rubber baby buggy bumpers.

The sixth sick sheik's sixth sheep's sick.

Red bug's blood and black bug's blood.

Soldiers' shoulders.

Thieves seize skis.

I'm a pleasant mother pheasant plucker. I pluck mother pheasants. I'm the most pleasant mother pheasant plucker that ever plucked a mother pheasant.

# Let's Talk Telephones

Smart travelers use the telephone every day to make hotel reservations, check on tourist information, or call home. The card-operated public phones are easier to use than coin-operated phones. In Spain or Portugal, buy a telephone card at post offices, tobacco shops, or newsstands. Your telephone card will work for local, long distance, and international calls made from card-operated public phones throughout the country where you purchase your card. When using a card-operated phone, pick up the receiver, insert your card in the slot in the phone, dial your number, make your call, then retrieve your card. The price of your call is automatically deducted from your card as you use it.

In Spain, a *Telefónica* is an easy-to-use "talk now, pay later" telephone office. You'll also find fair, metered phones in post offices in both Spain and Portugal.

Hotel room phones can be reasonable for local calls, but a terrible rip-off for long-distance calls. To avoid hassles, make your calls from a phone booth, phone office, or post office. European time is six/nine hours ahead of the east/west coast of the United States. Breakfast in Madrid is midnight in California.

For directory assistance in Spain, dial 1003 (for local numbers) or 025 (for pricey international assistance); in Portugal, dial 13.

## Dialing Direct

**Calling Between Countries:** Dial the international access code (usually 00 for most European countries, 011 for America), the country code of the country you're calling, the area code (if it it starts with zero, drop the zero), and then the local number.

**Calling Long Distance Within a Country:** First dial the area code (including its zero), then the local number. Spain is an exception; see below.

**Europe's Exceptions:** Some countries do not use area codes, such as Spain, France, Italy, Norway, and Denmark. To make an international call to these countries, dial the international access code, the country code, and then the local number in its entirety (okay, so there's one exception; for France, drop the initial zero of the local number). To make long-distance calls within any of these countries, simply dial the local number, whether you're calling across the country or across the street.

## International Access Codes
When dialing direct, first dial the international access code of the country you're calling from. For most countries, it's "00." The exceptions are Spain (07), Sweden (009), and the U.S.A./Canada (011).

## Country Codes
After dialing the international access code, dial the code of the country you're calling.

| | | |
|---|---|---|
| Austria—43 | France—33 | Netherlands—31 |
| Belgium—32 | Germany—49 | Norway—47 |
| Britain—44 | Greece—30 | Portugal—351 |
| Czech Rep.—420 | Ireland—353 | Spain—34 |
| Denmark—45 | Italy—39 | Sweden—46 |
| Estonia—372 | Latvia—371 | Switzerland—41 |
| Finland—358 | Lithuania—370 | U.S.A./Canada—1 |

## Dial away:

If you're dialing direct, here's the sequence of numbers you'd dial:

**USA to Spain:** 011 - 34 - local number
**Spain to USA:** 07 - 1 - area code - local number
**Long distance within Spain:** local number
**Spain to Portugal:** 07 - 351 - area code (without the initial 0) - local number
**USA to Portugal:** 011 - 351 - area code (without the initial 0) - local number
**Portugal to USA:** 00 - 1 - area code - local number
**Long distance within Portugal:** area code (including the initial 0) - local number
**Portugal to Spain:** 00 - 34 - local number

## U.S.A. Direct Services: Calling Card Operators

It's cheaper to call direct, but if you have a calling card and prefer to have an English-speaking operator dial for you, here are the numbers:

|  | ATT | MCI | Sprint |
|---|---|---|---|
| **Spain** | 900-99-0011 | 900-99-0014 | 900-99-0013 |
| **Portugal** | 0-800-111-1111 | 050-171-234 | 0800-800-187 |

## Metric conversions (approximate)

| | |
|---|---|
| 1 inch = 25 millimeters | 1 foot = .3 meter |
| 1 yard = .9 meter | 1 mile = 1.6 kilometers |
| 1 sq. yard = .8 sq. meter | 1 acre = 0.4 hectare |
| 1 quart = .95 liter | 1 ounce = 28 grams |
| 1 pound = .45 kilo | 1 kilo = 2.2 pounds |
| 1 centimeter = 0.4 inch | 1 meter = 39.4 inches |
| 1 kilometer = .62 mile | |

Miles = kilometers divided by 2 plus 10%
(120 km ÷ 2 = 60, 60 +12 = 72 miles)
Fahrenheit degrees = double Celsius + 30

32° F = 0° C, 82° F = about 28° C

## Weather
First line is average daily low (°F); second line is average
daily high (°F); third line, days of no rain.

|  | J | F | M | A | M | J | J | A | S | O | N | D |
|---|---|---|---|---|---|---|---|---|---|---|---|---|
| **Madrid** | 33 | 35 | 40 | 44 | 50 | 57 | 62 | 62 | 56 | 48 | 40 | 35 |
|  | 47 | 51 | 47 | 64 | 71 | 80 | 87 | 86 | 77 | 66 | 54 | 48 |
|  | 22 | 19 | 20 | 21 | 22 | 24 | 28 | 29 | 24 | 23 | 20 | 22 |
| **Barcelona** | 42 | 44 | 47 | 51 | 57 | 63 | 69 | 69 | 65 | 58 | 50 | 44 |
|  | 56 | 57 | 61 | 64 | 71 | 77 | 81 | 82 | 67 | 61 | 62 | 57 |
|  | 26 | 21 | 24 | 22 | 23 | 25 | 27 | 26 | 23 | 23 | 23 | 25 |
| **Costa del Sol** | 47 | 48 | 51 | 55 | 60 | 66 | 70 | 72 | 68 | 61 | 53 | 48 |
|  | 61 | 62 | 64 | 69 | 74 | 80 | 84 | 85 | 81 | 74 | 67 | 62 |
|  | 25 | 22 | 23 | 25 | 28 | 29 | 31 | 30 | 28 | 27 | 22 | 25 |
| **Lisbon** | 46 | 47 | 49 | 52 | 56 | 60 | 63 | 64 | 62 | 57 | 52 | 47 |
|  | 56 | 58 | 61 | 64 | 69 | 75 | 79 | 80 | 76 | 69 | 62 | 57 |
|  | 22 | 20 | 21 | 23 | 25 | 28 | 30 | 30 | 26 | 24 | 20 | 21 |
| **Algarve** | 47 | 57 | 50 | 52 | 56 | 60 | 64 | 65 | 62 | 58 | 52 | 48 |
|  | 61 | 61 | 63 | 67 | 73 | 77 | 83 | 84 | 80 | 73 | 66 | 62 |
|  | 22 | 19 | 20 | 24 | 27 | 29 | 31 | 31 | 28 | 26 | 22 | 22 |

# Faxing your hotel reservation

Most hotel managers know basic "hotel English." Photocopy
and enlarge this form, then fax away.

. . . . . . . . . . . . . . . . . . . . . . . . . . . . . . . . . . . . . . . . . . . . .

One page fax                              My fax #:_____
To:                                       Today's date: ___ / ___ / ___
From:                                              day  month  year
Dear Hotel _____,
      Please make this reservation for me:

Name: _____
Total # of people: ____  # of rooms: ____  # of nights: ____

Arriving: ___ / ___ / ___    Time of arrival (24-hour clock): _____
             day  month  year              (I will telephone if later)

Departing:  ___ / ___ / ___
             day  month  year

Room(s):  Single  Double  Twin    Triple   Quad   Quint
With:    Toilet Shower    Bathtub    Sink only
Special needs:   View    Quiet    Cheapest room   Ground floor

Credit card:  Visa    Mastercard    American Express

Card #: _____  Exp. date: _____
Name on card: _____

If a deposit is necessary, you may charge me for the first night. Please fax or mail
me confirmation of my reservation, along with the type of room reserved, the price,
and whether the price includes breakfast. Thank you.

Signature: _____
Name: _____
Address :_____
Phone: _____  E-mail: _____

# Spanish tear-out cheat sheet

| Hello. | Hola. | oh-lah |
|---|---|---|
| Do you speak English? | ¿Habla usted inglés? | ah-blah oo-**stehd** een-**glays** |
| Yes. / No. | Sí. / No. | see / noh |
| I don't speak Spanish. | No hablo español. | noh ah-bloh ay-spahn-**yohl** |
| I'm sorry. | Lo siento. | loh see-**ehn**-toh |
| Please. | Por favor. | por fah-**bor** |
| Thank you. | Gracias. | grah-**thee**-ahs |
| It's (not) a problem. | (No) hay problema. | (noh) ī proh-**blay**-mah |
| Very good. | Muy bien. | moo-ee bee-**yehn** |
| You are very kind. | Usted es muy amable. | oo-**stehd** ays moo-ee ah-**mah**-blay |
| Goodbye. | Adiós. | ah-dee-**ohs** |
| | | |
| Where is a...? | ¿Donde hay un...? | **dohn**-day ī oon |
| ...hotel | ...hotel | oh-**tel** |
| ...youth hostel | ...albergue de juventud | ahl-**behr**-gay day *h*oo-behn-**tood** |
| ...restaurant | ...restaurante | ray-stoh-**rahn**-tay |
| ...supermarket | ...supermercado | soo-pehr-mehr-**kah**-doh |
| ...bank | ...banco | **bahn**-koh |
| Where is the...? | ¿Dónde está la...? | **dohn**-day ay-**stah** lah |
| ...pharmacy | ...farmacia | far-mah-**thee**-ah |
| ...train station | ...estación de trenes | ay-stah-thee-**ohn** day **tray**-nays |
| ...tourist information office | ...Oficina de Turismo | oh-fee-**thee**-nah day too-rees-**moh** |
| Where are the toilets? | ¿Dónde están los aseos / servicios? | **dohn**-day ay-**stahn** lohs ah-**say**-ohs / sehr-bee-**thee**-ohs |
| men / women | hombres / mujeres | **ohm**-brays / moo-*h*eh-rays |
| How much is it? | ¿Cuánto cuesta? | **kwahn**-toh **kway**-stah |
| Write it? | ¿Me lo escribe? | may loh ay-**skree**-bay |

| | | |
|---|---|---|
| Cheap(er). | (Más) barato. | (mahs) bah-**rah**-toh |
| Cheapest. | El más barato. | ehl mahs bah-**rah**-toh |
| Is it free? | ¿Es gratis? | ays grah-**tees** |
| Is it included? | ¿Está incluido? | ay-**stah** een-kloo-**ee**-doh |
| Do you have...? | ¿Tiene...? | tee-**ehn**-ay |
| Where can I buy...? | ¿Dónde puedo comprar...? | **dohn**-day **pway**-doh kohm-**prar** |
| I want... | Quiero... | kee-**ehr**-oh |
| We want... | Queremos... | kehr-**ay**-mohs |
| ...this. | ...esto. | **ay**-stoh |
| ...just a little. | ...un poquito. | oon poh-**kee**-toh |
| ...more. | ...más. | mahs |
| ...a ticket. | ...un billete. | oon bee-**yeh**-tay |
| ...a room. | ...una habitación. | **oo**-nah ah-bee-tah-thee-**ohn** |
| ...the bill. | ...la cuenta. | lah **kwayn**-tah |
| | | |
| one | uno | **oo**-noh |
| two | dos | dohs |
| three | tres | trays |
| four | cuatro | **kwah**-troh |
| five | cinco | **theen**-koh |
| six | seis | says |
| seven | siete | see-**eh**-tay |
| eight | ocho | **oh**-choh |
| nine | nueve | **nway**-bay |
| ten | diez | dee-**ayth** |
| | | |
| At what time? | ¿A qué hora? | ah kay **oh**-rah |
| Just a moment. | Un momento. | oon moh-**mehn**-toh |
| Now. | Ahora. | ah-**oh**-rah |
| Soon. / Later. | Pronto. / Más tarde. | **prohn**-toh / mahs **tar**-day |
| Today. / Tomorrow. | Hoy. / Mañana. | oy / mahn-**yah**-nah |

# Portuguese tear-out cheat sheet

| | | |
|---|---|---|
| Hello. | Olá. | oh-lah |
| Do you speak English? | Fala inglês? | fah-lah een-glaysh |
| Yes. / No. | Sim. / Não. | seeng / now |
| I don't speak Portuguese. | Não falo português. | now fah-loo poor-too-gaysh |
| I'm sorry. | Desculpe. | dish-kool-peh |
| Please. | Por favor. | poor fah-vor |
| Thank you. | Obrigado[a]. | oh-bree-gah-doo |
| It's (not) a problem. | (Não) á problema. | (now) ah proo-blay-mah |
| Very good. | Muito bem. | mween-too bayn |
| You are very kind. | É muito simpático[a]. | eh mween-too seeng-pah-tee-koo |
| Goodbye. | Adeus. | ah-deh-oosh |
| Where is...? | Onde é que é...? | ohn-deh eh keh eh |
| ...a hotel | ...um hotel | oon oh-tehl |
| ...a youth hostel | ...uma pousada de juventude | oo-mah poh-zah-dah deh zhoo-vayn-too-deh |
| ...a restaurant | ...um restaurante | oon rish-toh-rahn-teh |
| ...a supermarket | ...um supermercado | oon soo-pehr-mehr-kah-doo |
| ...a pharmacy | ...uma farmácia | oo-mah far-mah-see-ah |
| ...a bank | ...um banco | oon bang-koo |
| ...the train station | ...a estação de comboio | ah ish-tah-sow deh kohn-boy-yoo |
| ...the tourist information office | ...a informação turística | ah een-for-mah-sow too-reesh-tee-kah |
| ...the toilet | ...a casa de banho | ah kah-zah deh bahn-yoo |
| men / women | homens / mulheres | aw-maynsh / mool-yeh-rish |
| How much is it? | Quanto custa? | kwahn-too koosh-tah |
| Write it? | Escreva? | ish-kray-vah |
| Cheap(er). | (Mais) barato. | (mish) bah-rah-too |

| | | |
|---|---|---|
| Cheapest. | **O mais barato.** | oo mīsh bah-**rah**-too |
| Is it free? | **É grátis?** | eh grah-teesh |
| Is it included? | **Está incluido?** | ish-tah een-kloo-ee-doo |
| Do you have...? | **Tem...?** | tay<u>n</u> |
| Where can I buy...? | **Onde posso comprar...?** | **ohn**-deh pos-soh koh<u>n</u>-**prar** |
| I would like... | **Gostaria...** | goosh-tah-**ree**-ah |
| We would like... | **Gostaríamos...** | goosh-tah-**ree**-ah-moosh |
| ...this. | **...isto.** | **eesh**-too |
| ...just a little. | **...só um bocadinho.** | saw oo<u>n</u> boo-kah-**deen**-yoo |
| ...more. | **...mais.** | mīsh |
| ...a ticket. | **...um bilhete.** | oo<u>n</u> beel-**yeh**-teh |
| ...a room. | **...um quarto.** | oo<u>n</u> **kwar**-too |
| ...the bill. | **...a conta.** | ah **koh<u>n</u>**-tah |

| | | |
|---|---|---|
| one | **um** | oo<u>n</u> |
| two | **dois** | doysh |
| three | **três** | traysh |
| four | **quatro** | **kwah**-troo |
| five | **cinco** | **seeng**-koo |
| six | **seis** | saysh |
| seven | **sete** | **seh**-teh |
| eight | **oito** | **oy**-too |
| nine | **nove** | **naw**-veh |
| ten | **dez** | dehsh |

| | | |
|---|---|---|
| At what time? | **A que horas?** | ah keh **aw**-rahsh |
| Just a moment. | **Um momento.** | oo<u>n</u> moo-**may<u>n</u>**-too |
| Now. | **Agora.** | ah-**goh**-rah |
| Soon. | **Em breve.** | ay<u>n</u> **bray**-veh |
| Later. | **Mais tarde.** | mīsh **tar**-deh |
| Today. | **Hoje.** | **oh**-zheh |
| Tomorrow. | **Amanhã.** | ah-**ming**-yah |

## Major Iberian transportation connections

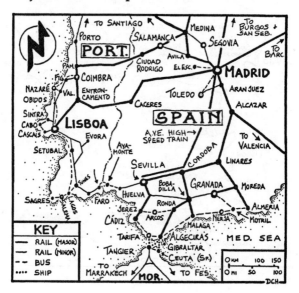

# Spain and Portugal

# More books by Rick Steves...

*Now more than ever, travelers are determined to get the most out of every mile, minute and dollar. That's what Rick's books are all about. He'll help you have a better trip because you're on a budget, not in spite of it. Each of these books is published by John Muir Publications, and is available through your local bookstore, or through Rick's free Europe Through the Back Door Travel Newsletter (call 425/771-8303 or go to www.ricksteves.com).*

## Rick Steves' Europe Through The Back Door

Updated every year, *ETBD* has given thousands of people the skills and confidence they needed to travel through the less-touristed "back doors" of Europe. You'll find chapters on packing, itinerary-planning, transportation, finding rooms, travel photography, keeping safe and healthy, plus chapters on Rick's favorite back door discoveries.

## Mona Winks: Self-Guided Tours of Europe's Top Museums

Let's face it, museums can ruin a good vacation. But *Mona* takes you by the hand, giving you fun and easy-to-follow self-guided tours through Europe's 20 most frightening and exhausting museums and cultural obligations. Packed with more than 200 maps and illustrations.

## Europe 101: History and Art for the Traveler

A lively, entertaining crash course in European history and art, *Europe 101* is the perfect way to prepare yourself for the rich cultural smorgasbord that awaits you.

## Rick Steves' Spain & Portugal

For a successful trip, raw information isn't enough. In this perfect companion to your phrase book, Rick Steves weeds through the region's endless possibilities to give you candid advice on what to see, where to sleep, how to manage your time, and how to get the most out of every dollar. Other regions covered in this series include...

**Rick Steves' Best of Europe**
**Rick Steves' France, Belgium & the Netherlands**
**Rick Steves' Paris**
**Rick Steves' Italy**
**Rick Steves' Germany, Austria & Switzerland**
        **(with Prague)**
**Rick Steves' Great Britain & Ireland**
**Rick Steves' London**
**Rick Steves' Scandinavia**
**Rick Steves' Russia & the Baltics**

**Rick Steves' European Phrase Books:**
**French, Italian, German, Spanish/Portuguese,**
**and French/Italian/German**
Finally, a series of phrase books written especially for the budget traveler! Each book gives you the words and phrases you need to communicate with the locals about room-finding, food, health and transportation—all spiced with Rick Steves' travel tips, and his unique blend of down-to-earth practicality and humor.

**Rick Steves' Postcards from Europe**
For twenty-five years Rick Steves has been exploring Europe, sharing his tricks and discoveries in guidebooks and on TV. Now, in *Postcards from Europe* he shares his favorite personal travel stories and his off-beat European friends – all told in that funny, down-to-earth style that makes Rick his Mom's favorite guidebook writer.

**www.ricksteves.com**
Rick Steves' popular Web site is sure to raise your European travel I.Q. You'll find a user-friendly online version of Rick's Guide to European Railpasses, a Graffiti Wall filled with advice from traveling readers, late-breaking book updates, and more.